MW01101424

"If you are looking for a job ... before you go to the newspapers and the help-wanted ads, listen to Bob Adams, editor of *The Metropolitan New York JobBank*."

-Tom Brokaw, NBC News

"One of the better publishers of employment almanacs is Bob Adams, Inc. ... publisher of *The Metropolitan New York JobBank* and similarly named directories of employers in Texas, Boston, Chicago, northern and southern California, and Washington DC. A good buy ..."

Wall Street Journal's
National Business Employment Weekly

"For those graduates whose parents are pacing the floor, conspicuously placing circled want ads around the house and typing up resumes,*[The Carolina JobBank]* answers job search questions."

-Greensboro News and Record

"Because our listing is seen by people across the nation it generates lots of resumes for us. We encourage unsolicited resumes. We'll always be listed [in *The Chicago JobBank*] as long as I'm in this career."

-Tom Fitzpatrick
Director of Human Resources
Merchandise Mart Properties, Inc.

"Job hunters can't afford to waste time. *The Minneapolis-St. Paul JobBank* contains information that used to require hours of research in the library."

-Carmella Zagone
Minneapolis Human Resources Administrator

"*The Florida JobBank* is an invaluable job search reference tool. It provides the most up-to-date information and contact names available for companies in Florida. I should know - it worked for me!"

-Rhonda Cody
Human Resources Consultant
Aetna Life and Casualty

"A powerful resume, *The Boston JobBank,* an aggressive job search strategy, and a positive attitude are the keys to landing the job you want."

-Anne M. Savas
Principal
The Competitive Edge

"*The Boston JobBank* provides a handy map of employment possibilities in Greater Boston. This book can help in the initial steps of a job search by locating major employers, describing their business activities, and for most firms, by naming the contact person and listing typical professional positions. For recent college graduates, as well as experienced professionals, *The Boston JobBank* is an excellent place to begin a job search."

-Juliet F. Brudney
Career Columnist
Boston Globe

"No longer can jobseekers feel secure about finding employment just through want ads. With the tough competition in the job market, particularly in the Boston area, they need much more help. For this reason, *The Boston JobBank* will have a wide and appreciative audience of new graduates, job changers, and people relocating to Boston. It provides a good place to start a search for entry-level professional positions."

-The Journal of College Placement

"*The Metropolitan Washington DC JobBank* is an excellent resource....A must have for the serious career hunter."

-Mel Rappleyea
Human Resource Director
Hit or Miss, Inc.

"*The Phoenix JobBank* provides the most convenient information source available to professionals with tight budgets and little time to waste."

-Jerry Mosqueda
President
Mosqueda & Mijas

"*The Phoenix JobBank* is a first-class publication. The information provided is useful and current."

-Lyndon Denton
Director of Human Resources and
Materials Management
Apache Nitrogen Products, Inc.

"I've had my firm listed in *The Denver JobBank* book for the past four editions and have been very pleased with the results."

-Jim Turner
President
J.Q. Turner & Associates, Inc.

"A good resource for the job hunter."

-Virginia Tyler
Human Resources Manager
Battelle Columbus Operations/Ohio

"*The Ohio JobBank* is a very helpful tool for locating and researching potential employers. It's easy to use and even gives advice on winning the job."

-Judith G. Bishop
Manager of Employment
Barberton Citizens Hospital

What makes the JobBank Series the nation's premier line of employment guides?

With vital employment information on thousands of employers across the nation, the JobBank Series is the most comprehensive and authoritative set of career directories available today.

Each book in the series provides information on **dozens of different industries** in a given city or area, with the primary employer listings providing contact information, telephone numbers, addresses, a thumbnail sketch of the firm's business, and in many cases descriptions of the firm's typical professional job categories, the principal educational backgrounds sought, and the fringe benefits offered.

In addition to the **detailed primary employer listings,** the new 1995 JobBank books give telephone numbers and addresses for **thousands of additional employers.**

All of the reference information in the JobBank Series is as up-to-date and accurate as possible. Every year, the entire database is thoroughly researched and verified, first by mail and then by telephone. Bob Adams Inc. publishes **more local JobBank books more often** than any other publisher of career directories.

In addition, the JobBank Series features important information about the local job scene--**forecasts on which industries are the hottest, overviews of local economic trends,** and even **lists of regional professional associations,** so you can get your job hunt started off right.

Hundreds of discussions with job hunters show that they prefer information organized geographically, because most people look for jobs in specific areas. The JobBank Series offers **twenty regional titles,** from Minneapolis to Houston, and from Washington, DC, to San Francisco. The future employee moving to a particular area can review the local employment data not only for information on the type of industry most common to that region, but also for names of specific employers.

A condensed, but thorough, review of the entire job search process is presented in the chapter **"The Basics of Job Winning"**, a feature which has received many compliments from career counselors. In addition, each JobBank directory is completed by a section on **resumes and cover letters** *The New York Times* has acclaimed as "excellent."

The JobBank Series gives job hunters the most comprehensive, most timely, and most accurate career information, organized and indexed to facilitate the job search. An entire career reference library, JobBank books are the consummate employment guides.

Published by Bob Adams, Inc.
260 Center Street, Holbrook, MA 02343

Manufactured in the United States of America.

Because addresses and telephone numbers of smaller companies change rapidly, we recommend you call each company and verify the information before mailing to the employers listed in this book. Mass mailings are not recommended.

While the publisher has made every reasonable effort to obtain accurate information and verify same, occasional errors are inevitable due to the magnitude of the data base. Should you discover an error, or if a company is missing, please write the editors at the above address so that we may update future editions.

"This publication is designed to provide accurate and authoritative information with regard to the subject matter covered. It is sold with the understanding that the publisher is not engaged in rendering legal, accounting, or other professional advice. If legal advice or other expert assistance is required, the services of a competent professional person should be sought."
--From a *Declaration of Principles* jointly adopted by a Committee of the American Bar Association and a Committee of Publishers and Associations

The appearance of a listing in the book does not constitute an endorsement from the publisher.

Cover design by Peter Gouck and Chris Ciaschini

Cover photo courtesy of: Mary Levin - The University of Washington

ISBN: 1-55850-460-5

This book is available at quantity discounts for bulk purchases.
For information, call 1-800-872-5627.

The
Seattle
JobBank
1 9 9 5

Managing Editor
Carter Smith

Series Editor
Steven Graber

Editorial Assistants
Isadora Beeler
Kenny Brooks
Jennifer B. Greene
Peter Hale
Matthew J. Horn
Jennifer J. Pfalzgraf

BOB ADAMS, INC.
Holbrook, Massachusetts

Top career publications from Bob Adams, Inc.

The Atlanta JobBank, 1995 ($15.95)
The Boston JobBank, 1995 ($15.95)
The Carolina JobBank, 2nd Edition
($15.95)
The Chicago JobBank, 1995 ($15.95)
The Dallas-Ft. Worth JobBank, 1995
($15.95)
The Denver JobBank, 6th Edition
($15.95)
The Detroit JobBank, 5th Edition
($15.95)
The Florida JobBank, 1995 ($15.95)
The Houston JobBank, 1995 ($15.95)
The Los Angeles JobBank, 1995 ($15.95)
The Minneapolis-St. Paul JobBank, 1995
($15.95)
The New York JobBank, 1995 ($15.95)
The Ohio JobBank, 1995 ($15.95)
The Philadelphia JobBank, 1995 ($15.95)
The Phoenix JobBank, 4th Edition
($15.95)
The San Francisco Bay Area JobBank,
1995 ($15.95)
The Seattle JobBank, 1995 ($15.95)
The St. Louis JobBank, 5th Edition
($15.95)
The Tennessee JobBank, 1st Edition
($15.95)
The Washington DC JobBank, 1995
($15.95)

The National JobBank, 1995
(Covers 50 states: $250.00)

The JobBank Guide to Employment
Services, 1994-1995
(Covers 50 states: $150.00)

OTHER CAREER TITLES:

The Adams Jobs Almanac, 1995 ($10.95)
The Adams Resume Almanac ($10.95)
America's Fastest Growing Employers,
2nd Edition ($16.00)

Career Shifting ($9.95)
Careers and the College Grad ($9.95)
Careers and the Engineer ($9.95)
Careers and the MBA ($9.95)
Cold Calling Techniques that Really
Work, 3rd Edition ($7.95)
Cover Letters that Knock 'em Dead, 2nd
Edition ($7.95)
The Elements of Job Hunting ($4.95)
Every Woman's Essential Job Hunting &
Resume Book ($10.95)
Harvard Guide to Careers in the Mass
Media ($7.95)
High Impact Telephone Networking for
Job Hunters ($6.95)
How to Become Successfully Self
Employed ($9.95)
The Job Hunter's Checklist ($5.95)
The Job Search Handbook ($6.95)
Job Search Networking ($9.95)
Knock 'em Dead--The Ultimate
Jobseeker's Handbook, 1995 ($9.95)
The Minority Career Book ($9.95)
The National Job Line Directory ($7.95)
Outplace Yourself ($25.00)
Over 40 and Looking for Work ($7.95)
The Resume Handbook, 2nd Edition
($5.95)
Resumes that Knock 'em Dead, 2nd
Edition ($7.95)
300 New Ways to Get A Better Job
($7.95)

To order these books or additional copies
of this book, send check or money order
(including $4.50 for postage) to:

Bob Adams, Inc.
260 Center Street
Holbrook MA 02343

Ordering by credit card?
Just call 1-800-USA-JOBS
(In Massachusetts, call 617-767-8100)

TABLE OF CONTENTS

SECTION FOUR: EMPLOYMENT SERVICES/297

Professional Employment Services/298
Includes the address, phone number, description of each company's services, contact name, and a list of positions commonly filled.

Executive Search Firms/302
Includes the address, phone number, description of each company's services, contact name, and a list of positions commonly filled.

SECTION FIVE: INDEX/305

An alphabetical index of primary employer listings only. Due to space constraints, employers that fall under the headings "Additional Employers" are not indexed here.

How to Use This Book

Right now, you hold in your hands one of the most effective job hunting tools available anywhere. In *The Seattle JobBank*, you will find a wide array of valuable information to help you to either launch or continue a rewarding career. But before you open to the book's employer listings and start calling about current job openings, take a few minutes to learn how best to put the resources presented in *The Seattle JobBank* to work for you.

The Seattle JobBank will help you to stand out from other jobseekers. While many people looking for a new job rely solely on newspaper help-wanted ads, this book offers you a much more effective job-search method -- direct contact. The direct contact method has been proven to be twice as effective as scanning the help-wanted ads. Instead of waiting for employers to come looking for you, you'll be far more effective going to them. While many of your competitors will use trial and error methods in trying to set up interviews, you'll learn not only how to get interviews, but what to expect once you've got them.

In the next few pages, we'll take you through each section of the book so you'll be prepared to get a jump-start on your competition:

The Seattle Job Market: An Overview

To get a feel for the state of Seattle's job scene, read the introductory section called *The Seattle Job Market*. In it, we'll recap the economy's recent performance, and the steps that local governments and business leaders are taking to bring new jobs to the area.

Even more importantly, you'll learn where things are headed. What are the prospects for the industries that form the core of the region's economy? Which new industries are growing fastest and which older ones are laying off? Are there any companies that are especially hot, and why?

To answer these questions for you, we've pored over local business journals and newspapers, and interviewed local business leaders and labor analysts. Whether you are new to the Emerald City and need a source of regional information, or are a life-long resident just looking for a fresh start in a new job, you'll find this section to be a concise thumbnail sketch of where Seattle's jobs are.

This type of information is potent ammunition to bring into an interview. Showing that you're well versed in current industry trends helps give you an edge over job applicants who haven't done their homework.

Basics of Job Winning

Preparation. Strategy. Time-Management. These are three of the most important elements of a successful job search. *The Basics of Job Winning* helps you address these and all the other elements needed to find the right job.

One of your first priorities should be to define your personal career objectives. What qualities make a job desirable to you? Creativity? High pay? Prestige? Use *Basics of Job Winning* to weigh these questions. Then use the rest of the chapter to design a strategy to find a job that matches your criteria.

In *Basics of Job Winning,* you'll learn which job hunting techniques work, and which don't. We've reviewed the pros and cons of mass mailings, help-wanted ads and direct contact. We'll show you how to develop and approach contacts in your field; how to research a prospective employer; and how to use that information to get an interview and the job.

Also included in *Basics*: interview dress code and etiquette, the "do's and don'ts" of interviewing, and sample interview questions. The often forgotten art of what to do <u>after</u> the interview is also discussed.

Resumes and Cover Letters

The approach you take to writing your resume and cover letter can often mean the difference between getting an interview and never being noticed. In this section, we discuss different formats, as well as what to put on (and what to leave off) your resume. It also reviews the benefits and drawbacks of professional resume writers, and the importance of a follow-up letter. Also included in this section are sample resumes and cover letters which you can use as models.

The Employer Listings

Employers are listed alphabetically by industry, and within industry, by company names. When a company does business under a person's name, like "John Smith & Co.", the company is usually listed by the surname's spelling (in this case 'S'). Exceptions occur when a company's name is widely recognized, like 'JCPenney' or 'Howard Johnson Motor Lodge'. In those cases, the company's first name is the key ('J' and 'H' respectively).

The Seattle JobBank covers thirty-six industries. Each company profile is assigned to one of the following:

Accounting/Management Consulting

Advertising/Marketing and Public Relations

Aerospace

Apparel and Textiles

Architecture, Construction and Engineering

Arts and Entertainment/Recreation

Automotive

Banking/Savings and Loans

Biotechnology/Pharmaceuticals/ Scientific R&D

Business Services and Non-Scientific Research

Charities/Social Services/Membership Organizations

Chemicals/Rubber and Plastics
Communications: Telecommunications/
Broadcasting
Computer Hardware, Software and
Services
Educational Services
Electronic/Industrial Electrical
Equipment
Environmental Services
Fabricated/Primary Metals and
Products
Financial Services
Food and Beverage/Agriculture
Government
Health Care: Service, Equipment and
Products
Hotels and Restaurants

Insurance
Legal Services
Manufacturing and Wholesaling: Misc.
Consumer
Manufacturing and Wholesaling: Misc.
Industrial
Mining/Gas/Petroleum/Energy Related
Paper and Wood Products
Personal Services
Printing and Publishing
Real Estate
Retail
Stone, Clay, Glass and Concrete
Products
Transportation
Utilities: Electric/Gas/Sanitation

While most of these industry headings are self-explanatory, a few may need clarification. *Business Services and Non-Scientific Research* contains companies that 1) provide services to other companies; and 2) aren't classified elsewhere (under advertising, or computer or financial services, for example). Examples include companies which do laundry for hotels, conduct personnel checks of job applicants, or provide security guards for warehouses. *Personal Services* addresses the services provided to individuals, such as hair stylists, house painters, or funeral homes.

Many of the company listings offer detailed company profiles. In addition to company names, addresses, and phone numbers, these listings also include contact names or hiring departments, and descriptions of each company's products and/or services. Many of these listings also include a variety of additional information including:

Common positions - A list of job titles that the company commonly fills when it is hiring. Note: keep in mind that *The Seattle JobBank* is a directory of major employers in the Seattle area, not a directory of openings currently available. Many of the companies listed will be hiring, others will not. However, since most professional job openings are filled without the placement of help-wanted ads, contacting the employers in this book directly is still a more effective method that browsing the Sunday papers.

Common positions are listed under many of the entries in alphabetical order, and range from Accountant to Wholesale Buyer.

Educational backgrounds sought - A list of educational backgrounds that companies seek when hiring.

Benefits - What kind of benefits packages are available from these employers? Here you'll find a broad range of benefits, from the relatively common (medical insurance) to those that are much more rare (health club membership; child daycare assistance).

Special programs - Does the company offer training programs, internships or apprenticeships? These programs can be important to first time job seekers and college students looking for practical work experience. Many employer profiles will include information on these programs.

Parent company - If an employer is a subsidiary of a larger company, the name of that parent company will often be listed here. Use this information to supplement your company research before contacting the employer.

Hires/layoffs in 1993 - This offers a quick glimpse at the company's recent employment trends. Some companies have given both local and national figures.

Number of employees: The number of workers a company employs.

Projected number of hires/layoffs - An estimate of hiring for the next year. Again, some firms have provided both national and local figures.

Companies may also include information on other U.S. locations, annual revenues, and any stock exchange the firm may be listed on.

Because so many job openings are with small and mid-sized employers, we've also included the addresses and phone numbers of additional Seattle employers. While none of these listings include any additional hiring information, many of them also offer rewarding career opportunities. These listings are also organized under each industry heading. Within each industry, they are organized by the type of product or service offered.

A note on all employer listings that appear in *The Seattle JobBank.* This book is intended as a starting point. It is not intended to replace any effort that you the jobseeker should devote to your jobhunt. Keep in mind that while a great deal of effort has been put into collecting and verifying company information that is provided in this book, addresses and contact names change regularly. Inevitably, some contact names listed herein have changed even before you read this. We recommend you contact a company before mailing your resume to insure nothing has changed.

At the end of each industry section, we have included a directory of other industry-specific resources to help you in your job search. These include: professional and industrial associations, many of which can provide employment advice and job search help; magazines that cover the industry; and additional directories that may supplement the employer listings in this book.

Employment Services and Executive Search Firms

Immediately following the employer listings section of this book are listings of Seattle's employment services and executive search firms. Many jobseekers supplement their own efforts by contracting "temp" services, head hunters, and other employment search firms to generate potential job opportunities.

This section is a comprehensive listing of such firms, arranged alphabetically under the headings Employment Agencies/Temporary Services, and Executive Search Firms. Each listing includes the firm's name, address, telephone number and contact person. Each listing may also include the firm's founding date, the areas it specializes in, whether an appointment is necessary, if unsolicited resumes are accepted, the type of positions the company commonly fills, how many jobs are filled annually, and who pays the finder's fee.

Index

The Seattle JobBank index is a straight alphabetical listing.

The Seattle Job Market:
An Economic Overview

While Seattle's economy has rebounded from the recessionary doldrums of the early '90s, the local job market has yet to return to full strength. The outlook for aerospace, which has long been Seattle's leading industry, remains cloudy. On the other hand, the region has a number of strengths that have helped it weather the economic storm. New company start-ups, an expanding high-tech scene, the region's role as a center of international trade, a highly diversified economy and a well-educated, professional work force have helped pulled the Emerald City out of the recession.

As home to nearly 40 percent of Washington's population, the Puget Sound region generates more than half of the state's jobs. Many of them are in international trade. Seattle is the same distance by air to Tokyo and London, and the Port of Seattle is the closest American seaport to the Far East. Each year, roughly 11 million metric tons of goods pass through the city. According to a study conducted by the consulting firm **Martin O'Connell Associates**, the billions in revenues that the port provides, coupled with the jobs it creates and moneys it injects into the local and state economy, are "the propellers of economic growth in the region."

Aerospace

While many other sectors of Seattle's economy have prospered, one should not understate havoc that layoffs in the aerospace industry have wreaked on the entire region. Historically, **The Boeing Company** --- which even today employs an astounding one out of every five workers in metro Seattle --- has been the backbone of the region's economy. Boeing has been critical in building the city's international port status, not only by providing the planes to carry goods, but also by creating over 100,000 jobs to build those planes. In recent years, however, the company has been hit hard by the one-two punch of defense cuts by the Federal government and airfare wars by the commercial airlines. With demand for new planes slowing beginning in the late '80s, Boeing was forced to cut back, and continues to do so. Roughly 15,000 people were laid off in 1993 alone, and 4,000 more were slated to be released by the end of 1994.

The worst may be over. For one, Boeing received some good news from Washington, D.C. when the Clinton Administration opted to renew China's Most Favored Nation (MFN) trading status. China has been one of the fastest-growing new markets for the American aerospace industry, and the loss of it's MFN status would probably have meant even more layoffs at Boeing and its suppliers.

A Growing Service Sector

According to regional analysts, Seattle's rising population will help to further strengthen the region's services industries through the mid-'90s. With more people living in the region, the opportunities for employees in industries that serve the growing population --- restaurants, retailers, utilities, construction, communications, finance, and many others --- will also increase.

The business services sector is also growing. One successful service company is **AEI Music Network**. Founded by Michael Malone in 1971, the company supplies customized tapes of original recordings to businesses across the country. The company has contracts to provide tapes of music targeted to specific markets with retailers like Limited Express and Pier 1; airlines including Delta, United and TWA; and various restaurants. Seattle is also home to **Muzak**, the much more widely known supplier of musical background tapes to businesses.

High-Tech and Multimedia

Seattle's high-tech sector is dominated by the same company that dominates much of the world's high-tech sector --- the Redmond-based **Microsoft**. As *The Seattle Times* puts it, Microsoft "virtually controls the market for operating systems." Microsoft single-handedly revolutionized personal computing by creating MS-DOS®, the operating system that virtually all IBM-compatible PCs use to operate. Since that time, Microsoft has strengthened its dominant position since that time by releasing its Windows® graphical interface. In addition to operating systems, Microsoft is also the leading producer of personal and business software. Microsoft's grip on the software industry has been so tight that for years, competitors like Lotus and Novell have cried foul. Competitors argued that Microsoft's software developers had unfair access to information on new versions of the company's own operating systems before their release to the public. In 1990, the Federal Trade Commission launched an anti-trust review of Microsoft. In July, 1994, the FTC announced that under an agreement with the federal government, Microsoft will make minor changes to its business and licensing practices, but will not have to pay any fines. These adjustments won't change the company's momentum into new markets, and the company should continue to grow.

While Microsoft employs only about one-tenth the number of workers that Boeing employs, the software giant's influence on the local job market has stretched beyond its corporate campus. Over the years, the company has attracted many of the best minds in the computer and high-tech fields to the Seattle area. Many of these workers have since left Microsoft to launch their own firms, thus creating a job-creating ripple effect. According to *Business Week*, Seattle has seen an explosion of new multimedia companies, many of which are headed by former Microsoft employees who cashed-in their stock options and struck out on their own.

The multimedia field, which combines video, sound and graphics in software, is expected to be a $1 billion market in 1995. Because of this potential, a great deal of money is flowing into the city from venture capitalists, industry watchers and other investors. Throughout 1994, multimedia companies collected millions of dollars from venture capital firms.

Why is Seattle such a fertile ground for multimedia? In addition to the high concentration of young computer professionals, the city is also home to a diverse culture of art, music and the like. As one start-up's co-founder put it, Seattle "has a very interesting approach to blending culture and technology, and that's what multimedia is all about."

Layoffs in Banking

While the software industry is booming, some banking employees are taking it on the chin. Portland-based **U.S. Bancorp,** the largest financial institution in the Pacific Northwest. recently announced it would close five branches in Washington and selling two more in order to cut costs and boost profitability. According to the *Seattle Post-Intelligencer,* "Although U.S. Bancorp is profitable, its financial performance lags behind major competitors." The company said attrition, early retirement and voluntary severance would cut total employment by 1,300, reducing the number of layoffs the company would have to make to reach its goal.

A State That Helps

The State of Washington has been innovative in creating new jobs and new businesses. According to *Home Office Computing* magazine, the Evergreen State was the first to try "the alternate use of unemployment insurance benefits as a potential for job creation and economic growth." The results of this experiment, called the **Self-Employment and Enterprise Development (SEED) Demonstration Project** are still being evaluated for future funding. Several of the participants of that program, however, are now nurturing fledgling businesses. One participant now runs a women's apparel wholesale company that manages 140 retail accounts in the U.S. and Canada.

There are also programs in operation to help minority entrepreneurs. *Black Enterprise* noted, "Last year, the state initiated the **Linked Deposits** program that will provide [minority and women] entrepreneurs with up to $100 million in low-interest loans." And while African-Americans only make-up 10 percent of Seattle's population, they are taking active measures to help promote business in the city. The **Black Dollar Days Task Force** is another nonprofit economic development organization which helps raise money for black-owned businesses and create inner-city jobs.

For more information contact:

Greater Seattle Chamber of Commerce, 1301 Fifth Avenue, Suite 2400, Seattle WA 98101-2603. 206/389-7200.

Employment Security Department, Job Service Center, P.O. Box 9765, Olympia WA 98507. 206/438-7800.

Washington State Business Assistance Center, Suite A, 919 Lakeridge Way SW, Olympia WA 98504-2516. 206/664-9501.

THE JOB SEARCH

THE BASICS OF JOB WINNING:
A CONDENSED REVIEW

The best way to obtain a better professional job is to contact the employer directly. Broad-based statistical studies by the Department of Labor show that job seekers find jobs more successfully by contacting employers directly than by using any other method.

However, given the diversity and the increasingly specialized nature of both industries and job tasks, in some situations other job seeking methods may also be successful. Three of the other most commonly used methods are: relying on personal contacts, using employment services, and following up help wanted advertisements. Many professionals have been successful in finding better jobs using one of these methods. However, the Direct Contact method boasts twice the success rate of any other method, and is used successfully by many more professionals. So unless you have specific reasons to believe that another method would work best for you, the Direct Contact method should form the foundation of your job search.

The Objective

With any business task, you must develop a strategy for meeting a goal. This is especially true when it comes to obtaining a better job. First you need to clearly define your objectives.

Setting your job objectives is better known as career planning (or life planning for those who wish to emphasize the importance of combining the two). Career planning has become a field of study in and of itself. Since many of our readers are probably well-entrenched in their career path, we will touch on career planning only briefly.

The first step in beginning your job search
is to clearly define your objectives

If you are thinking of choosing or switching careers, we particularly emphasize two things. First, choose a career where you will enjoy most of the day-to-day tasks. This sounds obvious, but most of us have at one point or another been attracted by a glamour industry or a prestigious job title without thinking of the most important consideration: Would we enjoy performing the everyday tasks the position entailed?

The second key consideration is that you are not merely choosing a career, but also a lifestyle. Career counselors indicate that one of the most common problems people encounter in job seeking is that they fail to consider how well-suited they are for a particular position or career. For example, some people, attracted to management consulting by good salaries, early responsibility, and high-level corporate exposure, do not adapt well to the long hours, heavy travel demands, and the constant pressure to produce. Be sure to ask yourself how you might adapt to not only the day-to-day duties and working environment that a specific position entails, but also how you might adapt to the demands of that career or industry choice as a whole.

Job hunting is intellectually demanding work that requires you to be at your best. So don't tire yourself out working around the clock

---

The Strategy

Assuming that you've established your career objectives, the next step of the job search is to develop a strategy. If you don't take the time to develop a strategy and lay out a plan, you will find yourself going in circles after several weeks of random searching for opportunities that always seem just beyond your reach.

Your strategy can be thought of as having three simple elements:

1. Choosing a method of contacting employers.

2. Allocating your scarce resources. (In most job searches the key scarce resource will be time, but financial considerations will become important in some searches, too.)

3. Evaluating how the selected contact method is working and then considering adopting other methods.

We suggest you consider using the Direct Contact method exclusively. However, we realize it is human nature to avoid putting all your eggs in one basket. So if you prefer to use other methods as well, try to expend at least half your effort on the Direct Contact method, spending the rest on all of the other methods combined. Millions of other jobseekers have already proven that Direct Contact has been twice as effective in obtaining employment, so why not benefit from their effort?

With your strategy in mind, the next step is to work out the details. The most important detail is setting up a schedule. Of course, since job searches aren't something most people do regularly, it may be hard to estimate how long each step will take. Nonetheless, it is important to have a plan so that you can see yourself progressing.

When outlining your job search schedule, have a realistic time frame in mind. If you will be job searching full-time, your search will probably take at least two months. If you can only devote part-time effort, it will probably take four months.

You probably know a few people who seem to spend their whole lives searching for a better job in their spare time. Don't be one of them. Once you begin your job search on a part-time basis, give it your whole-hearted effort. If you don't feel like devoting a lot of energy to job seeking right now, then wait. Focus on enjoying your present position, performing your best on the job, and storing up energy for when you are really ready to begin your job search.

Those of you currently unemployed should remember that job hunting is tough work physically and emotionally. It is also intellectually demanding work that requires you to be at your best. So don't tire yourself out by working on your job campaign around the clock. At the same time, be sure to discipline yourself. The most logical way to manage your time while looking for a job is to keep your regular working hours.

Try calling as early as 8 AM and as late as 6 PM. You'll be surprised how often you will be able to reach the executive you want during these times of the day

---

For those of you who are still employed, job searching will be particularly tiring because it must be done in addition to your regular duties. So don't work yourself to the point where you show up to interviews looking exhausted and start to slip behind at your current job. On the other hand, don't be tempted to quit your current job! The long hours are worth it. Searching for a job while you have one puts you in a position of strength.

If you are searching full-time and have decided to choose several different contact methods, we recommend that you divide up each week allowing some time for each method. For instance, you might devote Mondays to following up newspaper ads because most of them appear in Sunday papers. Then you might devote Tuesdays, and Wednesday mornings to working and developing the personal contacts you have, in addition to trying a few employment services. Then you could devote the rest of the week to the Direct Contact method. This is just one plan that may succeed for you.

By trying several methods at once, job-searching will be more interesting, and you will be able to evaluate how promising each of the methods seems, altering your schedule accordingly. Be very careful in your evaluation, however, and don't judge the success of a particular method just by the sheer number of interviews you obtain. Positions advertised in the newspaper, for instance, are likely to generate many more interviews per opening than positions that are filled without being advertised.

If you are searching part-time and decide to try several different contact methods, we recommend that you try them sequentially. You simply won't have enough time to put a meaningful amount of effort into more than one method at once. So estimate the length of your job search, and then allocate so many weeks or months for each contact method you will use. (We suggest that you try Direct Contact first.)

If you're expected to be in your office during the business day, then you have an additional problem to deal with. How can you work interviews into the business day? And if you work in an open office, how can you even call to set up interviews? As much as possible you should keep up the effort and the appearances on your present job. So maximize your use of the lunch hour, early mornings and late afternoons for calling. If you keep trying you'll be surprised how often you will be able to reach the executive you are trying to contact during your out-of-office hours. Also you can catch people as early as 8 AM and as late as 6 PM on frequent occasions. Jot out a plan each night on how you will be using each minute of your precious lunch break.

Your inability to interview at any time other than lunch just might work to your advantage. If you can, try to set up as many interviews as possible for your lunch hour. This will go a long way to creating a relaxed rapport. (Who isn't happy when eating?) But be sure the interviews don't stray too far from the agenda on hand.

Consider where your skills might be in demand, the degree of competition for employment, and the employment outlook at each particular firm

---

Lunchtime interviews are much easier to obtain if you have substantial career experience. People with less experience will often find no alternative to taking time off for interviews. If you have to take time off, you have to take time off. But try to do this as little as possible. Try to take the whole day off in order to avoid being blatantly obvious about your job search. Try to schedule in two to three interviews for the same day. (It is very difficult to maintain an optimum level of energy at more than three interviews in one day.) Explain to the interviewer why you might have to juggle your interview schedule -- he/she should honor the respect you're showing your current employer by minimizing your days off and will probably appreciate the fact that another prospective employer is interested in you.

We want to stress that if you are searching for a job -- especially part-time -- get out there and do the necessary tasks to the best of your ability and get it over with. Don't let your job search drag on endlessly.

And remember that all schedules are meant to be broken. The purpose of a job search schedule is not to rush you to your goal but to help you map out the road ahead, and then to periodically evaluate how you're progressing.

The Direct Contact Method

Once you have scheduled your time, you are ready to begin your search in earnest. We'll limit discussion here to the Direct Contact method.

The first step in preparing for Direct Contact is to develop a check list for categorizing the types of firms for which you'd like to work. You might categorize firms by product line, size, customer-type (such as industrial or consumer), growth prospects, or, by geographical location. Your list of important criteria might be very short. If it is, good! The shorter it is, the easier it will be to locate the company that is right for you.

DEVELOPING YOUR CONTACTS

Some career counselors feel that the best route to a better job is through somebody you already know or through somebody to whom you can be introduced. The counselors recommend that you build your contact base beyond your current acquaintances by asking each one to introduce you, or refer you, to additional people in your field of interest.

The theory goes like this: You might start with 15 personal contacts, each of whom introduces you to three additional people, for a total of 45 additional contacts. Then each of these people introduces you to three additional people, which adds 135 additional contacts. Theoretically, you will soon know every person in the industry.

Of course, developing your personal contacts does not usually work quite as smoothly as the theory suggests because some people will not be able to introduce you to anyone. The further you stray from your initial contact base, the weaker your references may be. So, if you do try developing your own contacts, try to begin with as many people you know personally as you can. Dig into your personal phone book and your holiday greeting card list and locate old classmates from school. Be particularly sure to approach people who perform your personal business such as your lawyer, accountant, banker, doctor, stockbroker, and insurance agent. These people develop a very broad contact base due to the nature of their professions.

Next, try to decide at which firms you're most likely to be able to find a job. Try matching your skills with those that a specific job demands. Consider where your skills might be in demand, the degree of competition for employment, and the employment outlook at each particular firm.

Now you'll want to assemble your list of potential employers. Build up your list to at least 100 prospects. Then separate your prospect list into three groups. The first tier of around 25 firms will be your primary target group, the second tier of another 25 firms will be your secondary group, and the remaining names you can keep in reserve.

After you form your prospect list begin work on your resume. Refer to the sample resumes included in the Resumes and Cover Letters section following this chapter in order to get ideas.

You should plan to spend an average of three or four hours researching each firm

Once your resume is complete, begin researching your first batch of 25 prospective employers. You will want to determine whether you would be happy working at the firms you are researching and also get a better idea of what their employment needs might be. You also need to obtain enough information to sound highly informed about the company during phone conversations and in mail correspondence. But don't go all out on your research yet! At some of these firms you probably will not be able to arrange interviews, so save your big research effort until you start to arrange interviews. Nevertheless, you should plan to spend an average of three to four hours researching each firm. Do your research in batches to save time and energy. Use one resource at a time and find out what you can about each of the 25 firms in the batch. Start with the easiest resources to use (such as this book). Keep organized. Maintain a folder on each firm.

If you discover something that really disturbs you about the firm (they are about to close their only local office), or if you discover that your chances of getting a job there are practically nil (they have just instituted a hiring freeze), then cross them off your prospect list.

If possible, supplement your research efforts with contacts to individuals who know the firm well. Ideally you should make an informal contact with someone at the particular firm, but often a contact at a direct competitor, or a major supplier or customer will be able to supply you with just as much information. At the very least, try to obtain whatever printed information that the company has available, not just annual reports, but product brochures and any other printed material the firm may have to offer. The company might have printed information about career opportunities.

DON'T BOTHER WITH MASS MAILINGS OR
BARRAGES OF PHONE CALLS

Direct Contact does not mean burying every firm within a hundred miles with mail and phone calls. Mass mailings rarely work in the job hunt. This also applies to those letters that are personalized -- but dehumanized -- on an automatic typewriter or computer. Don't waste your time or money on such a project; you will fool no one but yourself.

The worst part of sending out mass mailings -- or making unplanned phone calls to companies you have not researched -- is that you are likely to be remembered as someone with little genuine interest in the firm, who lacks sincerity, and as somebody that nobody wants to hire.

HELP WANTED ADVERTISEMENTS

Only a small fraction of professional job openings are advertised. Yet a majority of job seekers -- and a lot of people not in the job market -- spend a lot of time studying the help wanted ads. As a result, the competition for advertised openings is often very severe.

A moderate-sized employer told us about an experience advertising in the help wanted section of a major Sunday newspaper:

It was a disaster. We had over 500 responses from this relatively small ad in just one week. We have only two phone lines in this office and one was totally knocked out. We'll never advertise for professional help again.

If you insist on following up on help wanted ads, then research a firm before you reply to an ad. Preliminary research might help to separate you from all of the other professionals responding to that ad, many of whom will only have a passing interest in the opportunity, and will give you insight about a particular firm to help you determine if it is potentially a good match. That said, your chances of obtaining a job through the want-ads are still much smaller than they are if you use the Direct Contact method.

Getting The Interview

Now it is time to arrange an interview, time to make the Direct Contact. If you have read many books on job searching, you may have noticed that most of these books tell you to avoid the personnel office like the plague. It is said that the personnel office never hires people; they screen candidates. Unfortunately, this is often the case, but there are other options available to you. If you can identify the appropriate manager with the authority to hire you, contact that person directly. This will take a lot of time in each case, and often you'll be bounced back to personnel despite your efforts. So we suggest that initially you begin your Direct Contact campaign through personnel offices. If it seems that the firms on your prospect list do little hiring through personnel, you might consider some alternative courses of action. The three obvious means of initiating Direct Contact are:

-Showing up unannounced
-Mail
-Phone calls

Cross out the first one right away. You should never show up to seek a professional position without an appointment. Even if you are somehow lucky enough to obtain an interview, you will appear so unprofessional that you will not be seriously considered.

Mail contact seems to be a good choice if you have not been in the job market for a while. You can take your time to prepare a letter, say exactly what you want, and of course include your resume. Remember that employers receive many resumes every day. Don't be surprised if you do not get a response to your inquiry, so don't spend weeks waiting for responses that may never come. If you do send a cover letter, follow it up (or precede it) with a phone call. This will increase your impact, and because of the initial research you did, will underscore both your familiarity and your interest in the firm.

Always include a cover letter with your resume even if you are not specifically asked to do so

---

Another alternative is to make a "Cover Call." Your Cover Call should be just like your cover letter: concise. Your first sentence should interest the employer in you. Then try to subtly mention your familiarity with the firm. Don't be overbearing; keep your introduction to three sentences or less. Be pleasant, self-confident, and relaxed. This will greatly increase the chances of the person at the other end of the line developing the conversation. But don't press. When you are asked to follow up "with something in the mail", don't try to prolong the conversation once it has ended. Don't ask what they want to receive in the mail.

Always send your resume and a highly personalized follow-up letter, reminding the addressee of the phone conversation. Always include a cover letter if you are requested to send a resume.

Unless you are in telephone sales, making smooth and relaxed cover calls will probably not come easily. Practice them on your own and then with your friends or relatives.

If you obtain an interview as a result of a telephone conversation, be sure to send a thank you note reiterating the points you made during the conversation. You will appear more professional and increase your impact.

However, unless specifically requested, don't mail your resume once an interview has been arranged. Take it with you to the interview instead.

Preparing For The Interview

Once the interview has been arranged, begin your in-depth research. You should arrive at an interview knowing the company upside down and inside out. You need to know the company's products, types of customers, subsidiaries, the parent company, principal locations, rank in the industry, sales and profit trends, type of ownership, size, current plans, and much more. By this time you have probably narrowed your job search to one industry. If you haven't, then be familiar with the trends in the firm's industry, the firm's principal competitors and their relative performance, and the direction that the industry leaders are headed. Dig into every resource you can! Read the company literature, the trade press, the business press, and if the company is public, call your stockbroker (if you have one) and ask for additional information. If possible, speak to someone at the firm before the interview, or if not, speak to someone at a competing firm. The more time you spend, the better. Even if you feel extremely pressed for time, you should set aside at least 12 hours for pre-interview research.

You should arrive at an interview knowing the company upside down and inside out

---

If you have been out of the job market for some time, don't be surprised if you find yourself tense during your first few interviews. It will probably happen every time you re-enter the market, not just when you seek your first job after getting out of school.

Tension is natural during an interview, but if you can be relaxed you will have an advantage. Knowing you have done a thorough research job should put you more at ease. Make a list of questions that you think might be asked in an interview. Think out your answers carefully; practice reviewing

SOME FAVORITE INTERVIEW QUESTIONS

Tell me about yourself...

Why did you leave your last job?

What excites you in your current job?

What are your career goals?

Where would you like to be in 5 years?

What are your greatest strengths?

What are your greatest weaknesses?

Why do you wish to work for this firm?

Where else are you seeking employment?

Why should we hire you?

them with a friend. Tape record your responses to the problem questions. If you feel particularly unsure of your interviewing skills, arrange your first interviews at firms you are not as interested in. (But remember it is common courtesy to seem excited about the possibility of working for any firm at which you interview.) Practice again on your own after these first few interviews. Go over the difficult questions that you were asked.

How important is the proper dress for a job interview? Buying a complete wardrobe of Brooks Brothers pinstripes or Liz Claiborne suits, donning new wing tip shoes or pumps, and having your hair styled every morning is not enough to guarantee you a career position as an investment banker. But on the other hand, if you can't find a clean, conservative suit or a nice skirt and blouse, or won't take the time to wash your hair, then you are just wasting your time by interviewing at all.

Very rarely will the final selection of candidates for a job opening be determined by dress. So don't spend a fortune on a new wardrobe. But be sure that your clothes are adequate. Men applying for any professional position should wear a suit; women should either wear a dress or a suit (but not a pant suit). Your clothes should be at least as formal or slightly more formal and more conservative than the position would suggest.

Top personal grooming is more important than finding the perfect clothes for a job interview. Careful grooming indicates both a sense of thoroughness and self-confidence.

Be sure that your clothes fit well and that they are immaculate. Hair must be neat and clean. Shoes should be newly polished. Women need to avoid excessive jewelry and excessive makeup. Men should be freshly shaven, even if the interview is late in the day.

Be complete. Everyone needs a watch, a pen, and a notepad. Finally, a briefcase or a leather-bound folder (containing extra copies of your resume) will help complete the look of professionalism.

The very beginning of the interview is the most important part because it determines the rapport for the rest of it

Sometimes the interviewer will be running behind schedule. Don't be upset, be sympathetic. There is often pressure to interview a lot of candidates and to quickly fill a demanding position. So be sure to come to your interview with good reading material to keep yourself occupied. This will help you to relax.

The Interview

The very beginning of the interview is the most important part because it determines the rapport for the rest of it. Those first few moments are especially crucial. Do you smile when you meet? Do you establish enough eye contact, but not too much? Do you walk into the office with a self-assured and confident stride? Do you shake hands firmly? Do you make small talk easily without being garrulous? It is human nature to judge people by that first impression, so make sure it is a good one. But most of all, try to be yourself.

Often the interviewer will begin, after the small talk, by telling you about the company, the division, the department, or perhaps, the position. Because of your detailed research, the information about the company should be repetitive for you, and the interviewer would probably like nothing better than to avoid this regurgitation of the company biography. So if you can do so tactfully, indicate to the interviewer that you are very familiar with the firm. If he or she seems intent on providing you with background information, despite your hints, then acquiesce.

But be sure to remain attentive. If you can manage to generate a brief discussion of the company or the industry at this point, without being forceful, great. It will help to further build rapport, underscore your interests, and increase your impact.

If you are really unsure as to how detailed a response the interviewer is seeking, then ask

---

Soon (if it didn't begin that way) the interviewer will begin the questions. This period of the interview falls into one of two categories (or somewhere in between): either a structured interview, where the interviewer has a prescribed set of questions to ask; or an unstructured interview, where the interviewer will ask only leading questions to get you to talk about yourself, your experiences and your goals. Try to sense as quickly as possible which direction the interviewer wishes to proceed. This will make the interviewer feel more relaxed and in control of the situation.

Many of the questions will be similar to the ones that you were expecting and have practiced. Remember to keep attuned to the interviewer and make the length of your answers appropriate to the situation. If you are really unsure as to how detailed a response the interviewer is seeking, then ask.

As the interview progresses, the interviewer will probably mention some of the most important responsibilities of the position. If applicable, draw parallels between your experience and the demands of the position as detailed by the interviewer. Describe your past experience in the same manner that you did on your resume: emphasizing results and achievements and not merely describing activities. If you listen carefully (listening is a very important part of the interviewing process) the interviewer might very well imply the skills needed for the position. Don't exaggerate. Be on the level about your abilities.

Try not to cover too much ground during the first interview. This interview is often the toughest, where many candidates are screened out. If you are interviewing for a very competitive position, you will have to make an impression that will last. Focus on a few of your greatest strengths that are relevant to the position. Develop these points carefully, state them again in other words, and then try to summarize them briefly at the end of the interview.

Often the interviewer will pause towards the end and ask if you have any questions. Particularly in a structured interview, this might be the one chance to really show your knowledge of and interest in the firm. Have a list prepared of specific questions that are of real interest to you. Let your questions subtly show your research and your knowledge of the firm's activities. It is wise to have an extensive list of questions, as several of them may be answered during the interview.

YOU'RE FIRED!!

You are not the first and will not be the last to go through this traumatic experience. Thousands of professionals are fired every week. Remember, being fired is not a reflection on you as a person. It is usually a reflection of your company's staffing needs and its perception of your recent job performance. Share the fact with your relatives and friends. Being fired is not something of which to be ashamed.

Don't start your job search with a flurry of unplanned activity. Start by choosing a strategy and working out a plan. Now is not the time for major changes in your life. If possible, remain in the same career and in the same geographical location, at least until you have been working again for a while. On the other hand, if the only industry for which you are trained is leaving, or is severely depressed in your area, then you should give prompt consideration to moving or switching careers.

Register for unemployment compensation immediately. A thorough job search could take months. After all, your employers have been contributing to unemployment insurance specifically for you ever since your first job. Don't be surprised to find other professionals collecting unemployment compensation as well. Unemployment compensation is for everybody who is between jobs.

Be prepared for the question, "Why were you fired?", during job interviews. Avoid mentioning you were fired while arranging interviews. Try especially hard not to speak negatively of your past employer and not to sound particularly worried about your status of being temporarily unemployed. But don't spend much time reflecting on why you were fired or how you might have avoided it. Learn from your mistakes and then look ahead. Think positively. And be sure to follow a careful plan during your job search.

Do not turn your opportunity to ask questions into an interrogation. Avoid bringing your list of questions to the interview. Ask questions that you are fairly certain the interviewer can answer (remember how you feel when you cannot answer a question during an interview).

Even if you are unable to determine the salary range beforehand, do not ask about it during the first interview. You can always ask about it later. Above all, don't ask about fringe benefits until you have been offered a position. (Then be sure to get all the details.) You should be able to determine the company's policy on fringe benefits relatively easily before the interview.

Try not to be negative about anything during the interview. (Particularly any past employer or any previous job.) Be cheerful. Everyone likes to work with someone who seems to be happy.

Don't let a tough question throw you off base. If you don't know the answer to a question, say so simply -- do not apologize. Just smile. Nobody can answer every question -- particularly some of the questions that are asked in job interviews.

Before your first interview, you may be able to determine how many interviews there usually are for positions at your level. (Of course it may differ quite a bit even within the different levels of one firm.) Usually you can count on attending at least three or four interviews, although some firms, such as some of the professional partnerships, are well-known to give a minimum of six interviews for all professional positions. While you should be more relaxed as you return for subsequent interviews, the pressure will be on. The more prepared you are, the better.

Depending on what information you are able to obtain, you might want to vary your strategy quite a bit from interview to interview. For instance, if the first interview is a screening interview, then be sure a few of your strengths really stand out. On the other hand, if later interviews are primarily with people who are in a position to veto your hiring, but not to push it forward (and few people are weeded out at these stages), then you should primarily focus on building rapport as opposed to reiterating and developing your key strengths.

If it looks as though your skills and background do not match the position your interviewer was hoping to fill, ask him or her if there is another division or subsidiary that perhaps could profit from your talents.

After The Interview

Write a follow-up letter immediately after the interview, while it is still fresh in the interviewer's mind (see the sample follow-up letter format found in the Resumes and Cover Letters section). Then, if you have not heard from the interviewer within seven days, call to stress your continued interest in the firm, and the position, and request a second interview.

A parting word of advice. Again and again during your job search you will be rejected. You will be rejected when you apply for interviews. You will be rejected after interviews. For every job you finally receive, you will have probably been rejected a multitude of times. Don't let rejections slow you down. Keep reminding yourself that the sooner you go out and get started on your job search, and get those rejections flowing in, the closer you will be to obtaining the job you want.

RESUMES AND COVER LETTERS

RESUMES/OVERVIEW

When filling a position, a recruiter will often have 100 plus applicants, but time to interview only the 5 or 10 most promising ones. So he or she will have to reject most applicants after a brief skimming of their resume.

Unless you have phoned and talked to the recruiter -- which you should do whenever you can -- you will be chosen or rejected for an interview entirely on the basis of your resume and cover letter. So your resume must be outstanding. (But remember -- a resume is no substitute for a job search campaign. YOU must seek a job. Your resume is only one tool.)

RESUME PREPARATION

One page, usually

Unless you have an unusually strong background with many years of experience and a large diversity of outstanding achievements, prepare a one page resume. Recruiters dislike long resumes.

8-1/2 x 11 Size

Recruiters often get resumes in batches of hundreds. If your resume is on small sized paper it is likely to get lost in the pile. If oversized, it is likely to get crumpled at the edges, and won't fit in their files.

Typesetting

Modern photocomposition typesetting gives you the clearest, sharpest image, a wide variety of type styles and effects such as italics, bold facing, and book-like justified margins. Typesetting is the best resume preparation process, but is also the most expensive.

Word Processing

The most flexible way to get your resume typed is on a good quality word processor. With word processing, you can make changes almost instantly because your resume will be stored on a magnetic disk and the computer will do all the re-typing automatically. A word processing service will usually offer you a variety of type styles in both regular and proportional spacing. You can have bold facing for emphasis, justified margins, and clear, sharp copies.

Typing

Household typewriters and office typewriters with nylon or other cloth ribbons are NOT good for typing the resume you will have printed. If you can't get word processing or typesetting, hire a professional who uses a high quality office typewriter with a plastic ribbon (usually called a "carbon ribbon").

Printing

Find the best quality offset printing process available. DO NOT make your copies on an office photocopier. Only the personnel office may see the resume you mail. Everyone else may see only a copy of it. Copies of copies quickly become unreadable. Some professionally maintained, extra-high-quality photocopiers are of adequate quality, if you are in a rush. But top quality offset printing is best.

Proofread your resume

Whether you typed it yourself or had it written, typed, or typeset, mistakes on resumes can be embarrassing, particularly when something obvious such as your name is misspelled. No matter how much you paid someone else to type or write or typeset your resume, YOU lose if there is a mistake. So proofread it as carefully as possible. Get a friend to help you. Read your draft aloud as your friend checks the proof copy. Then have your friend read aloud while you check. Next, read it letter by letter to check spelling and punctuation.

If you are having it typed or typeset by a resume service or a printer, and you can't bring a friend or take the time during the day to proof it, pay for it and take it home. Proof it there and bring it back later to get it corrected and printed.

RESUME FORMAT (See samples)

Basic data

Your name, phone number, and a complete address should be at the top of your resume. (If you are a university student, you should also show your home address and phone number.)

Separate your education and work experience

In general, list your experience first. If you have recently graduated, list your education first, unless your experience is more important than your education. (For example, if you have just graduated from a teaching school, have some business experience and are applying for a job in business you would list your business experience first.) If you have two or more years of college, you don't need to list high schools.

Reverse chronological order

To a recruiter your last job and your latest schooling are the most important. So put the last first and list the rest going back in time.

Show dates and locations

Put the dates of your employment and education on the left of the page. Put the names of the companies you worked for and the schools you attended a few spaces to the right of the dates. Put the city and state, or the city and country where you studied or worked to the right of the page.

Avoid sentences and large blocks of type

Your resume will be scanned, not read. Short, concise phrases are much more effective than long-winded sentences. Keep everything easy to find. Avoid paragraphs longer than six lines. Never go ten or more lines in a paragraph. If you have more than six lines of information about one job or school, put it in two or more paragraphs.

<u>RESUME CONTENT</u>

Be factual

In many companies, inaccurate information on a resume or other application material will get you fired as soon as the inaccuracy is discovered. Protect yourself.

Be positive

You are selling your skills and accomplishments in your resume. If you achieved something, say so. Put it in the best possible light. Don't hold back or be modest, no one else will. But don't exaggerate to the point of misrepresentation.

Be brief

Write down the important (and pertinent) things you have done, but do it in as few words as possible. The shorter your resume is, the more carefully it will be examined.

Work experience

Emphasize continued experience in a particular type of function or continued interest in a particular industry. De-emphasize irrelevant positions. Delete positions that you held for less than four months. (Unless you are a very recent college grad or still in school.)

Stress your results

Elaborate on how you contributed to your past employers. Did you increase sales, reduce costs, improve a product, implement a new program? Were you promoted?

Mention relevant skills and responsibilities

Be specific. Slant your past accomplishments toward the type of position that you hope to obtain. Example: Do you hope to supervise people? Then state how many people, performing what function, you have supervised.

Education

Keep it brief if you have more than two years of career experience. Elaborate more if you have less experience. Mention degrees received and any honors or special awards. Note individual courses or research projects that might be relevant for employers. For instance, if you are a liberal arts major, be sure to mention courses in such areas as: accounting, statistics, computer programming, or mathematics.

Job objective

Leave it out. Even if you are certain of exactly the type of job that you desire, the inclusion of a job objective might eliminate you from consideration for other positions that a recruiter feels are a better match for your qualifications.

Personal data

Keep it very brief. Two lines maximum. A one-word mention of commonly practiced activities such as golf, skiing, sailing, chess, bridge, tennis, etc., can prove to be good way to open up a conversation during an interview. Do not include your age, weight, height, etc.

SHOULD YOU HIRE A RESUME WRITER?

If you write reasonably well, there are some advantages to writing your resume yourself. To write it well, you will have to review your experience and figure out how to explain your accomplishments in clear, brief phrases. This will help you when you explain your work to interviewers.

If you write your resume, everything in it will be in your own words -- it will sound like you. It will say what you want it to say. And you will be much more familiar with the contents. If you are a good writer, know yourself well, and have a good idea of what parts of your background employers are looking for, you may be able to write your own resume better than anyone else can. If you write your resume yourself, you should have someone who can be objective (preferably not a close relative) review it with you.

When should you have your resume professionally written?

If you have difficulty writing in "resume style" (which is quite unlike normal written language), if you are unsure of which parts of your background you should emphasize, or if you think your resume would make your case better if it did not follow the standard form outlined here or in a book on resumes, then you should have it professionally written.

There are two reasons even some professional resume writers we know have had their resumes written with the help of fellow professionals. First, when they need the help of someone who can be objective about their background, and second, when they want an experienced sounding board to help focus their thoughts.

If you decide to hire a resume writer

The best way to choose a writer is by reputation -- the recommendation of a friend, a personnel director, your school placement officer or someone else knowledgeable in the field.

You should ask, "If I'm not satisfied with what you write, will you go over it with me and change it?"

You should ask, "How long has the person who will write my resume been writing resumes?"

There is no sure relation between price and quality, except that you are unlikely to get a good writer for less than $50 for an uncomplicated resume and you shouldn't have to pay more than $300 unless your experience is very extensive or complicated. There will be additional charges for printing.

Few resume services will give you a firm price over the phone, simply because some people's resumes are too complicated and take too long to do at any predetermined price. Some services will quote you a price that applies to almost all of their customers. Be sure to do some comparative shopping. Obtain a firm price before you engage their services and find out how expensive minor changes will be.

COVER LETTERS

Always mail a cover letter with your resume. In a cover letter you can show an interest in the company that you can't show in a resume. You can point out one or two skills or accomplishments the company can put to good use.

Make it personal

The more personal you can get, the better. If someone known to the person you are writing has recommended that you contact the company, get permission to include his/her name in the letter. If you have the name of a person to send the letter to, make sure you have the name spelled correctly and address it directly to that person. Be sure to put the person's name and title on both the letter and envelope. This will ensure that your letter will get through to the proper person, even if a new person now occupies this position. But even if you are addressing it to the "Personnel Director" or the "Hiring Partner," send a letter.

Type cover letters in full. Don't try the cheap and easy ways like photocopying the body of your letter and typing in the inside address and salutation. You will give the impression that you are mailing to a multitude of companies and have no particular interest in any one. Have your letters fully typed and signed with a pen.

Bring extra copies of your resume to the interview

If the person interviewing you doesn't have your resume, be prepared. Carry copies of your own. Even if you have already forwarded your resume, be sure to take extra copies to the interview, as someone other than the interviewer(s) might now have the first copy you sent.

FUNCTIONAL RESUME
(Prepared on a word processor and laser printed.)

Michelle Hughes
430 Miller's Crossing
Essex Junction, VT 05452
802/555-9354

Solid background in plate making, separations, color matching, background definition, printing, mechanicals, color corrections, and personnel supervision. A highly motivated manager and effective communicator. Proven ability to:

*Create Commercial Graphic   ***Produce Embossing Drawings**
*Control Quality   ***Resolve Printing Problems**

Qualifications

Printing:
Black and white and color. Can judge acceptability of color reproduction by comparing it with original. Can make four or five color corrections on all media. Have long developed ability to restyle already reproduced four-color artwork. Can create perfect tone for black and white match fill-ins for resume cover letters.

Customer Relations:
Work with customers to assure specifications are met and customers are satisfied. Can guide work through entire production process and strike a balance between technical printing capabilities and need for customer approval.

Specialties:
Make silk screen overlays for a multitude of processes. Velo bind, GBC bind, perfect bind. Have knowledge to prepare posters, flyers, and personalized stationery.

Personnel Supervision:
Foster an atmosphere that encourages highly talented artists to balance high level creativity with a maximum of production. Meet or beat production deadlines. Instruct new employees, apprentices and students in both artistry and technical operations.

Experience
Graphic Arts Professor, University of Vermont, Burlington, VT (1987-present).
Assistant Manager (part time), Design Graphics, Barre, VT (1991-present).

Education
Massachusetts Conservatory of Art, Ph.D. 1987
University of Massachusetts, B.A. 1984

CHRONOLOGICAL RESUME
(Prepared on a word processor and laser printed.)

RICHARD FRAIN
412 Maple Court
Seattle, WA 98404
206/555-6584

EXPERIENCE

1992-present THE CENTER COMPANY, Seattle, WA
Systems Analyst, design systems for the manufacturing unit. Specifically, physical inventory, program specifications, studies of lease buy decisions, selection of hardware for the outside contractors and inside users. Wrote On-Site Computer Terminal Operators Manual. Adapted product mix problems to the LAPSP (Logistical Alternative Product Synthesis Program).

February 1990-February 1992
Industrial Engineer, designed computerized systems. Evaluated operations efficiency, productivity, and budget allocations. Analyzed material waste. Recommended solutions.

ADDITIONAL EXPERIENCE

1986-1990 *Graduate Research Assistant* at New York State Institute of Technology.
1984-1986 *Graduate Teaching Assistant* at Salem State University.

EDUCATION

1988-1990 NEW YORK STATE INSTITUTE OF TECHNOLOGY, Albany, NY
M.S. in Operations Research. GPA: 3.6. Graduate courses included Advanced Location and Queuing Theories, Forecasting, Inventory and Material Flow Systems, Linear and Nonlinear Determination Models, Engineering Economics and Integer Programming.

1986-1988 M.S. in Information and Computer Sciences. GPA: 3.8.
Curriculum included Digital Computer Organization & Programming. Information Structure & Process. Mathematical Logic, Computer Systems, Logic Design, and Switching Theory.

1982-1986 SALEM STATE UNIVERSITY, Salem, OR
B.A. in Mathematics. GPA: 3.6.

AFFILIATIONS

Member of the American Institute of Computer Programmers, Association for Computing Machinery and the Operations Research Society of America.

PERSONAL

Married, three dependents, able to relocate.

CHRONOLOGICAL RESUME
(Prepared on a office quality typewriter.)

Lorraine Avakian
70 Monback Avenue
Oshkosh, WI 54901
Phone: 414/555-4629

Business Experience

NATIONAL PACKAGING PRODUCTS, Princeton, WI
1991-present **District Sales Manager**
Improved 28-member sales group from a company rank in the bottom
thirty percent to the top twenty percent. Complete responsibility
for personnel, including recruiting, hiring and training. Developed
a comprehensive sales improvement program and advised its
implementation in eight additional sales districts.

1988-1990 **Marketing Associate**
Responsible for research, analysis, and presentation of marketing
issues related to long-term corporate strategy. Developed marketing
perspective for capital investment opportunities and acquisition
candidates, which was instrumental in finalizing decisions to make
two major acquisitions and to construct a $35 million canning
plant.

1986-1988 **Salesperson, Paper Division**
Responsible for a four-county territory in central Wisconsin.
Increased sales from $700,000 to over $1,050,000 annually in a 15
month period. Developed six new accounts with incremental sales
potential of $800,000. Only internal candidate selected for new
marketing program.

AMERICAN PAPER PRODUCTS, INC., Oshkosh, WI
1985-1986 **Sales Trainee**
Completed intensive six month training program and promoted to
salesperson status. Received the President's Award for superior
performance in the sales training program.

HENDUKKAR SPORTING GOODS, INC., Oshkosh, WI
1985 **Assistant Store Manager**
Supervised six employees on the evening shift. Handled accounts
receivable.

Education

1979-1984 **BELOIT COLLEGE**, Beloit, WI
Received Bachelor of Science Degree in Business Administration in
June 1982. Varsity Volleyball. Financed 50% of educational costs
through part-time and co-op program employment.

Personal Background

Able to relocate; Excellent health; Active in community activities.

CHRONOLOGICAL RESUME
(Prepared on a word processor and laser printed.)

Melvin Winter
43 Aspen Wall Lane
Wheaton, IL 60512
312/555-6923 (home)
312/555-3000 (work)

Related Experience

GREAT LAKES PUBLISHING COMPANY, Chicago, IL
Operations Supervisor (1990-present)
in the Engineering Division of large trade publishing house. Maintain on-line computerized customer files, title files, accounts receivable, inventory and sales files. Organize department activities, establish priorities and train personnel. Provide corporate accounting with monthly reports of sales, earned income from journals, samples, inventory levels/value and sales and tax data. Divisional sales average $3 million annually.

Senior Customer Service Representative (1988-1990)
in the Construction Division. Answered customer service inquiries regarding orders and accounts receivable, issued return and shortage credits and expedited special sales orders for direct mail and sales to trade schools.

Customer Service Representative (1986-1987)
in the International Division. Same duties as for construction division except that sales were to retail stores and universities in Europe.

B. DALTON, BOOKSELLER, Salt Lake City, UT
Assistant Manager (1984-1986)
of this retail branch of a major domestic book seller, maintained all paperback inventories at necessary levels, deposited receipts daily and created window displays.

Education

1980-1984 UNIVERSITY OF MAINE, Orono, ME
Awarded a degree of Bachelor of Arts in French Literature.

Languages

Fluent in French. Able to write in French, German and Spanish.

Personal

Willing to travel and relocate, particularly in Europe.

References available upon request.

General Model for a Cover Letter

Your address
Date

Contact Person Name
Title
Company
Address

Dear Mr./Ms._____:

Immediately explain why your background makes you the best candidate for the position that you are applying for. Keep the first paragraph short and hard-hitting.

Detail what you could contribute to this company. Show how your qualifications will benefit this firm. Remember to keep this letter short; few recruiters will read a cover letter longer than half a page.

Describe your interest in the corporation. Subtly emphasize your knowledge about this firm (the result of your research effort) and your familiarity with the industry. It is common courtesy to act extremely eager to work for any company that you interview with.

In the closing paragraph you should specifically request an interview. Include your phone number and the hours when you can be reached. Alternatively, you might prefer to mention that you will follow up with a phone call (to arrange an interview at a mutually convenient time within the next several days).

Sincerely,
(signature)

Your full name
(typed)

General Model for a Follow-Up Letter

Your Address
Date

Contact Person Name
Title
Company
Address

Dear Mr./Ms._____:

Remind the interviewer of the position for which you were interviewed, as well as the date. Thank him/her for the interview.

Confirm your interest in the opening and the organization. Use specifics to emphasize both that you have researched the firm in detail and considered how you would fit into the company and the position.

As in your cover letter, emphasize one or two of you strongest qualifications and slant them toward the various points that the interviewer considered the most important for the position. Keep the letter brief, a half-page is plenty.

If appropriate, close with a suggestion for further action, such as a desire to have additional interviews. Mention your phone number and the hours that you can best be reached. Alternatively, you may prefer to mention that you will follow up with a phone call in several days.

Sincerely yours,
(signature)

Your full name
(typed)

PRIMARY EMPLOYERS

ACCOUNTING/MANAGEMENT CONSULTING

Receipts for accounting and bookkeeping services have been climbing in recent years, up 5 percent from 1992 to 1993. And while the Big Six generate most of the industry's revenues, their growth has been slower than that of smaller accounting houses.

In the past few years, the industry has undergone some changes. Accounting firms are dropping clients that fall into high-risk categories, like savings and loans; and other accounting houses are refusing to take on new, risky clients. Auditors and accountants are being asked to play a bigger role in evaluating the way corporations are run, and improve their data in order to evaluate and project management's performance.

A new trend is evolving on the employment scene -- CPA firms, both large and small, are taking care of staffing needs by hiring accounting paraprofessionals. While billing rates remain the same because their skills are similar, there are significant in-house savings between the paraprofessionals and staff professionals. The cost of fringe benefits is reduced by hiring paraprofessionals, most of whom work part-time.

ARTHUR ANDERSEN & COMPANY
801 2nd Avenue, Suite 800
Seattle WA 98104
206/623-8023
Contact: Human Resources Department
Description: One of the nation's leading accounting firms.

R.W. BECK
2101 Fourth Avenue, Suite 600
Seattle WA 98121-2375
206/727-4484
Fax: 206/441-4960
Contact: Van Finger, Director of Human Resources
Description: R.W. Beck is a partnership of professional engineers and consultants that provides professional, technical, and management consulting services to the electric utility and other energy-intensive industries. Headquartered in Seattle, Washington, R.W. Beck has over 650 employees in its 10 regional offices. **Common positions include:** Civil Engineer; Designer; Economist/Market Research Analyst; Electrical/Electronic Engineer; Financial Analyst; Management Analyst/Consultant; Mechanical Engineer; Technical Writer/Editor. **Educational backgrounds include:** Economics; Engineering; Finance. **Benefits:** 401K; Dental Insurance;

Disability Coverage; Life Insurance; Medical Insurance; Pension Plan; Tuition Assistance. **Corporate headquarters location:** This Location. **Operations at this facility include:** Administration; Service. **Number of employees at this location:** 230. **Number of employees nationwide:** 650.

DELOITTE & TOUCHE
700 5th Avenue, Suite 4500
Seattle WA 98104-5044
206/292-1800
Contact: Human Resource Manager
Description: A certified public accounting firm.

ERNST & YOUNG
999 Third Avenue, Suite 3500
Seattle WA 98104
206/621-1800
Contact: Human Resources Department
Description: An international professional services firm. Other U.S. locations: 100+ different locations. **Common positions include:** Accountant/Auditor; Actuary; Computer Programmer; Financial Analyst; Systems Analyst. **Educational backgrounds include:** Accounting; Business Administration; Computer Science; Economics; Finance. **Benefits:** Dental Insurance; Life Insurance; Medical Insurance; Pension Plan. **Corporate headquarters location:** New York NY.

MILLIMAN & ROBERTSON INC.
1301 5th Avenue, Suite 3800
Seattle WA 98101-2605. 206/624-7940.
Contact: Personnel Department
Description: A nationwide actuarial service company. **Common positions include:** Actuary. **Educational backgrounds include:** Computer Science; Mathematics. **Benefits:** Life Insurance; Medical Insurance; Pension Plan; Profit Sharing; Savings Plan. **Corporate headquarters location:** This Location. **Operations at this facility include:** Administration; Service.

SHANNON & WILSON
P.O. Box 300303
Seattle WA 98103
206/632-8020
Contact: Roy Salley, President
Description: Provides geotechnical consulting services to a variety of industrial and governmental clients. Services include foundation engineering studies, waste management, and construction monitoring. **Corporate headquarters location:** This Location.

Note: Because addresses and telephone numbers of smaller companies change rapidly, we recommend you call each company and verify the information below before mailing to employers. Mass mailings are not recommended.

Additional employers with under 250 employees:

MANAGEMENT SERVICES

GTM Inc.
1801 Roeder Avenue, #208, Bellingham WA 98225-2200.
206/671-8900.

S&W Management Company
20062 19th Avenue, NW, Seattle WA 98155-1211.
206/362-2255.

MANAGEMENT CONSULTING SERVICES

Howard Johnson & Company
1111 3rd Avenue, Suite 1700, Seattle WA 98101-3275.
206/625-1040.

BUSINESS CONSULTING SERVICES

Education Systems Technology Corporation
18303 194th Avenue, NE, Woodinville WA 98072-8872.
206/788-4988.

For more information on career opportunities in accounting/management consulting:

Associations

AMERICAN ACCOUNTING ASSOCIATION
5717 Bessie Drive, Sarasota FL 34233. 813/921-7747.

AMERICAN INSTITUTE OF CERTIFIED PUBLIC ACCOUNTANTS
1211 Avenue, of the Americas, New York NY 10036. 212/596-6200.

AMERICAN MANAGEMENT ASSOCIATION
Management Information Service, 135 West 50th Street, New York NY 10020. 212/586-8100.

ASSOCIATION OF GOVERNMENT ACCOUNTANTS
2200 Mount Vernon Avenue, Alexandria VA 22301. 703/684-6931.

ASSOCIATION OF MANAGEMENT CONSULTING FIRMS
521 Fifth Avenue, 35th Floor, New York NY 10175. 212/697-9693.

COUNCIL OF CONSULTANT ORGANIZATIONS
521 Fifth Avenue, 35th Floor, New York NY 10175. 212/697-8262.

FEDERATION OF TAX ADMINISTRATORS
444 North Capital Street NW, Washington DC 20001. 202/624-5890.

INSTITUTE OF INTERNAL AUDITORS
49 Maitland Avenue, Altamont Springs FL 32701. 407/830-7600.

INSTITUTE OF MANAGEMENT CONSULTANTS
521 Fifth Avenue, 35th Floor, New York NY 10175. 212/697-8262.

INSTITUTE OF MANAGEMENT ACCOUNTING
10 Paragon Drive, Box 433, Montvale NJ 07645-1760. 201/573-9000.

NATIONAL ASSOCIATION OF TAX CONSULTORS
454 North 13th Street, San Jose CA 95112. 408/298-1458.

NATIONAL ASSOCIATION OF TAX PRACTITIONERS
720 Association Drive, Appleton WI 54914. 414/749-1040.

NATIONAL SOCIETY OF PUBLIC ACCOUNTANTS
1010 North Fairfax Street, Alexandria VA 22314. 703/549-6400.

Directories

AICPA DIRECTORY OF ACCOUNTING EDUCATION
American Institute of Certified Public Accountants, 1211 Avenue of the Americas, New York NY 10036. 212/596-6200.

ACCOUNTING FIRMS AND PRACTITIONERS
American Institute of Certified Public Accountants, 1211 Avenue of the Americas, New York NY 10036. 212/596-6200.

Magazines

CPA JOURNAL
200 Park Avenue, New York NY 10166. 212/719-8300.

CPA LETTER
American Institute of Certified Public Accountants, 1211 Avenue of the Americas, New York NY 10036. 212/575-6200.

JOURNAL OF ACCOUNTANCY
American Institute of Certified Public Accountants, 1211 Avenue of the Americas, New York NY 10036. 212/596-6200.

MANAGEMENT ACCOUNTING
Institute of Management Accounting, 10 Paragon Drive, Montvale NJ 07645. 201/573-9000.

WENDELL'S REPORT FOR CONTROLLERS
Warren, Gorham, and Lamont, Inc., 210 South Street, Boston MA 02111. 617/423-2020.

ADVERTISING, MARKETING AND PUBLIC RELATIONS

The long recession forced advertising firms to tighten their money belts as client companies slashed advertising budgets. Now PR firms and advertising houses are keeping employment levels at a minimum, hoping to boost efficiency. The industry should improve as the businesses inject more advertising dollars into the economy.

Analysts point to two factors which could make competition even tighter. One is television, which accounts for a quarter of all advertising expenditures. A new FCC rule will allow networks to make more money from syndication of shows on cable television, reducing their dependence on advertising dollars. Another factor is that Congress, in an effort to reduce the federal deficit, may eliminate business tax deductions for the cost of advertising certain products. Loss of this tax break could force some companies to cut advertising dollars. Affected products could include tobacco, pharmaceuticals, and children's products.

ACKERLY COMMUNICATIONS INC.
800 5th Avenue, Suite 3770
Seattle WA 98104
206/624-2888
Contact: Personnel Department
Description: Engaged in outdoor and airport advertising, professional basketball advertising, television advertising, and advertising for real estate agents and brokers.

AMERICAN PASSAGE MEDIA CORPORATION
215 West Harrison
Seattle WA 98119
206/282-8111
Contact: Human Resources Department
Description: Offers mail order and other advertising placement services.

BORDERS, PERRIN & NORRANDER
1008 Western Avenue, Suite 401
Seattle WA 98104
206/343-7741
Contact: Personnel Department
Description: An advertising agency.

BREMS EASTMAN GLADE, INC.
3131 Elliott Avenue, Suite 280
Seattle WA 98121
206/284-9400
Contact: Personnel Department
Description: An advertising agency.

COLE & WEBER INC.
308 Occidental Avenue South
Seattle WA 98104
206/447-9595
Contact: Personnel Department
Description: An advertising agency.

COLOR AND DESIGN EXHIBITS, INC.
2015 Airport Way South
Seattle WA 98134
206/622-7754
Contact: Human Resources
Description: Produces signs, exhibits, and other advertising media.

ELGIN SYFERD/DDB NEEDHAM
1008 Western Avenue, Suite 601
Seattle WA 98104
206/442-9900
Contact: Human Resources
Description: An advertising agency.

EVANS GROUP, INC.
190 Queen Anne North
Seattle WA 98109
206/285-2222
Contact: Personnel Department
Description: An advertising agency.

LIVINGSTON & COMPANY ADVERTISING
800 5th Avenue, Suite 3800
Seattle WA 98104
206/382-5500
Fax: 206/622-4532
Contact: Personnel Department
Description: An advertising agency. Privately held. **Common positions include:** Account Executive; Administrative Worker/Clerk; Art Director; Buyer; Copywriter; Layout Specialist; Production Coordinator; Secretary. **Benefits:** 401K; Medical Insurance. **Special Programs:** Internships.

McCANN-ERICKSON/SEATTLE
1011 Western Avenue, Suite 600
Seattle WA 98104
206/682-6360
Contact: Amanda Dwyer, Office Manager
Description: An advertising agency. **Common positions include:** Advertising Clerk. **Educational backgrounds include:** Advertising; Art/Design; Marketing. **Benefits:** Dental Insurance; Disability Coverage; Life Insurance; Medical Insurance; Savings Plan; Stock Option; Tuition Assistance. **Special Programs:** Internships. **Corporate headquarters location:** New York NY. **Parent company:** Interpublic Group of Companies, Inc. **Operations at this facility include:** Administration; Sales; Service. **Listed on:** New York Stock Exchange. **Number of employees at this location:** 50.

SHARP HARTWIG, INC.
1008 Western Avenue, Suite 201
Seattle WA 98119
206/282-6242
Contact: Personnel Department
Description: An advertising agency.

THOMPSON RECRUITMENT ADVERTISING INC.
720 Olive Way, Suite 1203
Seattle WA 98101
206/623-2620
Contact: Deborah Buckley, Branch Manager
Description: Nationally, the firm is an advertising agency specializing in personnel recruitment advertising, human resources management systems, and employee communications. **Corporate headquarters location:** Los Angeles CA.

WHITERUNKLE ASSOCIATES
505 West Riverside, Suite 300
Spokane WA 99201
509/747-6767
Contact: Jack C. White, President
Description: An advertising agency. **Common positions include:** Accountant/Auditor; Advertising Account Executive; Advertising Clerk; Commercial Artist; Marketing Specialist; Technical Writer/Editor. **Educational backgrounds include:** Accounting; Art/Design; Communications; Liberal Arts; Marketing. **Benefits:** Dental Insurance; Medical Insurance; Profit Sharing. **Special Programs:** Internships; Training Programs. **Corporate headquarters location:** This Location. **Operations at this facility include:** Administration; Service. **Annual Revenues:** $4,200,000. **Number of employees at this location:** 18.

WILLIAMS & HELDE
3161 Elliot Avenue, Suite 300
Seattle WA 98121
206/285-1940
Contact: Personnel Department
Description: An advertising agency.

Note: Because addresses and telephone numbers of smaller companies change rapidly, we recommend you call each company and verify the information below before mailing to employers. Mass mailings are not recommended.

Additional employers with under 250 employees:

PUBLIC RELATIONS SERVICES

Golin Harris Communications
800 Bellevue Way 400, Bellevue WA 98004. 206/462-4220.

SIGNS AND ADVERTISING SPECIALTIES

American Sign & Indicator Corporation
1013 South Mariam Street, Spokane WA 99206-3552. 509/926-6979.

Color & Design Exhibits
2015 Airport Way South, Seattle WA 98134-1602. 206/622-7754.

RADIO, TELEVISION AND PUBLISHING REPRESENTATIVES

KXLY Newsradio AM 920/FM 100
500 West Boone Avenue, Spokane WA 99201-2404. 509/328-6292.

McGavern-Guild Inc.
2505 2nd Avenue, Seattle WA 98121-1464. 206/441-3401.

DIRECT MAIL ADVERTISING SERVICES

Greater Seattle Printing
4528 150th Avenue NE, Redmond WA 98052-5303. 206/885-9015.

Kaye Smith Business Graphics
P.O. Box 956, Renton WA 98057-0956. 206/228-8600.

Laserdirect Inc.
19026 72nd Avenue South, Kent WA 98032-1005. 206/251-6688.

For more information on career opportunities in advertising, marketing, and public relations:

<u>Associations</u>

ADVERTISING RESEARCH FOUNDATION
641 Lexington Avenue, New York NY 10022. 212/751-5656.

AFFILIATED ADVERTISING AGENCIES INTERNATIONAL
2280 South Xanadu Way, Suite 300
Aurora CO 80014. 303/671-8551.

AMERICAN ASSOCIATION OF ADVERTISING AGENCIES
666 Third Avenue, New York NY 10017. 212/682-2500.

AMERICAN MARKETING ASSOCIATION
250 South Wacker Drive, Suite 200, Chicago IL 60606. 312/648-0536.

BUSINESS-PROFESSIONAL ADVERTISING ASSOCIATION
901 North Washington Street, Suite 206, Alexandria VA 22314. 703/683-2722.

DIRECT MARKETING ASSOCIATION
11 West 42nd Street, New York NY 10036. 212/768-7277

INTERNATIONAL ADVERTISING ASSOCIATION
342 Madison Avenue, Suite 2000, New York NY 10017. 212/557-1133.

LEAGUE OF ADVERTISING AGENCIES
2 South End Avenue #4C, New York NY 10280. 212/945-4991.

MARKETING RESEARCH ASSOCIATION
2189 Silas Deane Highway, Suite #5, Rocky Hill CT 06067. 203/257-4008.

PUBLIC RELATIONS SOCIETY OF AMERICA
33 Irving Place, New York NY 10003. 212/995-2230.

TELEVISION BUREAU OF ADVERTISING
850 3rd Avenue, 10th Floor, New York NY 10022-5892. 212/486-1111.

Directories

AAAA ROSTER AND ORGANIZATION
American Association of Advertising Agencies, 666 Third Avenue, New York NY 10017. 212/682-2500.

DIRECTORY OF MINORITY PUBLIC RELATIONS PROFESSIONALS
Public Relations Society of America, 33 Irving Place, New York NY 10003. 212/995-2230.

O'DWYER'S DIRECTORY OF PUBLIC RELATIONS FIRMS
J. R. O'Dwyer Company, 271 Madison Avenue, New York NY 10016. 212/679-2471.

PUBLIC RELATIONS CONSULTANTS DIRECTORY
American Business Directories, Division of American Business Lists, 5711 South 86th Circle, Omaha NE 68127. 402/593-4500.

PUBLIC RELATIONS JOURNAL REGISTER ISSUE
Public Relations Society of America, 33 Irving Place, New York NY 10003. 212/995-2230.

STANDARD DIRECTORY OF ADVERTISING AGENCIES
National Register Publishing Company, P.O. Box 31, New Providence NY 07974. 800/521-8110.

Magazines

ADVERTISING AGE
Crain Communications, 740 North Rush Street, Chicago IL 60611. 312/649-5316.

ADWEEK
1515 Broadway, 12th Floor, New York NY 10036. 212/536-5336.

BUSINESS MARKETING
Crain Communications, 740 North Rush Street, Chicago IL 60611. 312/649-5260.

JOURNAL OF MARKETING
American Marketing Association, 250 South Wacker Drive, Suite 200, Chicago IL 60606. 312/648-0536.

THE MARKETING NEWS
American Marketing Association, 250 South Wacker Drive, Suite 200, Chicago IL 60606. 312/648-0536.

PR REPORTER
PR Publishing Company, P.O. Box 600, Exeter NH 03833. 603/778-0514.

PUBLIC RELATIONS JOURNAL
Public Relations Society of America, 33 Irving Place, New York NY 10003. 212/995-2230.

PUBLIC RELATIONS NEWS
Phillips Publishing Inc., 1202 Seven Locks Road, Suite 300, Potomac MD 20854. 301/340-1520.

AEROSPACE

 *Despite some predictions that the aerospace industry would make a comeback in the '90s, aerospace manufacturers are still facing turbulent skies. Industry shipments are still dropping due to continued cuts in the defense budget, a weak global economy and growing competition from overseas.*

The downturn in the industry has caused severe job losses. According to the U.S. Bureau of Labor Statistics, between 1989 and 1993 total aerospace employment fell from 912,000 to 615,000. That translates to a layoff rate of almost 6,000 aerospace jobs lost every month from December 1989 to June 1993. The future does not look much better. In the words of the U.S. Department of Commerce, "Aerospace companies will continue to severely reduce their employment levels."

ALLIEDSIGNAL COMMERCIAL AVIONICS SYSTEMS
15001 NE 36th Street
Redmond WA 98073
206/885-3711
Contact: Personnel Department
Description: Designs and develops avionic systems for commercial and military aircraft. **Number of employees at this location: 950.**

THE BOEING COMPANY
P.O. Box 3707, Mail Stop 6H-PL
Seattle WA 98124
206/655-1131
Contact: Human Resources
Description: Manufactures aerospace, aircraft, and electronic systems for commercial and military applications.

BOEING FABRICATION DIVISION
P.O. Box 3707, MS 31-11
Seattle WA 98124-2207
206/931-2121
Contact: Human Resources Department
Description: A division of the aircraft manufacturer.

DOWTY AEROSPACE YAKIMA

P.O. Box 9907
Yakima WA 98909
509/248-5000
Contact: Bette Taylor, Personnel Director
Description: A manufacturer of aerospace components and equipment.
Common positions include: Bookkeeper; Buyer; Department Manager;
Draftsperson; Hydraulic Tester; Inspector/Tester/Grader; Marketing
Specialist; Mechanical Engineer; Personnel/Labor Relations Specialist;
Production Coordinator; Production Manager; Quality Control Supervisor.
Benefits: Dental Insurance; Disability Coverage; Life Insurance; Medical
Insurance; Pension Plan; Profit Sharing; Tuition Assistance. Corporate
headquarters location: This Location. Operations at this facility include:
Administration; Manufacturing; Sales.

EXOTIC METALS FORMING COMPANY

5411 South 226th Street
Kent WA 98032
206/395-3710
Contact: Human Resources
Description: Manufactures aircraft engine parts.

HEATH TECNA AEROSPACE COMPANY

P.O. Box 97004
Kent WA 98064-9704
206/872-7500
Contact: Human Resources Department
Description: An aircraft equipment parts and supplies company.

K&M ENTERPRISES

14666 NE 95th Street
Redmond WA 98052
206/869-9884
Contact: Human Resources
Description: An aircraft equipment manufacturer.

OLIN AEROSPACE

11441 Willows Road NE
Redmond WA 98052
206/885-5000
Contact: Employment Manager
Description: Olin Aerospace is comprised of two divisions. Rocket Research
Company is engaged in the research and development of liquid
monopropellant rocket engines/gas generators for space flight application
and solid propellant inflation devices. Pacific Electro Dynamics Company is
engaged in the research and development of analog power supply devices
and digital avionics ground test equipment for aerospace applications.
Common positions include: Aerospace Engineer; Buyer; Chemist;

Draftsperson; Electrical/Electronic Engineer; Industrial Engineer; Mechanical Engineer; Metallurgical Engineer. **Educational backgrounds include:** Business Administration; Engineering. **Benefits:** Dental Insurance; Disability Coverage; Employee Discounts; Life Insurance; Medical Insurance; Pension Plan; Savings Plan; Tuition Assistance. **Special Programs:** Internships. **Corporate headquarters location:** Stamford CT. **Parent company:** Olin Corporation. **Listed on:** New York Stock Exchange. **Number of employees nationwide:** 800.

TRAMCO, INC.
11323 30th Avenue West
Everett WA 98204
206/347-3030
Contact: Human Resources Department
Description: Manufactures aircraft engines and engine parts.

TWIN COMMANDER AIRCRAFT CORPORATION
19003 59th Drive NE
Arlington WA 98223
206/435-9797
Contact: Human Resources
Description: An aerospace company.

Note: Because addresses and telephone numbers of smaller companies change rapidly, we recommend you call each company and verify the information below before mailing to employers. Mass mailings are not recommended.

Additional employers with over 250 employees:

AIRCRAFT PARTS

Allfab Inc.
Building C-19 Paine Field, Everett WA 98204. 206/353-8080.

Northwest Composites
P.O. Box 1209, Marysville WA 98270-1209. 206/653-2211.

AIRCRAFT AND AEROSPACE PRODUCTS

Aero Specialty Manufacturing
100 Junior Point Court, Chelan WA 98816. 509/682-5082.

AEROSPACE PRODUCTS

Certified Holding Corporation
11410 Beverly Park Road, Everett WA 98204-3584. 206/356-2626.

Northwest Composites
501 North Newport Avenue, Newport WA 99156-9049. 509/447-4122.

Additional employers with under 250 employees:

AIRCRAFT PARTS

Aim Aviation Inc.
705 SW 7th Street,
Renton WA 98055-
2915. 206/235-2750.

Flight Structures Inc.
18810 59th Avenue
NE, Arlington WA
98223-8763.
206/435-8831.

Modern Manufacturing
2900 Lind Avenue
SW, Renton WA
98055-4036.
206/251-1515.

NTP Inc.
1820 West Valley
Highway, Auburn WA
98001-1645.
206/939-4936.

Precision Aerospace
1516 Fryar Avenue,
Sumner WA 98390-
1514. 206/863-7868.

Spectra-Lux Corp.
11825 120th Avenue
NE, Kirkland WA
98034-7108.
206/823-6857.

For more information on career opportunities in aerospace:

Associations

**AIR TRANSPORT ASSOCIATION
OF AMERICA**
1301 Pennsylvania Avenue NW,
Suite 1100, Washington DC 20004.
202/626-4000.

**AMERICAN INSTITUTE OF
AERONAUTICS AND
ASTRONAUTICS**
555 West 57th Street, New York NY
10019. 212/247-6500.

**FUTURE AVIATION
PROFESSIONALS OF AMERICA**
4959 Massachusetts Boulevard,
Atlanta GA 30337. 404/997-8097.

**NATIONAL AERONAUTIC
ASSOCIATION OF USA**
1815 North Fort Meyer Drive, Suite
700, Arlington VA 22209. 703/527-
0226.

**PROFESSIONAL AVIATION
MAINTENANCE ASSOCIATION**
500 NW Plaza, Suite 1016, Street.
Ann MO 63074. 314/739-2580.

APPAREL AND TEXTILES

After employment gains for four straight years in the late '80s, layoffs hit this industry hard as the '90s opened. And while shipments continued to increase in 1993, employment continued to drop. Production line work has dropped off for two reasons. First, foreign producers have increased their share of the U.S. market. Second, automation has replaced many positions, so future jobs will not consist of old-style production-line work. Jobseekers with technical and computer backgrounds have a distinct advantage.

CENTURY 21 PROMOTIONS INC.
2601 West Commodore Way
Seattle WA 98199
206/282-8827
Contact: Personnel Department
Description: An importer of hats, caps, and jackets.

PGL BUILDING PRODUCTS
P.O. Box 1049
Auburn WA 98071
206/941-2600
Contact: Human Resources
Description: A manufacturer of carpets and rugs.

PACIFIC TRAIL INC.
1310 Mercer Street
Seattle WA 98109
206/622-8730
Contact: Ann Sheldon, Merchandise Coordinator
Description: A manufacturer of jackets and related outerwear products.

PENDLETON WOOLEN MILLS
P.O. Box 145
Washougal WA 98671
206/835-2131
Contact: Human Resources
Description: A wool fabric mill.

Note: Because addresses and telephone numbers of smaller companies change rapidly, we recommend you call each company and verify the information below before mailing to employers. Mass mailings are not recommended.

Additional employers with over 250 employees:

WOMEN'S CLOTHING

KL Manufacturing Co.
703 North 7th Street,
Chewelah WA 99109.
509/935-8447

KL Manufacturing Co.
2726 North Monroe
Street, Spokane WA
99205-3355.
509/326-2350.

Additional employers with under 250 employees:

TEXTILE GOODS

Buffalo Industries
99 South Spokane
Street, Seattle WA
98134-2218.
206/682-9900.

MEN'S AND BOYS' NECKWEAR

Mallory & Church Corporation
6709 South Industrial
Way, Seattle WA
98108. 206/587-2100.

MEN'S AND BOYS' CLOTHING

Big Sky Washington
4020 South 56th
Street, Tacoma WA
98409-2610.
206/473-3096.

Down Products Corporation
1555 4th Avenue
South, Seattle WA
98134-1511.
206/223-2283.

Roffe Inc.
808 Howell Street,
Seattle WA 98101-1311. 206/622-0456.

Seattle Pacific Industries
P.O. Box 58710,
Seattle WA 98138-1710. 206/282-8889.

WOMEN'S AND MISSES' SUITS AND SKIRTS

Item House Inc.
2920 South Steele
Street, Tacoma WA
98409-7630.
206/627-7168.

WOMEN'S AND MISSES' OUTERWEAR

J Marcel Enterprises
5920 Martin Luther
King Jr. Way, Seattle
WA 98118-2626.
206/722-1412.

GIRLS' AND CHILDREN'S OUTERWEAR

Big Sky USA Inc.
4020 South 56th
Street, Tacoma WA
98409-2610.
206/471-9900.

CURTAINS AND DRAPERIES

American Drapery & Blind
3811 East Sprague
Avenue, Spokane WA
99202-4844.
509/534-8000.

FABRICATED TEXTILE PRODUCTS

Columbia Industries
P.O. Box 7346,
Kennewick WA
99336-0617.
509/582-4142.

Multifab SBI Inc.
3808 North Sullivan
Road Building 6,
Spokane WA 99216-
1618. 509/924-6631.

North Sails Seattle
6319 Seaview Avenue
NW, Seattle WA
98107-2664.
206/789-4950.

For more information on career opportunities in the apparel and textiles industries:

Associations

AFFILIATED DRESS MANUFACTURERS
225 West 39th, 5th Floor, New York
NY 10018.

AMERICAN APPAREL MANUFACTURERS ASSOCIATION
2500 Wilson Boulevard, Suite 301,
Arlington VA 22201. 703/524-1864.

AMERICAN CLOAK AND SUIT MANUFACTURERS ASSOCIATION
450 Seventh Avenue, New York NY
10123. 212/244-7300.

THE FASHION GROUP
597 5th Avenue, 8th Floor, New
York NY 10017. 212/593-1715.

INTERNATIONAL ASSOCIATION OF CLOTHING DESIGNERS
475 Park Avenue South, 17th Floor,
New York NY 10016. 212/685-
6602.

Directories

AAMA DIRECTORY
American Apparel Manufacturers
Association, 2500 Wilson
Boulevard, Suite 301, Arlington VA
22201. 703/524-1864.

APPAREL TRADES BOOK
Dun & Bradstreet Inc., 430
Mountain Avenue, New Providence
NJ 07974. 908/665-5000.

FAIRCHILD'S MARKET DIRECTORY OF WOMEN'S AND CHILDREN'S APPAREL
Fairchild Publications, 7 West 34th
Street, New York NY 10001.
212/630-4000.

Magazines

AMERICA'S TEXTILES
Billiam Publishing, 37 Villa Road,
Suite 111, P.O. Box 103 Greenville
SC 29615. 803/242-5300.

APPAREL INDUSTRY MAGAZINE
Shore Communications Inc., 6255
Barfield Road, Suite 200, Atlanta
GA 30328-4893. 404/252-8831.

ACCESSORIES
Business Journals, 50 Day Street,
P.O. Box 5550, Norwalk CT 06856.
203/853-6015.

BOBBIN
Bobbin Publications, P.O. Box
1986, 1110 Shop Road, Columbia
SC 29202. 803/771-7500.

WOMEN'S WEAR DAILY (WWD)
Fairchild Publications, 7 West 34th
Street, New York NY 10001.
212/630-4000.

ARCHITECTURE, CONSTRUCTION AND ENGINEERING

In the construction industry, home building is expected to stabilize, but commercial real estate construction -- particularly office buildings and hotels -- will continue to decline. Home improvement, hospitals, schools, water supply buildings, and public service buildings construction should offer the best opportunities.

Job prospects for engineers have been good for a number of years, and will continue to improve into the next century. Employers will need more engineers as they increase investment in equipment in order to expand output. In addition, engineers will find work improving the nation's deteriorating infrastructure.

ABAM ENGINEERS INC.
33301 Ninth Avenue South
Federal Way WA 98003
206/952-6100
Contact: Personnel Administrator
Description: A consulting and civil engineering firm specializing in the design of piers and waterfront structures, tanks and reservoirs, bridges, transit guideways, buildings, floating structures and offshore drilling platforms. In addition to design, the firm performs concrete material research, advanced computer design analysis, and construction management. **Common positions include:** Accountant/Auditor; Civil Engineer; Draftsperson; Marketing Specialist; Structural Engineer. **Educational backgrounds include:** Accounting; Business Administration; Computer Science; Engineering; Marketing. **Benefits:** Dental Insurance; Disability Coverage; Life Insurance; Medical Insurance; Tuition Assistance. **Corporate headquarters location:** This Location.

ANVIL CORPORATION
1675 West Bakerview Road
Bellingham WA 98226
206/755-9350
Contact: Human Resources Department
Description: An engineering corporation.

ROBERT E. BAYLEY CONSTRUCTION
P.O. Box 4567
Seattle WA 98104-0567
206/621-8884
Contact: Personnel Department
Description: A general building contractor, also specializing in commercial construction.

BROWN AND CALDWELL
100 West Harrison Street
Seattle WA 98119-4186
206/281-4000
Contact: Personnel Director
Description: A nationwide consulting firm offering technical services in environmental, engineering, planning, design, and construction management.

GORDON BROWN INC.
P.O. Box 18225
Seattle WA 98118
206/722-2100
Contact: Personnel Department
Description: Engaged in drywall plastering and acoustical tile contracting.

CH2M HILL
P.O. Box 91500
Bellevue WA 98009-2050
206/453-5000
Contact: Human Resources Department
Description: An engineering company.

THE CALLISON PARTNERSHIP, LTD.
1420 Fifth Avenue, Suite 2400
Seattle WA 98101
206/623-4646
Contact: Human Resources
Description: A firm involved in architecture, interior design, and space planning and programming.

CAPITAL DEVELOPMENT COMPANY
P.O. Box 3487
Lacey WA 98503-0487
206/491-6850
Contact: Gary Blume, Executive Vice President
Description: Engaged in a variety of construction activities, including contracting, leasing, and property development and management. Other activities include: lumber resource development.

CHRISTENSON RABER KIEF & ASSOCIATES
P.O. Box 3923
Seattle WA 98124-3923
206/762-4215
Contact: Personnel Department
Description: A construction company engaged in non-residential building construction, heavy construction, and contracting.

COCHRAN ELECTRIC COMPANY INC.
P.O. Box 33524
Seattle WA 98133-0524
206/367-1900
Contact: Personnel Department
Description: A company involved in commercial and industrial electrical work and power-line engineering.

EDAW INC.
1505 Western Avenue, Suite 601
Seattle WA 98101
206/622-1176
Contact: Jody Burroughs, Office Manager
Description: Provides landscape architecture, environmental planning, and urban design services throughout the United States and in many foreign countries. Number of employees worldwide: 250. **Benefits:** 401K; Dental Insurance; Life Insurance; Medical Insurance; Profit Sharing. **Corporate headquarters location:** San Francisco CA. **Other U.S. locations:** Irvine CA; Denver CO; Atlanta GA; Alexandria VA. **Operations at this facility include:** Administration; Service. **Listed on:** Privately held. **Number of employees at this location:** 14. **Number of employees nationwide:** 200.

FLETCHER CONSTRUCTION
P.O. Box 3764
Seattle WA 98124
206/447-7654
Contact: Personnel Department
Description: A general contracting company of non-residential buildings.

JOHN GRAHAM ASSOCIATES
Bank of California Building
900 Fourth Avenue, Suite 700
Seattle WA 98164
206/461-6000
Contact: Jonathan E. Pettit, Principal in the Firm
Description: Offers a wide range of planning, architectural, engineering, and design services, primarily for projects in the Pacific Northwest. Also offers

specialized consulting services. **Common positions include:** Architect; Civil Engineer; Construction and Building Inspector; Electrical/Electronic Engineer; Mechanical Engineer; Structural Engineer. **Educational backgrounds include:** Architecture; Engineering. **Benefits:** 401K; Dental Insurance; Disability Coverage; Life Insurance; Medical Insurance. **Special Programs:** Internships. **Other U.S. locations:** Phoenix AZ; Tampa FL; Minneapolis MN. **Operations at this facility include:** Regional Headquarters. **Listed on:** Privately held. **Number of employees at this location:** 50. **Number of employees nationwide:** 300.

KAISER ENGINEERS HANFORD COMPANY
1200 Jadwin Avenue, TCPC Building
Tri-City, Professional Building
Richland WA 99352
509/376-7452
Contact: Human Resources
Description: Offers engineering services.

LINDAL CEDAR HOMES INC.
P.O. Box 24426
Seattle WA 98124
206/725-0900
Contact: Personnel Department
Description: A prime manufacturer of pre-cut cedar homes and wholesalers of lumber and other building materials.

MEHRER DRYWALL INC.
2657 20th Avenue West
Seattle WA 98199
206/282-4288
Contact: Personnel Department
Description: A company engaged in drywall contracting.

LANCE MUELLER & ASSOCIATES
130 Lakeside, Suite 250
Seattle WA 98122
206/325-2553
Contact: Personnel Department
Description: An architectural commercial project company.

PARSONS BRINCKERHOFF
999 3rd Avenue, Suite 801
Seattle WA 98104
206/382-5200.
Contact: Personnel Director
Description: An engineering and design firm engaged in the design of bridges, tunnels, rapid transit systems, hydroelectric facilities, water supply

systems, and marine facilities. Maintains regional and branch offices throughout the United States and abroad. **Corporate headquarters location:** New York NY. **Listed on:** New York Stock Exchange.

PRIME CONSTRUCTION COMPANY INC.
P.O. Box 25749
Seattle WA 98125
206/820-6924
Contact: Personnel Department
Description: A warehouse and commercial building contractor.

SELLEN CONSTRUCTION COMPANY INC.
P.O. Box 9970
Seattle WA 98109
206/682-7770
Contact: Personnel Department
Description: A general contractor of non-residential and industrial buildings.

STRAND INC.
12015 115th Avenue NE, Suite 220
Kirkland WA 98034
206/746-8780
Contact: Human Resources
Description: A construction contractor.

URS CONSULTANTS
1100 Olive Way, Suite 200
Seattle WA 98101
206/623-1800
Contact: Human Resources Manager
Description: A full-service engineering and architectural company providing services to the private and public sectors.

VANGUARD MANAGEMENT
20230 Novelty Hill Road, Suite 100
Redmond WA 98053-5118
206/868-2020
Contact: Personnel Department
Description: An operative builder and property management company. *Note:* Applicants should have adequate computer skills. **Common positions include:** Bookkeeper; Receptionist. **Corporate headquarters location:** This Location. **Operations at this facility include:** Administration.

Note: Because addresses and telephone numbers of smaller companies change rapidly, we recommend you call each company and verify the information below before mailing to employers. Mass mailings are not recommended.

Additional employers with over 250 employees:

GENERAL CONTRACTORS

Baugh Enterprises
900 Poplar Place
South, Seattle WA
98144-2830.
206/726-8000.

GENERAL INDUSTRIAL CONTRACTORS

Lease Crutcher Lewis
107 Spring Street,
Seattle WA 98104-
1005. 206/622-0500.

ROAD CONSTRUCTION

NA Degerstrom Inc.
3303 North Sullivan
Road, Spokane WA
99216-1676.
509/928-3333.

BRIDGE, TUNNEL, AND HIGHWAY CONSTRUCTION

Wright Schuchart
P.O. Box 24665,
Seattle WA 98124-
0665. 206/447-7545.

ENGINEERING SERVICES

Ekono Inc.
1601 114th Avenue
SE, Suite 140,
Bellevue WA 98004-
6904. 206/455-5969.

Hart Crowser Inc.
1910 Fairview Avenue
East, Seattle WA
98102-3620.
206/324-9530.

Additional employers with under 250 employees:

PREFABRICATED METAL BUILDINGS AND COMPONENTS

Garco Building Systems
P.O. Box 19248,
Spokane WA 99219-
9248. 509/244-5611.

MOBILE HOMES

Fleetwood Homes Of Washington
P.O. Box 250,
Woodland WA 98674-
0250. 206/225-9461.

Glen River Industries
P.O. Box 810,
Centralia WA 98531-
0810. 206/736-1341.

ENGINEERING SERVICES

Pac-Tech Engineering
2601 South 35th
Street, Tacoma WA
98409-7479.
206/473-4491.

PTI Environmental Services
15375 SE 30th Place,
Suite 250, Bellevue
WA 98007-6500.
206/643-9803.

Sverdrup Corporation
3200 Carillon Point,
Kirkland WA 98033-
7354. 206/822-3330.

Applied Geotechnology
2930 Wetmore
Avenue, Everett WA
98201-4044.
206/339-8845.

Metrum Instrumentation Service
6500 Harbour Heights Parkway, Mukilteo WA 98275-4862.
206/356-3980.

Arc Professional Services Group
3100 NW Bucklin Hill Road, Silverdale WA 98383-9192.
206/692-3647.

Science Applications International Corporation
1845 Terminal Drive, Suite 202, Richland WA 99352-4959.
509/943-3133.

ARCHITECTURAL SERVICES

Architects Northwest
18915 142nd Avenue NE Suite 100, Woodinville WA 98072-8502.
206/485-4900.

GENERAL CONTRACTORS -- SINGLE FAMILY HOUSES

Osborne Construction Company
10628 NE 38th Place, Kirkland WA 98033-7902. 206/827-4221.

Standard Mechanical
1851 Alexander Avenue, Tacoma WA 98421-4107.
206/272-0129.

GENERAL CONTRACTORS -- INDUSTRIAL BUILDINGS

Dix Corporation
4024 South Grove Road, Spokane WA 99204-5320.
509/838-4455.

Lydig Construction
603 North Havana Street, Spokane WA 99202-4662.
509/534-0451.

GENERAL CONTRACTORS -- NONRESIDENTIAL BUILDINGS

Evergreen Mobile Company
P.O. Box 687, Redmond WA 98073-0687. 206/861-7400.

Strand Hunt Construction
12015 115th Avenue NE, Kirkland WA 98034-6925.
206/823-1954.

BRIDGE AND HIGHWAY CONSTRUCTION

Manson Construction & Engineering Company
P.O. Box 24067, Seattle WA 98124-0067. 206/762-0850.

PAINTING AND PAPER HANGING

RC Painting
16140 Woodinville Redmon Road NE, Woodinville WA 98072-6964.
206/869-2557.

ELECTRICAL WORK

Hooper Electric Company
16715 Aurora Avenue North, Seattle WA 98133-5310.
206/546-2491.

City Electric Inc.
3700 Rainier Avenue South, Seattle WA 98144-6911.
206/722-0700.

DW Close Company
3317 3rd Avenue South, Seattle WA 98134-1930.
206/623-8960.

PLASTERING AND DRYWALL

Allcity Drywall Inc.
10616 NE 14th
Street, Bellevue WA
98004-3623.
206/454-6811.

Monarch Construction
13838 1st Avenue
South, Seattle WA
98168-3438.
206/246-9618.

Coast Mechanical Insulation Service
545 108th Avenue NE
Suite 3, Bellevue WA
98004-5502.
206/451-0322.

State Mechanical Insulation Service
545 108th Avenue NE
Suite 3, Bellevue WA
98004-5502.
206/451-0309.

CARPENTRY WORK

Westmark Products
P.O. Box 44040,
Tacoma WA 98444-
0040. 206/531-3470.

INSTALLATION OF BUILDING EQUIPMENT

Sound Elevator Co.
506 7th Avenue
South, Kirkland WA
98033-6625.
206/828-3110.

For more information on career opportunities in architecture, construction and engineering:

<u>Associations</u>

AMERICAN ASSOCIATION OF COST ENGINEERS
209 Prairie Avenue, Suite 100, P.O.
Box 1557, Morgantown WV 26507-
1550. 304/296-8444. 800/858-
2678. Toll-free number provides
information on scholarships for
undergraduates.

AMERICAN CONSULTING ENGINEERS COUNCIL
1015 15th Street NW, Suite 802,
Washington DC 20005. 202/347-
7474.

AMERICAN INSTITUTE OF ARCHITECTS
1735 New York Avenue NW,
Washington DC 20006. 202/626-
7300. 800/365-2724. Toll-free
number for brochures.

AMERICAN SOCIETY FOR ENGINEERING EDUCATION
1818 NorthStreet NW, Suite 600,
Washington DC 20036. 202/331-
3500.

AMERICAN SOCIETY OF CIVIL ENGINEERS
345 East 47th Street, New York NY
10017. 212/705-7496.

AMERICAN SOCIETY OF HEATING, REFRIGERATING AND AIR CONDITIONING ENGINEERS
1791 Tullie Circle NE, Atlanta GA
30329. 404/636-8400.

AMERICAN SOCIETY OF LANDSCAPE ARCHITECTS
4401 Connecticut Avenue NW, Fifth
Floor, Washington DC 20008.
202/686-2752.

AMERICAN SOCIETY OF MECHANICAL ENGINEERS
345 East 47th Street, New York NY 10017. 212/705-7722.

AMERICAN SOCIETY OF NAVAL ENGINEERS
1452 Duke Street, Alexandria VA 22314. 703/836-6727.

AMERICAN SOCIETY OF PLUMBING ENGINEERS
3617 Thousand Oaks Boulevard, Suite 210, Westlake CA 91362. 805/495-7120.

AMERICAN SOCIETY OF SAFETY ENGINEERS
1800 East Oakton Street, Des Plaines IL 60018-2187. 708/692-4121.

ILLUMINATING ENGINEERING SOCIETY OF NORTH AMERICA
120 Wall Street, 17th Floor, New York NY 10005. 212/248-5000.

INSTITUTE OF INDUSTRIAL ENGINEERS
25 Technology Park, Norcross GA 30092. 404/449-0460.

NATIONAL ACTION COUNCIL FOR MINORITIES IN ENGINEERING
3 West 35th Street, New York NY 10001. 212/279-2626.

NATIONAL ASSOCIATION OF MINORITY ENGINEERING
435 North Michigan Avenue, Suite 1115, Chicago IL 60611. 312/661-1700, ext. 744.

JUNIOR ENGINEERING TECHNICAL SOCIETY
1420 King Street, Suite 405, Alexandria VA 22314. 703/548-JETS.

NATIONAL INSTITUTE OF CERAMIC ENGINEERS
735 Ceramic Place, Westerville OH 43081. 614/890-4700.

NATIONAL SOCIETY OF BLACK ENGINEERS
1454 Duke Street, Alexandria VA 22314. 703/549-2207.

NATIONAL SOCIETY OF PROFESSIONAL ENGINEERS
1420 King Street, Alexandria VA 22314-2715. 703/684-2800. 703/684-2830. Number provides scholarship information for students.

SOCIETY OF FIRE PROTECTION ENGINEERS
1 Liberty Square, Boston MA 02109-4825. 617/482-0686.

SOCIETY OF MANUFACTURING ENGINEERS
P.O. Box 930, One SME Drive, Dearborn MI 48121. 313/271-1500.

UNITED ENGINEERING TRUSTEES
345 East 47th Street, New York NY 10017. 212/705-7000.

Directories

DIRECTORY OF ENGINEERING SOCIETIES
American Association of Engineering Societies, 1111 19th Street NW, Suite 608, Washington DC 20036. 202/296-2237.

DIRECTORY OF ENGINEERS IN PRIVATE PRACTICE
National Society of Professional Engineers, 1420 King Street, Alexandria VA 22314. 703/684-2800.

ENCYCLOPEDIA OF PHYSICAL SCIENCES & ENGINEERING INFORMATION SOURCES
Gale Research Inc., 835 Penobscot Building, Detroit MI 48226. 313/961-2242.

Magazines

CAREERS AND THE ENGINEER
Bob Adams, Inc., 260 Center Street, Holbrook MA 02343. 617/767-8100.

COMPUTER-AIDED ENGINEERING
Penton Publishing, 1100 Superior Avenue, Cleveland OH 44114. 216/696-7000.

EDN CAREER NEWS
Cahners Publishing Company, 275 Washington Street, Newton MA 02158. 617/964-3030.

ENGINEERING TIMES
National Society of Professional Engineers, 1420 King Street, Alexandria VA 22314. 703/684-2800.

ARTS AND ENTERTAINMENT/RECREATION

Things are looking up for the entertainment industry. Revenues for film, music, cable, television and video rental have improved since 1991, when the recession dropped sales of movie tickets and prerecorded music. Technological advances continue to be a major variable in the industry's future. Multimedia interactive entertainment, or the use of digital technology to integrate audio, video, computers and telecommunications, has attracted investment from four major movie studios and companies from related industries.

Movie attendance continues to grow in the U.S., despite a decline in the number of new releases. Abroad, growth of U.S. exports has practically stopped. American films, however, continue to dominate the international film industry.

Prerecorded music sales are soaring. Some of the fastest sales have been of CD singles, which has shown faster sales growth than full-length CDs. Sales of cassette tapes are expected to slow, and, like CDs, cassette singles generate faster sales growth than full-length tapes.

ALPENTAL SKI ACRES SNOQUALMIE
7900 SE 28th Street
Mercer Island WA 98040
206/232-8182
Contact: Human Resources
Description: A ski resort.

CRYSTAL MOUNTAIN RESORT
1 Crystal Mountain Boulevard
Crystal Mountain WA 98022
206/663-2300
Contact: Human Resources Department
Description: A ski resort.

METROPOLITAN PARK DISTRICT OF TACOMA
4702 South 19th Street
Tacoma WA 98405
206/305-1003
Contact: Human Resources
Description: Provides park and recreational programs and services.

NATIONAL PARK SERVICE, OLYMPIC NATIONAL PARK
600 East Park Avenue
Port Angeles WA 98362
206/452-4501
Contact: Human Resources
Description: National park service managing nearly one million acres of coast, rain forest, and mountains. **Common positions include:** Biological Scientist/Biochemist; Blue-Collar Worker Supervisor; Branch Manager; Computer Programmer; Construction Contractor and Manager; Electrician; Forester/Conservation Scientist; Interpreter; Investigator; Landscape Architect; Personnel/Labor Relations Specialist; Public Relations Specialist; Purchasing Agent and Manager; Science Technologist. **Educational backgrounds include:** Biology; Business Administration; Communications; Computer Science; Engineering; History. **Benefits:** 401K; Dental Insurance; Disability Coverage; Life Insurance; Medical Insurance; Pension Plan. **Special Programs:** Internships. **Corporate headquarters location:** Washington DC. **Operations at this facility include:** Administration; Research and Development; Service. **Number of employees at this location:** 300.

PIERCE COLLEGE THEATER
9401 Farwest Drive SW
Tacoma WA 98498
Contact: Director
Description: A theater.

SEATTLE GROUP THEATRE
305 Harrison
Seattle WA 98109
Contact: Producing Director
Description: A multi-cultural theater.

SEATTLE SYMPHONY
4th Floor, Seattle Center
305 Harrison
Seattle WA 98109
Contact: Personnel
Description: The city's symphony orchestra.

SUNRISE RESORT & RECREATION
P.O. Box 4100
Renton WA 98057
206/656-2861
Contact: Personnel Department
Description: An operator of a recreational campground.

THOUSAND TRAIL NACO
12301 NE 10th Place
Bellevue WA 98005
206/455-3155
Contact: Tita Jones, Personnel Director
Description: Provides camping memberships and related services.

Note: Because addresses and telephone numbers of smaller companies change rapidly, we recommend you call each company and verify the information below before mailing to employers. Mass mailings are not recommended.

Additional employers with under 250 employees:

AMUSEMENT AND RECREATION SERVICES

Golf Park Inc.
2405 Carillon Point, Kirkland WA 98033-7353. 206/828-7412.

Mount Clements Archery Range
10223 US Highway 12, Naches WA 98937-9786.
509/653-1117.

Trout Meadows Inc.
2241 South Naches Road, Naches WA 98937-9618.
509/965-3863.

For more information on career opportunities in arts, entertainment and recreation:

Associations

ACTOR'S EQUITY ASSOCIATION
165 West 46th Street, New York NY 10036. 212/869-8530.

AFFILIATE ARTISTS
45 West 60th Street, New York NY 10023. 212/246-3889.

AMERICAN ALLIANCE FOR THEATRE AND EDUCATION
Division of Performing Arts, Virginia Tech, Blacksburg VA 24061-0141. 703/231-5335.

AMERICAN ASSOCIATION OF MUSEUMS
1225 I Street NW, Suite 200, Washington DC 20005. 202/289-1818.

AMERICAN ZOO AND AQUARIUM ASSOCIATION
Oglebay Park, Wheeling WV 26003. 304/242-2160.

AMERICAN COUNCIL FOR THE ARTS
1 East 53rd Street, New York NY 10022. 212/223-2787.

AMERICAN CRAFTS COUNCIL
72 Spring Street, New York NY 10012. 212/274-0630.

AMERICAN DANCE GUILD
31 West 21st Street, New York NY 10010. 212/627-3790.

AMERICAN FEDERATION OF MUSICIANS
1501 Broadway, Suite 600, New York NY 10036. 212/869-1330.

AMERICAN FEDERATION OF TELEVISION AND RADIO ARTISTS
260 Madison Avenue, New York NY 10016. 212/532-0800. Membership required.

AMERICAN FILM INSTITUTE
John F. Kennedy Center for the Performing Arts, Washington DC 20566. 202/828-4000.

AMERICAN GUILD OF MUSICAL ARTISTS
1727 Broadway, New York NY 10019. 212/265-3687.

AMERICAN MUSIC CENTER
30 West 26th Street, Suite 1001, New York NY 10010. 212/366-5260.

AMERICAN SOCIETY OF COMPOSERS, AUTHORS, AND PUBLISHERS (ASCAP)
1 Lincoln Plaza, New York NY 10023. 212/595-3050.

AMERICAN SYMPHONY ORCHESTRA LEAGUE
777 14th Street NW, Suite 500, Washington DC 20005. 202/628-0099.

ASSOCIATION OF INDEPENDENT VIDEO AND FILMMAKERS
625 Broadway, 9th Floor, New York NY 10012. 212/473-3400.

NATIONAL ARTISTS' EQUITY ASSOCIATION
P.O. Box 28068, Central Station, Washington DC 20038-8068. 202/628-9633.

NATIONAL DANCE ASSOCIATION
1900 Association Drive, Reston VA 22091. 703/476-3436.

NATIONAL ENDOWMENT FOR THE ARTS
1100 Pennsylvania Avenue NW, Washington DC 20506. 202/682-5400.

NATIONAL ORGANIZATION FOR HUMAN SERVICE EDUCATION
Brookdale Community College, Newman Springs Road, Lyncroft NJ 07738. 908/842-1900, ext. 546.

NATIONAL RECREATION AND PARK ASSOCIATION
2775 South Quincy Street, Suite 300, Arlington VA 22206. 703/820-4940.

PRODUCERS GUILD OF AMERICA
400 South Beverly Drive, Suite 211, Beverly Hills CA 90212. 310/557-0807.

SCREEN ACTORS GUILD
5757 Wilshire Boulevard, Hollywood CA 90036-3600. 213/954-1600.

THEATRE COMMUNICATIONS GROUP
355 Lexington Avenue, New York NY 10017. 212/697-5230.

WOMEN'S CAUCUS FOR ART
Moore College of Art, 20th & The
Parkway, Philadelphia PA 19103.
215/854-0922.

Directories

ARTIST'S MARKET
Writer's Digest Books, 1507 Dana
Avenue, Cincinnati OH 45207.
513/531-2222.

CREATIVE BLACK BOOK
866 3rd Avenue, 3rd Floor, New
York NY 10022. 212/254-1330.

PLAYERS GUIDE
165 West 46th Street, New York NY
10036. 212/869-3570.

ROSS REPORTS TELEVISION
Television Index, Inc., 40-29 27th
Street, Long Island City NY 11101.
718/937-3990.

Magazines

AMERICAN ARTIST
One Astor Place, 1515 Broadway,
New York NY 10036. 212/764-
7300. 800/346-0085, ext. 477.

AMERICAN CINEMATOGRAPHER
American Society of
Cinematographers, P.O. Box 2230,
Hollywood CA 90028. 213/969-
4333.

ART BUSINESS NEWS
Myers Publishing Company, 19 Old
Kings Highway South, Darien CT
06820. 203/656-3402.

ART DIRECTION
10 East 39th Street, 6th Floor, New
York NY 10016. 212/889-6500.

ARTFORUM
65 Bleecker Street, New York NY
10012. 212/475-4000.

ARTWEEK
12 South First Street, Suite 520,
San Jose CA 95113. 408/279-2293.

AVISO
American Association of Museums,
1225 I Street NW, Suite 200,
Washington DC 20005. 202/289-
1818.

BACK STAGE
1515 Broadway, New York NY
10036. 212/764-7300.

BILLBOARD
Billboard Publications, Inc., 1515
Broadway, New York NY 10036.
212/764-7300.

CASHBOX
157 West 57th Street, Suite 503,
New York NY 10019. 212/245-
4224.

CRAFTS REPORT
300 Water Street, Wilmington DE
19801. 302/656-2209.

DRAMA-LOGUE
P.O. Box 38771, Los Angeles CA
90038. 213/464-5079.

HOLLYWOOD REPORTER
5055 Wilshire Boulevard, 6th Floor,
Los Angeles CA 90036. 213/525-
2000.

VARIETY

249 West 17th Street, New York NY 10011. 212/779-1100.800/323-4345. Customer Service.

WOMEN ARTIST NEWS

300 Riverside Drive, New York NY 10025. 212/666-6990.

AUTOMOTIVE

The motor vehicle and parts industry is a key component of the U.S. economy, and makes up a large percentage of the country's direct and indirect employment and industrial output. Because the market for new passenger cars and light trucks in the U.S. is essentially saturated, sales from year to year shouldn't grow much faster than 1 or 2 percent. This saturation level has spurred intense competition. According to the U.S. Department of Commerce, severe competition has taken its toll on domestic profit, but it has also caused the industry to take painful, but beneficial, steps to reduce operating costs through improvements in manufacturing technology and productivity, and reductions in overhead expenses.

KENWORTH TRUCK COMPANY
P.O. Box 1000
Kirkland WA 98083-1000
206/828-5000
Contact: Director of Human Resources
Description: Manufacturers of Class 8 trucks. **Common positions include:** Accountant/Auditor; Administrator; Advertising Clerk; Civil Engineer; Claim Representative; Computer Programmer; Credit Manager; Customer Service Representative; Department Manager; Draftsperson; Electrical/Electronic Engineer; Financial Analyst; General Manager; Industrial Engineer; Management Trainee; Manufacturer's/Wholesaler's Sales Rep.; Marketing Specialist; Mechanical Engineer; Metallurgical Engineer; Operations/ Production Manager; Personnel/Labor Relations Specialist; Quality Control Supervisor; Systems Analyst; Technical Writer/Editor. **Educational backgrounds include:** Business Administration; Computer Science; Engineering; Finance; Liberal Arts; Marketing. **Benefits:** Dental Insurance; Disability Coverage; Life Insurance; Medical Insurance; Pension Plan; Savings Plan; Tuition Assistance. **Special Programs:** Internships; Training Programs. **Corporate headquarters location:** Bellevue WA. **Parent company:** Paccaar, Inc. **Operations at this facility include:** Administration; Divisional Headquarters; Sales; Service. **Listed on:** NASDAQ. **Number of employees nationwide:** 2,500.

PACCAR INC.
777 106th Avenue NE
Bellevue WA 98004
206/455-7400
Contact: Human Resources
Description: A manufacturer of heavy duty trucks and other equipment for industrial and commercial use. Brand names include Peterbilt and Kenworth.
Corporate headquarters location: This Location.

Note: Because addresses and telephone numbers of smaller companies change rapidly, we recommend you call each company and verify the information below before mailing to employers. Mass mailings are not recommended.

Additional employers with under 250 employees:

TRUCK TRAILERS

Comet Trailer Corporation
P.O. Box 460, Selah WA 98942-0460.
509/697-4800.

AUTOMOBILES AND OTHER MOTOR VEHICLES WHOLESALE

Clearwater & Company
20220 Pacific Highway South, Seattle WA 98198-5703
206/433-5911.

MOTOR VEHICLE SUPPLIES WHOLESALE

Mar-Lac Distributing Company
1426 South Dearborn Street, Seattle WA 98144-2890
206/322-2626.

Seattle Automotive Distributing Inc.
1264 South King Street, Seattle WA 98144-2025.
206/323-6700.

TRAVEL TRAILERS AND CAMPERS

Western Recreational Vehicles Inc.
3401 West Washington Avenue, Yakima WA 98903-1138. 509/457-4133.

MOTOR VEHICLE PARTS

Six States Distributors
3711 East Trent Avenue, Spokane WA 99202-4420.
509/535-7671.

For more information on career opportunities in the automotive industry:

Associations

ASSOCIATION OF INTERNATIONAL AUTOMOBILE MANUFACTURERS
1001 19th Street North, Suite 1200, Arlington VA 22209. 703/525-7788.

AUTOMOTIVE AFFILIATED REPRESENTATIVES
25 Northwest Point Boulevard, Suite 425, Elk Grove Village IL 6007-1035. 708/228-1310

AUTOMOTIVE SERVICE ASSOCIATION
1901 Airport Freeway, Suite 100, P.O. Box 929, Bedford TX 76095. 817/283-6205

MOTOR VEHICLE MANUFACTURERS ASSOCIATION
7430 2nd Avenue, Suite 300, Detroit MI 48202. 313/872-4311.

NATIONAL AUTOMOTIVE PARTS ASSOCIATION
2999 Circle 75 Parkway, Atlanta GA 30339. 404/956-2200.

NATIONAL INSTITUTE FOR AUTOMOTIVE SERVICE EXCELLENCE
13505 Dulles Technology Drive, Herndon VA 22071. 703/713-3800.

Directories

AUTOMOTIVE NEWS MARKET DATA BOOK
Automotive News, 1400 Woodbridge Avenue, Detroit MI 48207-3187. 313/446-6000.

WARD'S AUTOMOTIVE YEARBOOK
Ward's Communications, 3000 Town Center, Suite 2750, Southville, MI 48075. 810/357-0800.

Magazines

AUTOMOTIVE INDUSTRIES
Chilton Book Company, 201 King of Prussia Road, Radnor PA 19089. 800/695-1214.

AUTOMOTIVE NEWS
1400 Woodbridge Avenue, Detroit MI 48207. 313/446-6000.

WARD'S AUTO WORLD
Ward's Communications, Inc., 3000 Town Center, Suite 2750, Southville MI 48075. 810/357-0800.

WARD'S AUTOMOTIVE REPORTS
Ward's Communications, Inc., 3000 Town Center, Suite 2750, Southville MI 48075. 810/357-0800.

BANKING/SAVINGS AND LOANS

Heading into the mid-1990s, the banking industry is continuing to evolve. The industry began the decade with a series of mega-mergers aimed at solidifying its strongest institutions, which resulted in a series of major layoffs. By the end of 1991, however, commercial banks had rebounded, and the recovery continued through 1992 and 1993. Even so, there is still pressure on legislators and regulators alike to address the banking industry's problems.

Inc.reasingly, banks are facing new competition from mutual funds and other financial services. Competition will most likely take the form of innovation, such as new products and delivery systems; of securitization, such as converting assets into marketable certificates; and of internationalization, such as the elimination of geographic barriers.

BELLINGHAM NATIONAL BANK
101 East Holly Street, Mail Stop 3111
Bellingham WA 98225
206/676-6300
Contact: Human Resources
Description: A bank.

FIRST INTERSTATE BANK OF WASHINGTON
P.O. Box 160
Seattle WA 98111
206/292-3111
Contact: Personnel Department
Description: A bank.

GREAT WESTERN FEDERAL SAVINGS BANK
11201 Southeast 8th Street, Suite 110
Bellevue WA 98004
Contact: Human Resources
Description: A financial institution with strong emphasis on mortgage banking. Jobseekers: Please apply to the department of your interest. **Common positions include:** Accountant/Auditor; Administrator; Bank Officer/Manager; Bank Teller; Marketing Specialist; Personnel/Labor Relations Specialist; Purchasing Agent and Manager; Secretary; Systems Analyst; Underwriter/Assistant Underwriter. **Educational backgrounds include:** Accounting; Business Administration; Computer Science; Economics;

Finance. **Benefits:** Dental Insurance; Disability Coverage; Life Insurance; Medical Insurance; Pension Plan; Profit Sharing; Tuition Assistance. **Corporate headquarters location:** This Location. **Operations at this facility include:** Administration; Research and Development; Sales; Service. **Listed on:** American Stock Exchange.

INTERWEST SAVINGS BANK
P.O. Box 1649
Oak Harbor WA 98277
206/675-0788
Contact: Human Resources
Description: A bank.

KEY BANK
1536 NW Market
Seattle WA 98107
206/789-4000
Contact: Personnel Department
Description: A bank.

KEY BANK OF WASHINGTON
P.O. Box 90, MS 0248
Seattle WA 98111
206/684-6000
Contact: Human Resources Office
Description: A bank. Company encourages candidates interested in equal employment opportunities to call its 24-hour job hotline at 206/684-6189.

KEY BANK OF WASHINGTON
P.O. Box 11500
Tacoma WA 98411-5500
206/593-3790
Contact: Ms. Sandy Hedington, Personnel Director
Description: A bank holding company whose subsidiaries offer a wide range of financial services. **Number of employees nationwide:** 1,000.

METROPOLITAN FEDERAL SAVINGS & LOAN ASSOCIATION
1520 4th Avenue
Seattle WA 98101-1648
206/625-1818
Contact: Personnel Department
Description: A savings and loan association.

U.S. BANK OF WASHINGTON

P.O. Box 720
Seattle WA 98111-0720
206/344-3619
Contact: Human Resources
Description: A bank offering a wide range of financial services to its customers. **Number of employees nationwide:** 3,500.

U.S. BANK OF WASHINGTON

West 428 Riverside Avenue
Spokane WA 99220
509/353-5008
Contact: Senior Vice President of Personnel
Description: A bank. **Parent company:** ONB Corporation. **Number of employees nationwide:** 1,600.

UNITED SAVINGS AND LOAN BANK

601 South Jackson Street
Seattle WA 98104
206/624-7581
Contact: Personnel Department
Description: A savings and loan association. **Common positions include:** Customer Service Representative; Management Trainee. **Educational backgrounds include:** Accounting; Finance. **Benefits:** Dental Insurance; Life Insurance; Medical Insurance; Savings Plan. **Special Programs:** Training Programs. **Corporate headquarters location:** This Location. **Operations at this facility include:** Administration; Service. **Number of employees at this location:** 48.

UNIVERSITY SAVINGS BANK

6400 Roosevelt Way North East
Seattle WA 98115
206/526-1000
Contact: Barbara Bales, Vice President/Human Resources
Description: A bank. **Common positions include:** Accountant/Auditor; Branch Manager; Computer Programmer; Draftsperson; Underwriter/Assistant Underwriter. **Benefits:** Dental Insurance; Disability Coverage; Life Insurance; Medical Insurance; Pension Plan; Profit Sharing; Savings Plan. **Special Programs:** Training Programs. **Corporate headquarters location:** This Location. **Parent company:** Glendale Federal. **Operations at this facility include:** Service. **Listed on:** New York Stock Exchange. **Number of employees at this location:** 250.

WASHINGTON MUTUAL
1191 2nd Avenue
P.O. Box 834, SAS 0108
Seattle WA 98111
206/383-2511
Contact: Personnel Department
Description: A savings bank. **Number of employees nationwide:** 734.

YAKIMA FEDERAL SAVINGS AND LOAN ASSOC.
P.O. Box 1526
Yakima WA 98907
509/248-2634
Contact: Human Resources
Description: A savings and loan.

Note: Because addresses and telephone numbers of smaller companies change rapidly, we recommend you call each company and verify the information below before mailing to employers. Mass mailings are not recommended.

Additional employers with over 250 employees:

CREDIT UNIONS

Kenworth Employees Credit Union
P.O. Box 80222,
Seattle WA 98108-0222. 206/767-8585.

Bemis Credit Union
P.O. Box 1178,
Vancouver WA 98666-1178.
206/695-1251.

WTN Credit Union
4302 Chambers Creek Road, Steilacoom WA 98388-1528.
206/588-2115.

Virginia Mason Credit Union
P.O. Box 1930,
Seattle WA 98111-1930. 206/223-6369.

Inland Dairy Credit Union
33 East Francis Avenue, Spokane WA 99207-1034.
509/489-8600.

BANKS

Puget Sound National Bank
1119 Pacific Avenue, Tacoma WA 98402-4374. 206/593-3600.

Farm Credit Bank Of Spokane
601 West 1st Avenue, Spokane WA 99204-0317. 509/838-9223.

SAVINGS INSTITUTIONS

Sterling Savings Association Spokane
120 North Wall Street, Spokane WA 99201-0612. 509/624-4121.

Additional employers with under 250 employees:

STATE COMMERCIAL BANKS

Frontier Bank
9620 271st Street NW, Stanwood WA 98292-8096. 206/652-5605.

Washington Mutual Savings Bank
4279 Guide Meridian Road, Bellingham WA 98226-8791. 206/647-5980.

Continental Savings Bank
601 Union Street, Suite 2000, Seattle WA 98101-2326. 206/623-3050.

First Savings Bank Of Washington
P.O. Box 907, Walla Walla WA 99362-0265. 509/527-3636.

FEDERALLY CHARTERED SAVINGS INSTITUTIONS

Cascade Savings Bank FSB
2828 Colby Avenue Everett WA 98201-3537. 206/339-5500.

Cascade Savings Bank FSB
303 Front Street, Issaquah WA 98027. 206/391-5500.

SAVINGS INSTITUTIONS, NOT FEDERALLY CHARTERED

Pioneer Savings Bank
4111 200th Street SW, Lynnwood WA 98036-6727. 206/771-2525.

Puget Sound Savings Bank
1325 4th Avenue, Floor 12, Seattle WA 98101-2509. 206/447-5700.

FEDERALLY CHARTERED CREDIT UNIONS

Rohr Federal Credit Union
3130 D Street SE, Auburn WA 98002-8034. 206/833-2380.

PERSONAL CREDIT UNIONS

North Sound Bank
901 West Washington Street, Sequim WA 98382-3266. 206/681-2590.

Metlife Capital Corporation
10900 NE 4th Street, Bellevue WA 98004-5841. 206/451-0090.

MISCELLANEOUS BUSINESS CREDIT INSTITUTIONS

Great Western Leasing Company
18210 Redmond Way, Redmond WA 98052-5090. 206/451-8688.

MORTGAGE BANKERS

Action Mortgage
303 Diagonal Street, Clarkston WA 99403-1936. 509/758-1023.

Directors Mortgage Loan Corporation
4114 198th Street SW, Lynnwood WA 98036-6742. 206/778-3410.

Gold Seal Financial
19125 Northcreek
Plaza, Bothell WA
98011. 206/483-
6669.

**Phoenix Mortgage &
Investment Inc.**
3500 188th Street
SW, Lynnwood WA
98037-4716.
206/778-7988.

**SECURITY BROKERS
AND DEALERS**

**Interpacific Investors
Service**
600 University Street,
Seattle WA 98101-
1129. 206/623-2784.

**National Securities
Corporation**
1001 4th Avenue,
Suite 2200, Seattle
WA 98154-1100.
206/622-7200.

**OFFICES OF BANK
HOLDING
COMPANIES**

Central Bancorporation
301 North Chelan
Avenue, Wenatchee
WA 98801-2106.
509/663-0733.

**Frontier Financial
Corporation**
6623 Evergreen Way
Everett WA 98203-
4552. 206/347-0600.

**GNW Financial
Corporation**
500 Pacific Avenue,
Bremerton WA 98310-
1904. 206/479-1551.

For more information on career opportunities in the banking/savings and loan industry:

Associations

**AMERICAN BANKERS
ASSOCIATION**
1120 Connecticut Avenue NW,
Washington DC 20036. 202/663-
5221.

**INDEPENDENT BANKERS
ASSOCIATION OF AMERICA**
One Thomas Circle NW, Suite 950,
Washington DC 20005. 202/659-
8111.

**U.S. LEAGUE OF SAVINGS AND
LOAN INSTITUTIONS**
900 19th Street NW, Suite 400,
Washington DC 20006. 202/857-
3100.

Directories

AMERICAN BANK DIRECTORY
Thomson Financial Publications,
6195 Crooked Creek Road,
Norcross GA 30092. 404/448-1011.

**AMERICAN SAVINGS
DIRECTORY**
McFadden Business Publications,
6195 Crooked Creek Road,
Norcross GA 30092. 404/448-1011.

**BUSINESS WEEK/TOP 200
BANKING INSTITUTIONS ISSUE**
McGraw-Hill, Inc., 1221 Avenue of
the Americas, 39th Floor, New York
NY 10020. 212/512-4776.

MOODY'S BANK AND FINANCE MANUAL
Moody's Investors Service, Inc., 99 Church Street, First Floor, New York NY 10007. 212/553-0300.

POLK'S BANK DIRECTORY
R.L. Polk & Co., P.O. Box 305100, Nashville TN 37320-5100. 615/889-3350.

RANKING THE BANKS/ THE TOP NUMBERS
American Banker, Inc., 1 State Street Plaza, New York NY 10004. 212/943-6700.

Magazines

ABA BANKING JOURNAL
American Bankers Association, 1120 Connecticut Avenue NW, Washington DC 20036. 202/663-5221.

BANK ADMINISTRATION
1 North Franklin, Chicago IL 60606. 800/323-8552.

BANKERS MAGAZINE
Warren, Gorham & Lamont, Park Square Building, 31 Street. James Avenue, Boston MA 02116-4112. 617/423-2020.

JOURNAL OF COMMERCIAL BANK LENDING
Robert Morris Associates, P.O. Box 8500 S-1140, Philadelphia PA 19178. 215/851-9100. Cover letter required.

BIOTECHNOLOGY, PHARMACEUTICALS, AND SCIENTIFIC R&D

The biotechnology industry continues to grow, and industry analysts expect it to be a $50 billion industry by the year 2000. Most biotech firms are relatively small -- 99 percent employ fewer than 500 people, and 76 percent have fewer than 50 employees.

Observers expected the pharmaceutical industry to sustain steady real growth of roughly 2 percent during 1994. The long-term outlook will depend on the level of research and development, further expansion into foreign markets, and the result of the current national health care reform debate.

Skilled science technicians should find excellent employment opportunities in the '90s, largely due to the increased emphasis on the research and development of technical products.

BATTELLE PACIFIC NORTHWEST LABORATORIES
P.O. Box 999, Dept. 942041
Richland WA 99352
509/376-7149
Fax: 509/376-9099
Contact: Gil Lopez, Staffing Team Manager
Description: A national laboratory engaged in basic and applied research in energy, material and chemical sciences, earth and environmental engineering, waste technology, environmental restoration, and nuclear-related areas. **Common positions include:** Architect; Biological Scientist/Biochemist; Ceramics Engineer; Chemical Engineer; Civil Engineer; Computer Programmer; Computer Systems Analyst; Designer; Draftsperson; Electrical/Electronic Engineer; Electrician; Geologist/Geophysicist; Industrial Engineer; Management Analyst/Consultant; Mathematician; Mechanical Engineer; Meteorologist; Nuclear Engineer; Quality Control Supervisor; Software Engineer; Statistician; Structural Engineer; Technical Writer/Editor. **Educational backgrounds include:** Biology; Chemistry; Computer Science; Electronics; Energy; Engineering; Geology; Mathematics; Physics. **Benefits:** 401K; Dental Insurance; Disability Coverage; Employee Discounts; Life Insurance; Medical Insurance; Pension Plan; Savings Plan; Tuition Assistance. **Special Programs:** Internships. **Corporate headquarters location:** Columbus OH. **Operations at this facility include:** Research and Development. **Number of employees at this location:** 4,800.

CANTRELL & ASSOCIATES
1050 Larrabee Avenue, Suite 701
Bellingham WA 98225
206/738-4725
Contact: Human Resources
Description: A research and development lab.

IMMUNEX CORPORATION
Immunex Building, 51 University Street
Seattle WA 98101
206/587-0430
Contact: Human Resources Department
Description: A biopharmaceutical company focused on the discovery, manufacture, and marketing of products to treat cancer and auto immune diseases. **Common positions include:** Biological Scientist/Biochemist; Chemist; Clinical Lab Technician. **Educational backgrounds include:** Biology; Business Administration; Chemistry; Marketing. **Benefits:** Dental Insurance; Disability Coverage; Life Insurance; Medical Insurance; Pension Plan; Savings Plan; Tuition Assistance. **Corporate headquarters location:** This Location. **Other U.S. locations:** Bothell WA. **Operations at this facility include:** Administration; Manufacturing; Research and Development; Sales. **Listed on:** NASDAQ. **Number of employees nationwide:** 800.

LABORATORY OF PATHOLOGY
1229 Madison Street, Suite 600
Seattle WA 98104
206/386-2672
Contact: Human Resources Department
Description: A medical laboratory.

WHITMIRE DISTRIBUTING CORPORATION
P.O. Box 4959
Federal Way WA 98063-4959
206/838-7661
Contact: Sally Tice-Corter, Personnel Director
Description: Primarily engaged in the distribution of pharmaceutical products to medical facilities and retail drug outlets.

ZYMOGENETICS INC.
4225 Roosevelt Way NE, Suite 100
Seattle WA 98105
206/547-8080
Contact: Human Resources Coordinator
Description: Engaged in genetic research.

Note: Because addresses and telephone numbers of smaller companies change rapidly, we recommend you call each company and verify the information below before mailing to employers. Mass mailings are not recommended.

Additional employers with over 250 employees:

PHARMACEUTICAL PREPARATIONS

Receptech Corporation
51 University Street,
Seattle WA 98101-
2936. 206/587-0430.

RESEARCH AND TESTING

Bristol Myers Squibb
3005 1st Avenue,
Seattle WA 98121-
1035
206/728-4800.

Innovative Technology Lab Inc.
3100 George
Washington Way,
Richland WA 99352-
1663. 509/375-3123.

Panlabs Inc.
11804 North Creek
Parkway South,
Bothell WA 98011.
206/487-8200.

EM Factors
530 Lee Boulevard,
Richland WA 99352-
4225. 509/946-3353.

Failure Analysis Associates
8411 154th Avenue
NE, Redmond WA
98052-3863.
206/881-1807.

SCS Engineers
2950 Northup Way,
Bellevue WA 98004-
1402. 206/822-5800.

BIOLOGICAL PRODUCTS

Miles Inc.
P.O. Box 3145,
Spokane WA 99220-
3145. 509/489-5656.

Additional employers with under 250 employees:

PHARMACEUTICAL PREPARATIONS

Icos Corporation
22021 20th Avenue
SE, Bothell WA
98021-4423.
206/485-1900.

IN VITRO AND IN VIVO DIAGNOSTIC SUBSTANCES

Genetic Systems Corporation
P.O. Box 97016,
Redmond WA 98073-
9716. 206/881-8300.

COMMERCIAL, PHYSICAL AND BIOLOGICAL RESEARCH

Asymetrix Corporation
110 110th Avenue NE
Suite 700, Bellevue
WA 98004-5840.
206/462-0501.

Teague
14727 NE 87th
Street, Redmond WA
98052-6598.
206/883-8684.

Combustion Research Institute
600 Stewart Street,
Seattle WA 98101-
1217. 206/728-5138.

EMCON Northwest
18912 North Creek
Parkway, Suite 100,
Bothell WA 98011-
8028. 206/485-5000.

Environmental Issues Management
720 Olive Way
#1625, Seattle WA
98101-1853.
206/322-3245.

Mental Inc.
89 Virginia Street,
Seattle WA 98101-
1012. 206/728-6061.

**PRC Environmental
Management Inc.**
1411 4th Avenue,
Suite 720, Seattle WA
98101-2216.
206/624-2692.

**TESTING
LABORATORIES**

**Remediation
Technologies Inc.**
1011 SW Klickitat
Way Suite 207,
Seattle WA 98134-
1162. 206/624-9349.

Shannon & Wilson
1354 North
Grandridge Boulevard,
Kennewick WA
99336-1037.
509/946-6309.

For more information on career opportunities in biotechnology, pharmaceuticals, and scientific R&D:

Associations

**AMERICAN ASSOCIATION FOR
CLINICAL CHEMISTRY**
2029 K Street NW, 7th Floor,
Washington DC 20006. 202/857-
0717.

**AMERICAN ASSOCIATION OF
COLLEGES OF PHARMACY**
1426 Prince Street, Alexandria VA
22314. 703/739-2330.

**AMERICAN COLLEGE OF
CLINICAL PHARMACY (ACCP)**
3101 Broadway, Suite 380, Kansas
City MO 64111. 816/531-2177.
Operates ClinNet jobline at
412/648-7893 for both members
and nonmembers, for a fee.

**AMERICAN COUNCIL ON
PHARMACEUTICAL EDUCATION**
311 West Superior Street, Chicago
IL 60610. 312/664-3575.

**AMERICAN PHARMACEUTICAL
ASSOCIATION**
2215 Constitution Avenue NW,
Washington DC 20037. 202/628-
4410.

**AMERICAN SOCIETY FOR
BIOCHEMISTRY AND
MOLECULAR BIOLOGY**
9650 Rockville Pike, Bethesda MD
20814. 301/530-7145.

**AMERICAN SOCIETY OF
HOSPITAL PHARMACISTS**
7272 Wisconsin Avenue, Bethesda
MD 20814. 301/657-3000.

**BIOMEDICAL INDUSTRY
COUNCIL**
225 Broadway, Suite 1600,
San Diego, CA 92101. 619/236-
1322.

**BIOTECHNOLOGY INDUSTRY
ORGANIZATION**
1625 K Street NW, Suite 1100,
Washington DC 20006-1604.
202/857-0244.

**GEORGIA SOCIETY OF
HOSPITAL PHARMACISTS
(GSHP)**
2786 North Decatur Road, Suite
260, Decatur GA 30033. 404/508-
1700

NATIONAL ASSOCIATION OF PHARMACEUTICAL MANUFACTURERS
747 Third Avenue, New York NY 10017. 212/838-3720.

NATIONAL PHARMACEUTICAL COUNCIL
1894 Preston White Drive, Reston VA 22091. 703/620-6390.

Directories

DRUG TOPICS RED BOOK
Medical Economics Company, 5 Paragon Drive, Montvale, NJ 07645. 201/358-7200.

Magazine

DRUG TOPICS
Medical Economics Co., 5 Paragon Drive, Montvale NJ 07645. 201/358-7200.

PHARMACEUTICAL ENGINEERING
International Society of Pharmaceutical Engineers, 3816 West Linebaugh Avenue, Suite 412, Tampa FL 33624. 813/960-2105.

BUSINESS SERVICES AND NON-SCIENTIFIC RESEARCH

 *This industry covers a broad spectrum of services and careers. Here's a sampling: Guards and Security Officers: Openings for applicants should be plentiful through the year 2005. Most of these openings can be attributed to the high turnover within the industry. The greatest competition will be for the full-time, in-house positions, which are generally the higher paying positions.*

Data Processing Services: Performing such services as credit card authorization, data entry and payroll processing, revenues of data processing companies have grown as other companies choose not to maintain staff to provide these services in-house.

LOOMIS CORPORATION
720 Olive Way, Suite 625
Seattle WA 98101
206/223-4900
Contact: Personnel Department
Description: Provides armored car services, guard and patrol services, alarm service, and other security services. **Parent company:** Mayne Nickless Limited. **Number of employees nationwide:** 600.

LYNDEN INC.
P.O. Box 3757
Seattle WA 98124
206/241-8778
Contact: Personnel Department
Description: A holding company for transportation and construction companies.

MUZAK
200 South Orcas
Seattle WA 98108
206/763-2517
Contact: Personnel Department
Description: A company engaged in sound and video contracting services to businesses. **Common positions include:** Credit Manager; Customer Service Representative; Department Manager; Electrical/Electronic Engineer; Electronics Technician; Manufacturer's/Wholesaler's Sales Rep.; Operations/

Production Manager. **Educational backgrounds include:** Business Administration; Communications; Engineering; Liberal Arts; Marketing. **Benefits:** Dental Insurance; Disability Coverage; Life Insurance; Medical Insurance; Pension Plan; Profit Sharing; Savings Plan; Tuition Assistance.

MUZAK
400 North 34th Street, Suite 200
Seattle WA 98103
206/633-3000
Contact: Personnel Department
Description: Provides satellite deliverance and on-premises music services to commercial and retail establishments directly and through franchised dealers in the U.S. and internationally. **Common positions include:** Accountant/ Auditor; Broadcast Technician; Collector; Computer Programmer; Computer Systems Analyst; Customer Service Representative; Electrical/Electronic Engineer; Personnel/Labor Relations Specialist. **Educational backgrounds include:** Accounting; Business Administration; Communications; Finance; Liberal Arts. **Benefits:** 401K; Dental Insurance; Disability Coverage; Life Insurance; Medical Insurance; Profit Sharing; Tuition Assistance. **Corporate headquarters location:** This Location. **Operations at this facility include:** Administration; Research and Development. **Listed on:** Privately held. **Number of employees at this location:** 140. **Number of employees nationwide:** 650.

NBBJ
111 South Jackson
Seattle WA 98104
206/223-5555
Contact: Scott B. Johnson, Associate and Personnel Manager
Description: A professional service firm engaged in the fields of architecture, interior design, planning, economics and related fields to serve the needs of public and private clients throughout the world. NBBJ is an Equal Opportunity Employer and qualified females and minorities are encouraged to apply for employment. **Common positions include:** Architect; Draftsperson; Economist/Market Research Analyst; Interior Designer. **Educational backgrounds include:** Architecture; Interior Design. **Benefits:** Daycare Assistance; Dental Insurance; Disability Coverage; Life Insurance; Medical Insurance; Profit Sharing; Savings Plan. **Other U.S. locations:** Phoenix AZ; Los Angeles CA; San Francisco CA; Columbus NY. **Operations at this facility include:** Service. **Number of employees nationwide:** 450.

NORTHWEST PROTECTIVE SERVICE INC.
2700 Elliott Avenue
Seattle WA 98121
206/448-4040
Contact: Maggie Ricketts, Manager of Human Resources
Description: Provides contract security services. **Common positions include:** Security Officer; Store Detective. **Benefits:** Disability Coverage; Life

Insurance; Medical Insurance. **Other U.S. locations:** Portland OR; Spokane WA; Tacoma WA. **Operations at this facility include:** Service. **Number of employees nationwide:** 600.

SEATTLE CENTER
305 Harrison Street
Seattle WA 98109
206/684-7202
Contact: Human Resources Department
Description: A convention hall.

Note: Because addresses and telephone numbers of smaller companies change rapidly, we recommend you call each company and verify the information below before mailing to employers. Mass mailings are not recommended.

Additional employers with under 250 employees:

LINEN SUPPLY

Cintas Corporation
773 Valley Street,
Seattle WA 98109-
4321. 206/285-2000.

**BUILDING CLEANING
AND MAINTENANCE**

**Dependable Building
Maintenance Company
Washington**
4817 Aurora Avenue
North, Seattle WA
98103-6517.
206/547-8787.

**DETECTIVE, GUARD
AND ARMORED CAR
SERVICES**

**Hi Way Prevention
Patrol**
3845 East McKinley
Avenue, Tacoma WA
98404-2941.
206/927-1780.

**International
Protective Agency**
1022 72nd Street
East, Tacoma WA
98404-1732.
206/536-0991.

**Northwest Protective
Service**
3514 East McKinley
Avenue, Tacoma WA
98404-2163.
206/383-4040.

**Northwest Security
Services**
521 NE 165th Street,
Seattle WA 98155-
5828. 206/365-0760.

**Pinkerton Security
Services**
W1719 Northwest
Boulevard, Spokane
WA 99205. 509/325-
1544.

Sarah Thorson Little
P.O. Box 55541,
Seattle WA 98155-
0541. 206/368-8393.

**American Detective
Agency**
1001 4th Avenue,
Seattle WA 98154-
1101. 206/622-1212.

Allied Investigations
19936 Ballinger Way
NE, Seattle WA
98155-1223.
206/367-3780.

Hoover Investigations
3202 East M Street,
Tacoma WA 98404-
4027. 206/272-5090.

**Rosa Sub
Investigations**
1001 4th Avenue,
Suite 3200, Seattle
WA 98154-1075.
206/623-5169.

ECONOMIC, SOCIOLOGICAL AND EDUCATIONAL RESEARCH

Dick Conway & Associates
2323 Eastlake Avenue East Rm 410, Seattle WA 98102-3393. 206/324-0700.

Thomas Lane & Associates
117 East Louisa Street #141, Seattle WA 98102-3279. 206/523-6140.

BUSINESS SERVICES

Zetec Inc.
1370 NW Mall Street, Issaquah WA 98027-8921. 206/392-5316.

Greyhound Exposition Service
4060 Lind Avenue SW, Renton WA 98055-4902. 206/251-6565.

REFRIDGERATION AND AIR-CONDITIONING SERVICE AND REPAIR

CRRR Building Service
6118 East 6th Avenue, Spokane WA 99212-0435. 509/624-9952.

For more information on career opportunities in business services:

Associations

AMERICAN SOCIETY OF APPRAISERS
P.O. Box 17265, Washington DC 20041. 703/478-2228.

EQUIPMENT LEASING ASSOCIATION OF AMERICA
1300 17th Street, North Arlington VA 22209. 703/527-8655.

INTERACTIVE SERVICES ASSOCIATION
Suite 865, 8403 Colesville Road, Silver Springs MD 20910. 301/495-4955.

Directories

WORLD LEASING YEARBOOK
Euromoney, Inc., 145 Hudson Street, 7th Floor, New York NY 10012. 212/941-5880.

CHARITIES/SOCIAL SERVICES/ MEMBERSHIP ORGANIZATIONS

The outlook for social services workers is better than average. In fact, opportunities for qualified applicants are expected to be excellent, partly due to the rapid turnover in the industry, the growing number of older citizens, and an increased awareness of the needs of the mentally and physically handicapped.

LONGSHORE SEATTLE
3440 East Marginal Way South
Seattle WA 98134
206/623-7844
Contact: Human Resources
Description: Seattle local for the labor organization.

OVERLAKE SERVICE LEAGUE
167 Bellevue Square
Bellevue WA 98004
Contact: Human Resources
Description: A social service organization.

**TACOMA GOODWILL INDUSTRIES
REHABILITATION CENTER INC.**
714 South 27th Street
Tacoma WA 98409
206/272-5166
Contact: Norma Carolyn, Personnel Director
Description: Providers of vocational rehabilitation programs. **Common positions include:** Blue-Collar Worker Supervisor; Cashier; Chef/Cook/Kitchen Worker; Industrial Manager; Payroll Clerk; Restaurant/Food Service Manager; Retail Manager; Retail Sales Worker; Transportation/Traffic Specialist. **Educational backgrounds include:** Accounting; Business Administration; Rehabilitative Teaching. **Benefits:** Dental Insurance; Life Insurance; Medical Insurance. **Corporate headquarters location:** This Location. **Operations at this facility include:** Administration; Regional Headquarters. **Number of employees at this location:** 400.

UNITED CEREBRAL PALSY ASSOCIATION
4409 Interlake Avenue North
Seattle WA 98103
206/632-2827
Fax: 206/633-6670
Contact: Teri Ano, Director of Human Resources
Description: Offices of the national association. **Common positions include:** Accountant/Auditor; Dental Assistant/Dental Hygienist; Human Service Worker; Licensed Practical Nurse; Personnel/Labor Relations Specialist; Physical Therapist; Social Worker; Speech-Language Pathologist; Teacher. **Benefits:** 403B; Dental Insurance; Life Insurance; Medical Insurance. **Corporate headquarters location:** This Location. **Operations at this facility include:** Administration; Service. **Number of employees at this location:** 335.

YMCA ACCOMMODATIONS
909 4th Avenue
Seattle WA 98104
206/382-5000
Contact: Personnel
Description: A YMCA shelter.

Note: Because addresses and telephone numbers of smaller companies change rapidly, we recommend you call each company and verify the information below before mailing to employers. Mass mailings are not recommended.

Additional employers with under 250 employees:

LIBRARIES

Timberland Regional Library
415 Airdustrial Way SW, Olympia WA 98501-5717.
206/943-5001.

INDIVIDUAL AND FAMILY SOCIAL SERVICES

Amerasian Project
606 Maynard Avenue South, Seattle WA 98104-2957.
206/340-0345.

CHILD DAY CARE SERVICES

Childrens World Learning Centers
5030 168th Street SW, Lynnwood WA 98037-6826.
206/742-3422.

La Petite Academy
20415 Poplar Way, Lynnwood WA 98036-7840.
206/778-2864.

Tulalip Tribes Daycare
8223 Verle Hatch Drive, Marysville WA 98271-9611.
206/653-0324.

SOCIAL SERVICES

Catholic Community Services SW
4109 Bridgeport Way West, Tacoma WA 98466-4328.
206/566-8669.

Fremont Public Association
2326 6th Avenue
#240, Seattle WA
98121-1817.
206/441-5686.

Metropolitan Development Council
622 Tacoma Avenue
South, Tacoma WA
98402-2323.
206/383-3921.

Yakima Valley OIC
325 Highway 12,
Sunnyside WA 98944.
509/839-2717.

CIVIC, SOCIAL AND FRATERNAL ASSOCIATIONS

Environmental Careers Organization Inc.
1218 3rd Avenue,
Suite 1515, Seattle
WA 98101-3021.
206/625-1750.

The Trust For Public Land
506 2nd Avenue
#1510, Seattle WA
98104-2311.
206/587-2447.

BUSINESS ASSOCIATIONS

American Plywood Association
P.O. Box 11700,
Tacoma WA 98411-
0700. 206/565-6600.

CHEMICALS/RUBBER AND PLASTICS

 *Historically, growth has been cyclical for the chemicals industry. The industry is currently coming out of the low end of a cycle. The U.S. Commerce Department reports that an upturn in the domestic and foreign economies is needed to stimulate the chemical industry. Following this, the American chemical industry is expected to grow at a rate just above GNP over the next five years. Jobseekers with chemical engineering experience will benefit from the current shortage of workers in the industry.*

The rubber and plastic industries will do better as well, with growth in the 4 to 5 percent range. The highest growth rates will be for high-value, small-volume elastomers. In fabricated rubber, the big trend is toward customized production. Jobseekers with experience in Computer-Aided Design Manufacturing will reap the benefits of this trend. Demand for commodity plastics is expected to rise, as the market grows in North America but shrinks overseas. Competition in Europe, for example, is forcing many companies there to close their doors.

ACHILLES USA
P.O. Box 2287
Everett WA 98203
206/353-7000
Contact: Human Resources Department
Description: Produces unsupported plastic film and sheets.

ALLIED CORPORATION
Port of Longview, Warehouse 22
Longview WA 98632
Contact: Human Resources
Description: Manufactures cyclic organic crudes.

ATOCHEM NORTH AMERICA
P.O. Box 1297
Tacoma WA 98401
206/627-9101
Contact: Human Resources
Description: Manufactures chemicals.

AUTO CHLOR SYSTEM OF WASHINGTON
4315 7th Avenue
South Seattle WA 98108
206/622-0900
Contact: Personnel Department
Description: A company engaged in the wholesale and retail of chemicals.
Also provides dishwashing services.

BP CHEMICALS
3016 Auburn Way North
Auburn WA 98002
206/854-3000
Contact: Human Resources Department
Description: A chemicals company.

GACO WESTERN INC.
P.O. Box 88698
Seattle WA 98138-2698
206/575-0450
Contact: Personnel Department
Description: A manufacturer of elastomeric coatings.

PREMIER INDUSTRIES INC.
1019 Pacific Avenue
Tacoma WA 98402
206/572-5111
Contact: Human Resources
Description: Manufactures foam plastic products.

PRESERVATIVE PAINT COMPANY
5502 Airport Ways South
Seattle WA 98108
206/763-0300
Contact: Personnel Department
Description: A company engaged in the manufacture and retail of industrial
paint coatings.

UNIVAR
VAN WATERS AND ROGERS, INC.
P.O. Box 34325
Seattle WA 98124-1325
206/889-3400
Contact: Personnel Department
Description: A company engaged in the wholesale of industrial and textile
chemicals and pesticides.

VAUPELL INDUSTRIAL PLASTICS
1144 NW 53rd Street
Seattle WA 98107
206/784-9050
Contact: Human Resources Department
Description: Manufactures plastic products.

Note: Because addresses and telephone numbers of smaller companies change rapidly, we recommend you call each company and verify the information below before mailing to employers. Mass mailings are not recommended.

Additional employers with over 250 employees:

CHEMICALS AND CHEMICAL PREPARATIONS

Allied Kelite Division
3231 17th Avenue West, Seattle WA 98119-1708.
206/284-5032.

ITT Rayonier Inc. Seattle
P.O. Box 34162, Seattle WA 98124-1162. 206/246-3400.

INDUSTRIAL GASES

Airco Gases
4715 NE 78th Street, Vancouver WA 98665-0905.
206/695-1255.

Airco Welding Products
7700 14th Avenue South, Seattle WA 98108-3507.
206/767-3888.

Liquid Air Corporation
RR 2 Box 2838A, Kennewick WA 99337-7702.
509/582-5168.

Liquid Air Corporation Industrial
4230 East Trent Avenue, Spokane WA 99202-4453.
509/536-7484.

FERTILIZERS

Unocal
P.O. Box 5797, Kennewick WA 99336-0618.
509/586-5500.

The McGregor Company
P.O. Box 740, Colfax WA 99111-0740.
509/397-4355.

Crop Production Services
1529 West Lee Road, Othello WA 99344-9416. 509/488-5227.

Crop Production Services Inc.
6551 Road 170, Mesa WA 99343-9797.
509/269-4217.

INORGANIC CHEMICALS

General Chemical Corporation
P.O. Box 40, Anacortes WA 98221-0040. 206/293-2171.

The PQ Corporation
1202 Taylor Way, Tacoma WA 98421-4110. 206/627-1131.

PLASTICS PRODUCTS

Elixir Industries Custom
P.O. Box 1926, Vancouver WA 98668-1926.
206/693-1471.

Johnson Controls
P.O. Box 98949, Tacoma WA 98498-0949. 206/581-0417.

Northwest Containers
635 East 15th Street,
Tacoma WA 98421-
1691. 206/627-2151.

The Furon Company
P.O. Box 18319,
Seattle WA 98118-
0319. 206/723-5600.

Lasco Bathware
P.O. Box 1180, Yelm
WA 98597-1180.
206/458-3900.

Mikron Industries
1034 6th Avenue
North, Kent WA
98032-2991.
206/226-8020.

Puget Corporation
2101 Mildred Street
West, Tacoma WA
98466-6135.
206/564-3632.

**PLASTIC MATERIALS
WHOLESALE**

Laird Plastics
650 South Industrial
Way, Seattle WA
98108-5236.
206/623-4900.

**CHEMICALS AND
ALLIED PRODUCTS
WHOLESALE**

Univar Corporation
P.O. Box 34325,
Seattle WA 98124-
1325. 206/889-3400.

Additional employers with under 250 employees:

**INDUSTRIAL
INORGANIC
CHEMICALS**

**Occidental Chemical
Corporation**
605 Alexander
Avenue, Tacoma WA
98421-4209.
206/383-2661.

**PLASTICS
MATERIALS AND
SYNTHETIC RESINS**

Neste Resins
Spokane Industrial
Park Building North,
Spokane WA 99204.
509/924-8800.

**INDUSTRIAL
ORGANIC
CHEMICALS**

Kalama Chemical Inc.
1296 3rd Street NW,
Kalama WA 98625-
9799. 206/673-2550.

Kalama Chemical Inc.
1110 Bank Of
California Center,
Seattle WA 98164.
206/682-7890.

FERTILIZERS

Pacific Topsoils Inc.
14002 35th Avenue
SE, Bothell WA
98012-4699.
206/486-3201.

**PAINTS, VARNISHES
AND LACQUERS**

**Columbia Paint
Company**
112 North Haven
Street, Spokane WA
99202-3822.
509/535-9741.

**Forest Technical
Coatings**
9514 East
Montgomery Avenue,
Building 34, Spokane
WA 99206-4160.
509/924-3785.

**Wolfkill Feed &
Fertilizer Corporation**
P.O. Box 578, Monroe
WA 98272-0578.
206/794-7065.

CHEMICALS AND CHEMICAL PREPARATIONS

Chemithon Surface Finishing
5430 West Marginal Way SW, Seattle WA 98106-1517.
206/937-9954.

Pace International
500 7th Avenue South
Kirkland WA 98033-6625. 206/827-8711.

MOLDED, EXTRUDED AND LATHE-CUT RUBBER

Pyrotek Inc.
9601 East Montgomery Avenue, Spokane WA 99206-4117. 509/926-6212.

UNSUPPORTED PLASTICS PROFILE SHAPES

Fleck Company Inc.
P.O. Box 398, Auburn WA 98071-0398.
206/833-5900.

PLASTIC BOTTLES

Quintex Corporation
Spokane Industrial Park, Building 8, Spokane WA 99216.
509/924-7900.

PLASTICS FOAM PRODUCTS

Dolco Packaging Corporation
1121 South Columbia Street, Wenatchee WA 98801-3007.
509/663-8541.

Richter Northwest Corporation
21327 88th Avenue South, Kent WA 98031-1919.
206/872-8848.

PLASTICS PRODUCTS

A&B Plastics Inc.
50 West Arlington Avenue, Yakima WA 98902-4618.
509/248-9166.

Ershigs Inc.
742 Marine Drive, Bellingham WA 98225-1530.
206/733-2620.

La Valley Inds Inc.
7600 NE 47th Avenue, Vancouver WA 98661-1343.
206/696-2588.

Livingston Inc.
25 37th Street NE, Auburn WA 98002-1751. 206/852-7374.

McCawley Precision Machine
8825 South 184th Street, Kent WA 98031-1232.
206/251-3740.

Triquest Precision Plastics
P.O. Box 66008, Vancouver WA 98666-2008.
206/695-1234.

Pac Western Extruded Plastic Company
1820 Midvak Road, Sunnyside WA 98944.
509/837-7800.

PLASTICS MATERIALS WHOLESALE

Fiberchem Inc.
22239 76th Avenue South, Kent WA 98032-1924.
206/872-7777.

Perstorp Xytec Inc.
P.O. Box 99057, Tacoma WA 98499-0997. 206/582-0644.

CHEMICALS WHOLESALE

Full Circle Inc.
1175 South 1st Avenue, Othello WA 99344-1824.
509/488-2641.

For more information on career opportunities in the chemicals/rubber and plastics industries:

Associations

AMERICAN CHEMICAL SOCIETY
Career Services, 1155 16th Street NW, Washington DC 20036. 202/872-4600.

AMERICAN INSTITUTE OF CHEMICAL ENGINEERING
345 East 47th Street, New York NY 10017. 212/705-7338.

AMERICAN INSTITUTE OF CHEMISTS
7315 Wisconsin Avenue, Suite 502 E, Bethesda MD 20814. 301/652-2447.

CHEMICAL MANUFACTURERS ASSOCIATION
2501 M Street NW, Washington DC 20037. 202/887-1100.

CHEMICAL MARKETING RESEARCH ASSOCIATION
60 Bay Street, Suite 702, Staten Island NY 10301. 718/876-8800.

SOCIETY OF PLASTICS ENGINEERS
14 Fairfield Drive, P.O. Box 0403, Brookfield CT 06804-0403. 203/775-0471.

SOCIETY OF PLASTICS INDUSTRY
1275 K Street NW, Suite 400, Washington DC 20005. 202/371-5200.

Directories

CHEMICAL INDUSTRY DIRECTORY
State Mutual Book and Periodical Service, Order Department, 17th Floor, 521 5th Avenue, New York NY 10175. 516/537-1104.

CHEMICALS DIRECTORY
Cahners Publishing, 275 Washington Street, Newton MA 02158. 617/964-3030.

DIRECTORY OF CHEMICAL ENGINEERING CONSULTANTS
American Institute of Chemical Engineering, 345 East 47th Street, New York NY 10017. 212/705-7338.

DIRECTORY OF CHEMICAL PRODUCERS
SRI International, 333 Ravenswood Avenue, Menlo Park CA 94025. 415/326-6200.

Magazines

CHEMICAL & ENGINEERING NEWS
1155 16th Street NW, Washington DC 20036. 202/872-4600.

CHEMICAL MARKETING REPORTER
Schnell Publishing Company, 80 Brot Street, 23rd Floor, New York NY 10004. 212/248-4177.

CHEMICAL PROCESSING
Putnam Publishing Co., 301 East
Erie Street, Chicago IL 60611.
312/644-2020.

CHEMICAL WEEK
888 7th Avenue, 26th Floor, New
York NY 10106. 212/621-4900.

COMMUNICATIONS: TELECOMMUNICATIONS & BROADCASTING

Broadcasting: Competition for jobs in broadcasting, especially announcers and newscasters, is extremely intense because there are often more people looking to enter the field than there are positions. The smaller the station, the more duties an announcer has, while many specialize in weather, sports or news once they get to larger stations. Broadcasting technicians face a tough labor market because of technical advances. Computer controlled programming and remote control of transmitters are two examples of advances which cut directly into the job of a technician. The U.S. Department of Labor expects employment in radio and television broadcasting to decline for broadcast technicians in the future.

Telecommunications: While the demand for telecommunications equipment was sluggish in 1993, shipments should slowly start to take-off again. Product areas leading this growth will be network equipment, wireless communications equipment and satellite communications. The telecommunications services industry should continue to expand. Revenues generated from international services are expected to climb by 20 percent. Information services are expected to remain among the most active sectors of the U.S. economy.

AMERICAN KOTUBIKI ELECTRONICS
P.O. Box 61427
Vancouver WA 98666
206/695-1338
Contact: Human Resources
Description: Manufactures broadcasting equipment.

APPLIED VOICE TECHNOLOGY
11410 NE 122nd Way
Kirkland WA 98034
206/820-6000
Contact: Human Resources
Description: Manufactures communications apparatus.

CSC
3160 Fairview Park Drive
VTCA Building
Church WA 22042
703/876-1000
Fax: 703/573-9311
Contact: Human Resources
Description: Provides telecommunication and information processing services. **Common positions include:** Accountant/Auditor; Administrative Services Manager; Aerospace Engineer; Attorney; Biomedical Engineer; Budget Analyst; Chemical Engineer; Clerical Supervisor; Computer Programmer; Computer Systems Analyst; Construction and Building Inspector; Construction Contractor and Manager; Editor; Electrical/Electronic Engineer; Financial Analyst; General Manager; Mechanical Engineer; Nuclear Engineer; Personnel/Labor Relations Specialist; Purchasing Agent and Manager; Technical Writer/Editor. **Educational backgrounds include:** Accounting; Business Administration; Communications; Computer Science; Economics; Engineering; Finance; Liberal Arts; Marketing; Physical Science. **Benefits:** 401K; Dental Insurance; Disability Coverage; Employee Discounts; Life Insurance; Medical Insurance; Pension Plan; Tuition Assistance. **Special Programs:** Internships. **Operations at this facility include:** Administration; Divisional Headquarters; Regional Headquarters. **Number of employees nationwide:** 28,000.

CELLULAR ONE
617 East Lake Avenue East
Seattle WA 98109
206/339-7777
Contact: Human Resources Department
Description: A mobile telephone service company.

FISHER BROADCASTING INC.
100 Fourth Avenue North
Seattle WA 98109
206/443-4000
Contact: Sharon Greenfield, Vice President of Personnel
Description: Engaged in radio and television broadcasting. **Parent company:** Fisher Companies, Inc. **Number of employees at this location:** 479.

GTE NORTHWEST
P.O. Box 1003
Everett WA 98206
206/261-5321
Contact: Human Resources Department
Description: A telephone company.

KCTS-TV CHANNEL 9
401 Mercer Street
Seattle WA 98109
Contact: Pamela Sampel, Director of Personnel and Employee Relations
Description: A television station.

KEZX AM/FM RADIO
2615 4th Avenue, Suite 150
Seattle WA 98121
206/441-3699
Fax: 206/441-6322
Contact: Jill Kenly, E.E.O. Officer
Description: A radio station. **Common positions include:** Accountant/Auditor; Electrical/Electronic Engineer; General Manager; Operations/Production Manager; Radio/TV Announcer/Newscaster; Services Sales Representative. **Educational backgrounds include:** Accounting; Business Administration; Communications; Economics; Engineering; Liberal Arts; Marketing. **Benefits:** 401K; Dental Insurance; Disability Coverage; Life Insurance; Medical Insurance. **Special Programs:** Internships. **Corporate headquarters location:** Ithaca NY. **Parent company:** Park Broadcasting. **Operations at this facility include:** Administration; Sales; Service. **Listed on:** NASDAQ. **Number of employees at this location:** 30.

KOMO-TV CHANNEL 4 ABC
100 4th Avenue North
Seattle WA 98109
206/443-4000
Contact: Human Resources
Description: Seattle's ABC-affiliated television station.

KING 5 TELEVISION
333 Dexter Avenue North
Seattle WA 98109
Contact: Human Resources
Description: A television station, the local NBC affiliate. Programming includes daily newscasts, Evening Magazine, Almost Live, and Watch This!. **Number of employees nationwide:** 225.

KIRO, INC.
2807 Third Avenue
Seattle WA 98121
206/728-5068
Contact: Personnel Department
Description: A radio and television broadcasting company. **Parent company:** Bonneville International Corporation. **Number of employees nationwide:** 375.

LIN BROADCASTING
5295 Carillon Point
Kirkland WA 98033
206/828-1902
Contact: Office Manager
Description: A broadcasting company which operates as a group owner of several television stations.

McCAW CELLULAR COMMUNICATIONS, INC.
5400 Carillon Point
Kirkland WA 98033
206/827-4500
Contact: Personnel Department
Description: A cellular telephone and paging business.

NORTHLAND CABLE PROPERTIES FOUR LTD.
1201 3rd Avenue, Suite 3600
Seattle WA 98101
206/621-1351
Contact: Personnel Department
Description: A cablevision service.

PACIFIC TELECOM INC.
P.O. Box 9901
Vancouver WA 98668-8701
206/696-0983
Contact: Manager of Employment and Administration
Description: A holding company supplying administrative and other services to subsidiary companies, whose operations include providing telephone services to customers. **Common positions include:** Accountant/Auditor; Attorney; Budget Analyst; Buyer; Computer Programmer; Computer Systems Analyst; Economist/Market Research Analyst; Financial Analyst; Personnel/ Labor Relations Specialist; Purchasing Agent and Manager. **Educational backgrounds include:** Accounting; Business Administration; Computer Science. **Benefits:** 401K; Dental Insurance; Life Insurance; Medical Insurance; Pension Plan; Tuition Assistance. **Other U.S. locations:** Anchorage AK; Kalispell MT; Lebanon OR; Cheney WA; Gig Harbor WA; Tomah WI. **Operations at this facility include:** Administration. **Listed on:** NASDAQ. **Number of employees at this location:** 500. **Number of employees nationwide:** 3,000.

PROCTOR & ASSOCIATES COMPANY
15050 Northeast 36th Street
Redmond WA 98052
206/881-7000
Contact: Personnel Administrator
Description: A manufacturer of electronic equipment for the telephone industry. **Common positions include:** Electrical/Electronic Engineer; Hardware

Engineer; Software Engineer; Technical Representative. **Educational backgrounds include:** Engineering. **Benefits:** Dental Insurance; Life Insurance; Medical Insurance; Profit Sharing; Savings Plan; Tuition Assistance. **Operations at this facility include:** Administration; Manufacturing; Research and Development; Sales; Service. **Number of employees at this location:** 60.

TELTONE CORPORATION
22121 20th Avenue SE
Bothell WA 98021
206/487-1515
Contact: Ms. Marnie Vitt, Human Resources Manager
Description: A manufacturer of telecommunications equipment. **Common positions include:** Accountant/Auditor; Buyer; Computer Programmer; Credit Manager; Customer Service Representative; Electrical/Electronic Engineer; Financial Analyst; Manufacturer's/Wholesaler's Sales Rep.; Marketing Specialist; Public Relations Specialist; Quality Control Supervisor; Systems Analyst; Technical Writer/Editor. **Educational backgrounds include:** Accounting; Business Administration; Communications; Computer Science; Engineering; Finance; Marketing; Mathematics; Physics. **Benefits:** Dental Insurance; Disability Coverage; Employee Discounts; Life Insurance; Medical Insurance; Profit Sharing; Savings Plan; Stock Option; Tuition Assistance. **Special Programs:** Internships; Training Programs. **Corporate headquarters location:** This Location. **Operations at this facility include:** Administration; Manufacturing; Research and Development; Sales; Service. **Annual Revenues:** $10,000,000. **Number of employees at this location:** 76.

TONE COMMANDER SYSTEMS INC.
P.O. Box 97039
Redmond WA 98073-9739
206/883-3600
Contact: Personnel
Description: A manufacturer of telecommunications equipment, small PBX systems, and related electronic equipment. **Common positions include:** Accountant/Auditor; Blue-Collar Worker Supervisor; Buyer; Draftsperson; Electrical/Electronic Engineer; Manufacturer's/Wholesaler's Sales Rep.; Marketing Specialist; Purchasing Agent and Manager; Quality Control Supervisor; Technical Writer/Editor. **Educational backgrounds include:** Business Administration; Engineering; Finance; Marketing. **Benefits:** Dental Insurance; Life Insurance; Medical Insurance; Paid Vacation. **Corporate headquarters location:** This Location. **Operations at this facility include:** Administration; Manufacturing; Research and Development; Sales; Service.

U.S. INTELCO NETWORKS, INC.
4501 Intelco Loop, P.O. Box 2909
Olympia WA 98507
206/493-6000
Contact: Ms. Jamie Allison, Manager/Human Resources
Description: Provides services to the telecommunications industry; develops computer software. **Common positions include:** Computer Programmer; Customer Service Representative; Financial Analyst; Systems Analyst. **Educational backgrounds include:** Computer Science; Engineering; Marketing. **Benefits:** Dental Insurance; Disability Coverage; Life Insurance; Medical Insurance; Profit Sharing; Tuition Assistance. **Corporate headquarters location:** This Location. **Operations at this facility include:** Administration; Research and Development; Sales; Service. **Number of employees at this location:** 150.

U.S. WEST COMMUNICATIONS
1600 7th Avenue, Room 210
Seattle WA 98911
206/345-1234
Contact: Employment
Description: A telephone service. **Parent company:** U.S. West, Inc. **Number of employees nationwide:** 14,117.

U.S. WEST, NEW VECTOR GROUP
3350 161st Avenue East South
P.O. Box 7329
Bellevue WA 98008-1329
206/747-4900
Contact: Personnel Department
Description: Company specializing in cellular mobile commercial products and services.

VIACOM CABLEVISION
900 132nd Street SW
Everett WA 98204
206/743-5300
Contact: Human Resources
Description: A cable television broadcaster.

Note: Because addresses and telephone numbers of smaller companies change rapidly, we recommend you call each company and verify the information below before mailing to employers. Mass mailings are not recommended.

Additional employers with over 250 employees:

TELEPHONE AND TELEGRAPH APPARATUS

Applied Voice Technology
11410 NE 122nd Way, Kirkland WA 98034-6927.
206/820-6000.

Digital Systems International Inc.
6464 185th Avenue NE, Redmond WA 98052-6736.
206/881-7544.

Joslyn Electronic Systems
Sip Building N-1, Spokane WA 99216.
509/922-0483.

Voice Communication Systems
400 108th Avenue NE, Suite 615, Bellevue WA 98004-5508. 206/455-2636.

TELEPHONE COMMUNICATIONS

LDDS Inc.
422 West Riverside Avenue Suite 628, Spokane WA 99201-0302. 509/455-9595.

MCI Telecommunications Corporation
601 West 1st Avenue, Suite 508, Spokane WA 99204-0317.
509/455-6103.

MCI Telecommunications Corporation
701 5th Avenue, Suite 500, Seattle WA 98104-7016.
206/624-9933.

Northwest Telecommunications
2001 6th Avenue, Seattle WA 98121-2522. 206/441-9574.

Sprint International
520 Pike Street, Suite 2100, Seattle WA 98101-4001.
206/621-7600.

Additional employers with under 250 employees:

RADIO AND TELEVISION BROADCASTING AND COMMUNICATION EQUIPMENT

Augat Communication Group Inc.
23315 66th Avenue South, Kent WA 98032-1827.
206/854-9802.

RADIOTELEPHONE COMMUNICATIONS

U.S. West Cellular
2211 Rimland Boulevard, #202, Bellingham WA 98226-5662.
206/733-2159.

CABLE AND OTHER PAY TV SERVICES

Cox Cable Spokane
E1717 East Buckeye Avenue, Spokane WA 99207-4908.
509/484-4931.

**TELEPHONE AND
TELEGRAPH
APPARATUS**

**Active Voice
Corporation**
2901 3rd Avenue,
Suite 500, Seattle WA
98121-1049.
206/441-4700.

**Motorola/Mobile Data
Division**
19807 North Creek
Parkway, Bothell WA
98011-8214.
206/487-1234.

**TELEPHONE
COMMUNICATIONS**

**US West
Communications**
1313 Broadway,
Tacoma WA 98402-
3418. 206/597-5275.

American Sharecom
316 West Boone
Avenue Suite 584,
Spokane WA 99201-
2346. 509/455-5030.

STS Communications
720 Olive Way,
Seattle WA 98101-
1853. 206/447-9613.

**Telephone Utilities Of
Washington Inc.**
111 A Street, Cheney
WA 99004-1798.
509/235-5171.

**Enhanced
Telemanagement**
Tacoma Financial
Center, Suite 52,
Tacoma WA 98402.
206/383-0590.

Maxcom Inc.
916 111th Avenue
NE, Bellevue WA
98004-4410.
206/450-0560.

**Mid-Com
Communications**
1601 5th Avenue,
Suite 1000, Seattle
WA 98101-1619.
206/628-8000.

Pruden & Associates
10006 NE 9th
Avenue, Vancouver
WA 98685-5569.
206/576-8243.

Seattle Long Distance
10900 NE 4th Street,
Suite 600, Bellevue
WA 98004-5847.
206/637-2810.

**Active Voice
Corporation**
1336 98th Avenue
NE, Bellevue WA
98004-3413.
206/454-7828.

Telegenisys Systems
600 West Olympic
Place, Seattle WA
98119-3636.
206/284-4151.

Voice Net Inc.
83 South King Street
#100 A, Seattle WA
98104-2875.
206/682-8723.

CDI Telcom Inc.
1800 112th Avenue
NE, Bellevue WA
98004-2939.
206/637-8580.

**Contel Office
Communications**
1201 3rd Avenue
#1090, Seattle WA
98101-3000.
206/223-8900.

**Delta Communications
Systems**
P.O. Box 4736,
Federal Way WA
98063-4736.
206/952-2211.

Electric Lightwave
1218 3rd Avenue,
Suite 410, Seattle WA
98101-3021.
206/441-8400.

**First Federated
Communications**
600 Stewart Street
#1124, Seattle WA
98101-1217.
206/443-8605.

**In-Touch
Communications**
15334 SE 307th
Street, Kent WA
98042-5526.
206/630-2825.

In-Touch Communications
1911 SW Campus Drive, Suite 195, Federal Way WA 98023-6441. 206/630-2825.

Metronet
800 Stewart Street, Suite 300, Seattle WA 98101-1312. 206/223-1400.

Northwest Microwave
W421 West Riverside Avenue, Spokane WA 99201-0401. 509/838-7552.

Novacom
999 3rd Avenue, Seattle WA 98104-4001. 206/624-9601.

Realcom Office Communications Inc.
777 108th Avenue NE, Bellevue WA 98004-5118. 206/646-3200.

Verdan Technology
16715 Meridian E, Puyallup WA 98373-9616. 206/848-1843.

For more information on career opportunities in the communications industries:

Associations

ACADEMY OF TELEVISION ARTS & SCIENCES
5220 Lankershim Boulevard, North Hollywood CA 91601. 818/752-1870 (Research Library).

AMERICAN WOMEN IN RADIO AND TV, INC.
1650 Tysons Boulevard, Suite 200, McLean VA 22102. 703/506-3290.

BROADCAST PROMOTION AND MARKETING EXECUTIVES
6255 Sunset Boulevard, Suite 624, Los Angeles CA 90028. 213/465-3777.

INTERNATIONAL TELEVISION ASSOCIATION
6311 North O'Connor Road, LB51, Suite 236, Irving TX 75309. 214/869-1112. Membership required.

NATIONAL ASSOCIATION OF BROADCASTERS
1771 NorthStreet NW, Washington DC 20036. 202/429-5300, ext. 5490 (Research Library). 202/429-5497. Provides further employment information.

NATIONAL CABLE TELEVISION ASSOCIATION
1724 Massachusetts Avenue NW, Washington DC 20007. 202/775-3550.

UNITED STATES TELEPHONE ASSOCIATION
900 19th Street NW, Suite 800, Washington DC 20006. 202/326-7300.

Magazines

BROADCASTING AND CABLE
Broadcasting Publications Inc., 1705 DeSales Street NW, Washington DC 20036. 202/659-2340.

ELECTRONIC MEDIA

Crain Communications, 220 East
42nd Street, New York NY 10017.
212/210-0100.

COMPUTER HARDWARE, SOFTWARE AND SERVICES

 *Computer Services: Computer professional services perform three activities: systems integration, custom programming and consulting/training. During both 1992 and 1993, most companies failed to meet their own growth expectations, so many were more willing to reduce both inventory and employment. The recent shortage of venture capital has continued to reduce the size of start-up firms offering computer professional services.*

Equipment and Software: The U.S. computer industry continues on the road to recovery from the 1990-91 recession, led by an increase in domestic demand. The U.S. Department of Commerce notes the "mix of shipments was towards cheaper and increasingly more powerful workstations and personal computers, as users continue to shift many of their applications from mainframes and minicomputers." Revenues of the U.S. software industry should also continue to grow steadily, benefiting from its leading position in the world market and the continuing demand from users to more effectively harness the power of their PCs.

ALDUS CORPORATION
411 First Avenue South
Seattle WA 98104
206/622-5500
Contact: Personnel
Description: Aldus develops computer software for Apple Macintosh, Windows, and OS/2 compatible computers. **Number of employees nationwide:** 809.

APPLIED MICROSYSTEMS CORPORATION
P.O. Box 97002
Redmond WA 98073-9702
Contact: Human Resources
Description: A manufacturer and supplier of high-quality software development tools and in-circuit emulators for embedded system development.

ATTACHMATE CORPORATION
3617 131st Avenue SE
Bellevue WA 98006
206/644-4010
Contact: Personnel
Description: A manufacturer of high technology and information processing components and support products, including PC expansion boards and data communication equipment.

HEWLETT-PACKARD/VANCOUVER DIVISION
P.O. Box 8906
Vancouver WA 98668-8906
206/254-8110
Contact: Personnel Manager
Description: Produces workstation printers including serial impact and serial inkjet printers. Parent company is engaged in the design and manufacture of measurement and computation products and systems used in business, industry, engineering, science, health care, and education. Principal products are integrated instrument and computer systems (including hardware and software), computer systems and peripheral products, and medical electronic equipment and systems. **Parent company:** Hewlett Packard.

IBM CORPORATION
P.O. Box 1830
Seattle WA 98111
206/587-4400
Contact: Central Employment Office
Description: A manufacturer and supplier of information technology. Products include data processing machines and systems, telecommunications systems and products, information distributors, office systems, typewriters, copiers, educational and testing materials, and related supplies and services. Operates worldwide through the following groups, each comprised of several operating divisions: Information Systems Group; Information Systems and Technology Group; and Information Systems and Communications Group. Subsidiaries include: IBM Credit Corporation; IBM Instruments, Inc.; and IBM World Trade Corporation. **Corporate headquarters location:** Armonk NY. **Listed on:** New York Stock Exchange.

IBM CORPORATION
3600 Carillon Point
Kirkland WA 98033
206/803-0600
Contact: Human Resources Department
Description: A programming center.

INFOMETRIX INC.
2200 6th Avenue, Suite 833
Seattle WA 98121
206/441-6616
Contact: Personnel Department
Description: A company engaged in the manufacture and development of statistical software and microbial detection systems. **Common positions include:** Biological Scientist/Biochemist; Chemist; Technical Writer/Editor. **Educational backgrounds include:** Biology; Chemistry; Computer Science. **Benefits:** Dental Insurance; Life Insurance; Medical Insurance; Profit Sharing. **Special Programs:** Internships. **Corporate headquarters location:** This Location. **Operations at this facility include:** Administration; Manufacturing; Research and Development; Sales; Service. **Number of employees at this location:** 15.

INTERMEC CORPORATION
P.O. Box 4280
Everett WA 98203
206/348-2600
Contact: Human Resources Department
Description: A computer peripheral equipment company.

KEY TRONIC CORPORATION
P.O. Box 14687
Spokane WA 99214
509/928-8000
Fax: 509/927-5248
Contact: Employment Administrator
Description: The world's largest independent manufacturer of computer keyboards and computer peripherals. The company employs 2,400 people worldwide, at locations such as Juarez, Mexico, Taiwan, and Ireland. **Common positions include:** Accountant/Auditor; Adjuster; Attorney; Blue-Collar Worker Supervisor; Budget Analyst; Buyer; Collector; Computer Programmer; Computer Systems Analyst; Credit Manager; Customer Service Representative; Designer; Draftsperson; Economist/Market Research Analyst; Electrical/Electronic Engineer; Electrician; Industrial Manager; Investigator; Mechanical Engineer; Operations Research Analyst; Public Relations Specialist; Purchasing Agent and Manager; Quality Control Supervisor; Services Sales Representative; Software Engineer; Transportation/Traffic Specialist; Travel Agent. **Educational backgrounds include:** Accounting; Business Administration; Computer Science; Engineering; Marketing. **Benefits:** 401K; Bonus Award/Plan; Dental Insurance; Disability Coverage; Employee Discounts; Life Insurance; Medical Insurance; Profit Sharing; Tuition Assistance. **Corporate headquarters location:** This Location. **Other U.S. locations:** Las Cruces NM; El Paso TX. **Operations at this facility include:** Administration; Manufacturing; Research and Development; Sales; Service. **Listed on:** NASDAQ. **Number of employees nationwide:** 850.

MANNESMANN TALLY CORPORATION
P.O. Box 97018
Kent WA 98064-9718
206/251-5500
Contact: Personnel Department
Description: Manufactures laser, serial, and line matrix printers.

MICROSOFT CORPORATION
One Microsoft Way
Redmond WA 98052-6399
206/882-8080
Contact: Recruiting Department-NJB
Description: Designs, develops and supports a product line of systems and applications microcomputer software for business and professional use.

NCR CORPORATION
AT&T GLOBAL INFORMATION SOLUTIONS
15400 Southeast 30th Place
Bellevue WA 98007
206/643-4150
Contact: John McGinnis, Administrative Manager
Description: Nationally, the company develops, manufactures, markets, installs, and services business information processing systems for worldwide markets. Products include general purpose computer systems, industry-specific occupational workstations, and computer components and equipment.

OLIVETTI NORTH AMERICA, INC.
22425 East Appleway Avenue
Liberty Lake WA 99019
509/927-5600
Contact: Stan Dahlin, Staffing and Employee Relations Manager
Description: Provides branch automation solutions, systems, and services to the financial industry and is a major vendor for third party maintenance. **Common positions include:** Accountant/Auditor; Budget Analyst; Buyer; Computer Programmer; Computer Systems Analyst; Dispatcher; Electronics Technician; Financial Manager; General Manager; Inspector/Tester/Grader; Marketing Research Analyst; Marketing/Advertising/PR Manager; Personnel/ Labor Relations Specialist; Secretary; Software Engineer; Technical Writer/Editor. **Educational backgrounds include:** Accounting; Business Administration; Computer Science; Marketing. **Benefits:** Dental Insurance; Disability Coverage; Life Insurance; Medical Insurance; Pension Plan; Savings Plan; Tuition Assistance. **Corporate headquarters location:** This Location. **Other U.S. locations:** San Mateo CA; Shelton CT; Atlanta GA; Chicago IL. **Parent company:** Olivetti. **Operations at this facility include:** Administration; Sales; Service. **Listed on:** Privately held. **Annual Revenues:** $170,000,000. **Number of employees at this location:** 500. **Number of employees nationwide:** 1,100.

Note: Because addresses and telephone numbers of smaller companies change rapidly, we recommend you call each company and verify the information below before mailing to employers. Mass mailings are not recommended.

Additional employers with over 250 employees:

COMPUTERS AND COMPUTER EQUIPMENT WHOLESALE

Iomega Corporation
19125 North Creek
Parkway #112, Bothell
WA 98011-8000.
206/487-0045.

PC Craft Inc.
15325 NE 90th
Street, Redmond WA
98052-3562.
206/867-9651.

Altos Computer Systems Inc.
1611 116th Avenue
NE, Bellevue WA
98004-3045.
206/646-4909.

COMPUTER SERVICES

Analysts International Corporation
10655 NE 4th Street,
Suite 804, Bellevue
WA 98004-5022.
206/454-2500.

BCS Richland Inc.
P.O. Box 300,
Richland WA 99352-
0300. 509/376-1874.

Cap Gemini America
6840 Southcenter
Boulevard, Suite 325,
Seattle WA 98188-
2555. 206/433-9088.

Information Builders
1001 4th Avenue
#810, Seattle WA
98154-1101.
206/628-6494.

Intermetrics
1750 112th Avenue
NE, Suite D 151,
Bellevue WA 98004-
3789. 206/451-1120.

Legent Corporation
1111 3rd Avenue,
#2900, Seattle WA
98101-3207.
206/623-9344.

Must Software International
11911 NE 1st Street,
Suite 308, Bellevue
WA 98005-3032.
206/453-8125.

North American Morpho Systems
1145 Broadway, Suite
300, Tacoma WA
98402-3523.
206/383-3617.

Oracle Corporation
500 108th Avenue
NE, Suite 1300,
Bellevue WA 98004-
5535. 206/646-0200.

Project Software & Development
777 108th Avenue
NE, Suite 600,
Bellevue WA 98004-
5195. 206/646-4818.

Sybase
800 Bellevue Way NE
Suite 400, Bellevue
WA 98004-4229.
206/462-7428.

Walker Richer & Quinn
P.O. Box 31876,
Seattle WA 98103-
1876. 206/324-0350.

Computervision
11400 SE 8th Street,
Suite 350, Bellevue
WA 98004-6431.
206/455-0774.

Esca Corporation
11120 NE 33rd Place,
Bellevue WA 98004-
1448. 206/822-6800.

**Gasboy Development
Systems**
12525 Willows Road
NE, Suite 100,
Kirkland WA 98034-
8700. 206/821-5030.

**Mini-Systems
Associates**
12509 Bel Red Road,
Suite 100, Bellevue
WA 98005-2535.
206/637-0102.

Harris Adacom
10800 NE 8th Street,
Bellevue WA 98004-
4428. 206/455-5523.

Unisys Corporation
104 South Freya
Street, Suite 117,
Spokane WA 99202-
4896. 509/535-0909.

**Frank Russell
Company**
909 A Street, Tacoma
WA 98402-5111.
206/572-9500.

**COMPUTERS AND
RELATED EQUIPMENT**

**Bull HN Information
Systems**
P.O. Box 3647,
Bellevue WA 98009-
3647. 206/646-7400.

Computervision
445 SW 41st Street,
Renton WA 98055-
4926. 206/251-0652.

Computing Devices
40 Lake Bellevue
Drive, Suite 100,
Bellevue WA 98005-
2480. 206/453-7658.

**Concurrent Computer
Corporation**
13555 SE 36th
Street, Suite 260,
Bellevue WA 98006-
1485. 206/827-1484.

Itron Inc.
P.O. Box 15288,
Spokane WA 99215-
5288. 509/924-9900.

**Motorola Computer
Systems**
11911 NE 1st Street,
Suite 304, Bellevue
WA 98005-3032.
206/455-2442.

**Network Computing
Devices Inc.**
10900 NE 8th Street,
Suite 900, Bellevue
WA 98004-4400.
206/635-0849.

Calcomp Inc.
568 Industry Drive #6,
Seattle WA 98188-
3404. 206/575-7422.

**Network Systems
Corporation**
500 108th Avenue NE
Suite 485, Bellevue
WA 98004-5500.
206/454-5699.

Additional employers with under 250 employees:

**COMPUTER
PERIPHERAL
EQUIPMENT**

**Output Technology
Corporation**
2310 North Fancher
Road, Spokane WA
99212-1329.
509/536-0468.

**ELECTRONIC
COMPUTERS**

General Automation
12826 SE 40th Lane
#101, Bellevue WA
98006-5266.
206/562-2743.

**PERIPHERAL
EQUIPMENT AND
SOFTWARE
WHOLESALE**

Agena Corporation
9709 3rd Avenue NE,
Seattle WA 98115-
2027. 206/525-0005.

Encore Computer Corporation
4010 Lake Washington Boulevard NE 1, Kirkland WA 98033-7866. 206/828-3987.

COMPUTER PROGRAMMING SERVICES

ATC Graphics
24863 Norman Road NE, Kingston WA 98346-9305. 206/297-4648.

Interconnections
14711 NE 29th Place Suite 100, Bellevue WA 98007-7666. 206/881-5773.

R-Squared
9757 NE Juanita Drive, #128, Kirkland WA 98034-4205. 206/883-3116.

Scitor Corporation
631 Strander Boulevard, Seattle WA 98188-2922. 206/394-4800.

Scott & Scott Systems
2101 4th Avenue, Suite 303, Seattle WA 98121-2375. 206/441-1804.

Sierra Systems Consultants Inc.
1200 Westlake Avenue North, Suite 612, Seattle WA 98109-3530. 206/286-1205.

Syspro Inc.
300 120th Avenue NE Suite 10, Bellevue WA 98005-3020. 206/462-5776.

Wall Data Inc.
17769 NE 78th Place, Redmond WA 98052-4962. 206/883-4777.

CNA Manufacturing Systems Inc.
6675 185th Avenue NE, Redmond WA 98052-6734. 206/861-4065.

COMPUTER INTEGRATED SOFTWARE DESIGN

ESCA Corporation
11120 NE 33rd Place, Bellevue WA 98004-1448. 206/822-6800.

Phamis Inc.
401 2nd Avenue South, #200, Seattle WA 98104-2862. 206/622-9558.

COMPUTER PROCESSING AND DATA PREPARATION

US Intelco Networks
P.O. Box 2909, Olympia WA 98507-2909. 206/493-6000.

Lasergraphics
17791 Fjord Drive NE, Poulsbo WA 98370-8481. 206/697-3717.

Electronic Data Systems
19351 8th Avenue NE Building B, Poulsbo WA 98370-8710. 206/697-3330.

COMPUTER MAINTENANCE AND REPAIR

Ballard Computer
5424 Ballard Avenue NW, Seattle WA 98107-4028. 206/781-7000.

NCR Corporation
15400 SE 30th Place, Bellevue WA 98007-6546. 206/643-4150.

COMPUTER RELATED SERVICES

Cimlinc Inc.
130 Andover Park East Suite 200, Seattle WA 98188-2948. 206/431-7980.

**NW/Six Sigma
Washington**
4918 20th Street E,
Tacoma WA 98424-
1922. 206/922-9393.

**Computer Sciences
Corporation**
2817 Wheaton Way
Suite 203, Bremerton

WA 98310-3440.
206/373-1032.

For more information on career opportunities in the computer industry:

Associations

**ASSOCIATION FOR COMPUTING
MACHINERY**
1515 Broadway, 17th Floor, New
York NY 10036. 212/869-7440.
Membership required.

**INFORMATION AND
TECHNOLOGY ASSOCIATION OF
AMERICA**
1616 North Fort Myer Drive, Suite
1300, Arlington VA 22209. 703/522-
5055.

Directories

**INFORMATION INDUSTRY
DIRECTORY**
Gale Research Inc., 835 Penobscot
Building, Detroit MI 48226.
313/961-2242.

Magazines

**COMPUTER-AIDED
ENGINEERING**
Penton Publishing, 1100 Superior
Avenue, Cleveland OH 44114.
216/696-7100

COMPUTERWORLD
CW Communications, 375
Cochituate Road, P.O. Box 01701-
9171. 508/879-0700.

DATA COMMUNICATIONS
McGraw-Hill, 1221 Avenue of the
Americas, New York NY 10020.
212/512-2000.

DATAMATION
Cahners Publishing, 275
Washington Street, Newton MA
02158. 617/964-3030.

IDC REPORT
International Data Corporation, Five
Speen Street, Framingham MA
01701. 508/872-8200.

EDUCATIONAL SERVICES

Job prospects for college faculty will increase at average speed during the '90s. Most openings will result from retirements. The best prospects are in business, engineering, health sciences, physical sciences, and mathematics. Among kindergarten and elementary school teachers, the best opportunities await those with training in special education. Among high school teachers, opportunities will increase rapidly. Increased teacher involvement and higher salaries will attract new applicants.

BAINBRIDGE SCHOOL DISTRICT
8489 Madison Avenue NE
Bainbridge Island WA 98110
206/842-4714
Contact: Human Resources
Description: A five-school district in Bainbridge Island.

BATTLE GROUND PUBLIC SCHOOLS
204 West Main Street
Battle Ground WA 98604
206/687-6534
Contact: Human Resources
Description: A 16-school district in Battle Ground.

BELLEVUE COMMUNITY COLLEGE
3000 Landerholm Circle SE
Bellevue WA 98007
206/641-2222
Contact: Human Resources Department
Description: A community college.

BETHEL SCHOOL DISTRICT
516 East 176th Street
Spanaway WA 98387
206/536-7272
Contact: Human Resources
Description: A 26-school district in Spanaway.

CENTRAL KITSAP SCHOOL DISTRICT
9210 Silverdale Way NW, P.O. Box 8
Silverdale WA 93838
206/692-3118
Contact: Human Resources
Description: A 18-school district in Silverdale.

CENTRAL WASHINGTON UNIVERSITY
400 East 8 Avenue
Ellensburg WA 98926-7425
509/963-1202
Fax: 509/963-1733
Contact: Personnel Services
Description: A university. **Common positions include:** Accountant/Auditor; Actuary; Adjuster; Administrative Services Manager; Architect; Blue-Collar Worker Supervisor; Broadcast Technician; Budget Analyst; Buyer; Clerical Supervisor; Collector; Computer Programmer; Computer Systems Analyst; Construction Contractor and Manager; Cosmetologist; Education Administrator; Electrician; Financial Analyst; General Manager; Health Services Manager; Human Service Worker; Investigator; Librarian; Library Technician; Licensed Practical Nurse; Materials Engineer; Operations/Production Manager; Personnel/Labor Relations Specialist; Physician; Preschool Worker; Public Relations Specialist; Purchasing Agent and Manager; Restaurant/Food Service Manager; Statistician; Teacher. **Benefits:** Dental Insurance; Disability Coverage; Life Insurance; Medical Insurance; Pension Plan; Tuition Assistance.

CLOVER PARK SCHOOL DISTRICT
10903 Gravelly Lake Drive
Tacoma WA 98499
206/589-7433
Fax: 206/589-7440
Contact: Human Resources
Description: A 28-school district in Tacoma. **Common positions include:** Licensed Practical Nurse; Occupational Therapist; Physical Therapist; Registered Nurse; Speech-Language Pathologist; Teacher. **Educational backgrounds include:** Accounting; Education. **Benefits:** Dental Insurance; Disability Coverage; Life Insurance; Medical Insurance. **Corporate headquarters location:** This Location. **Operations at this facility include:** Administration. **Number of employees at this location:** 1,800.

EASTERN WASHINGTON UNIVERSITY
MS 114, Eastern Washington University
Cheney WA 99004-2431
509/359-2381
Contact: Human Resources
Description: A public university.

EDMONDS COMMUNITY COLLEGE
20000 68th Avenue West
Lynnwood WA 98036
206/640-1400.
Fax: 206/640-1359
Contact: Pauline Rita, Human Resources Assistant
Description: A community college which is part of the Washington State Public Higher Education System. **Common positions include:** Accountant/Auditor; Budget Analyst; Buyer; Cashier; Clerical Supervisor; Commercial Artist; Computer Operator; Computer Programmer; Computer Systems Analyst; Counselor; Customer Service Representative; Editor; Education Administrator; Electrician; Financial Manager; Librarian; Library Technician; Payroll Clerk; Preschool Worker; Public Relations Specialist; Purchasing Agent and Manager; Receptionist; Secretary; Sociologist; Stenographer; Stock Clerk; Teacher; Teacher Aide; Technical Writer/Editor; Typist/Word Processor. **Educational backgrounds include:** Accounting; Art/Design; Biology; Business Administration; Chemistry; Communications; Computer Science; Economics; Engineering; Finance; Liberal Arts; Marketing; Mathematics; Physics. **Benefits:** Daycare Assistance; Dental Insurance; Disability Coverage; Life Insurance; Medical Insurance; Pension Plan; Tuition Assistance. **Corporate headquarters location:** This Location. **Number of employees at this location:** 1,000.

EDMONDS SCHOOL DISTRICT
20420 68th Avenue
Lynnwood WA 98036
206/670-7020
Contact: Human Resources
Description: A 38-school district.

EVERETT COMMUNITY COLLEGE
801 Wetmore Avenue
Everett WA 98201
206/388-9100
Contact: Human Resources Department
Description: A community college.

EVERETT SCHOOL DISTRICT
4730 Colby Avenue
Everett WA 98203
206/339-4245
Contact: Human Resources
Description: A 26-school district.

EVERGREEN SCHOOL DISTRICT
13905 NE 28th Street
Vancouver WA 98686
206/256-6011
Contact: Human Resources
Description: A 25-school district.

FEDERAL WAY SCHOOL DISTRICT
31405 18th Avenue
Federal Way WA 98003
206/941-0100
Contact: Human Resources
Description: A 33-school district.

MILTON FIFE COOPERATIVE PRESCHOOL
2303 54th Avenue East
Tacoma WA 98424
206/922-3076
Contact: Human Resources
Description: A preschool.

FRANKLIN PIERCE SCHOOL DISTRICT
315 South 129th Street
Tacoma WA 98444
206/537-0211
Contact: Greg Roberts, Executive Director of Personnel
Description: A K-12 school district. **Common positions include:** Education Administrator; Librarian; Library Technician; Licensed Practical Nurse; Preschool Worker; Teacher. **Educational backgrounds include:** Education. **Benefits:** Dental Insurance; Disability Coverage; Medical Insurance; Pension Plan; Savings Plan. **Operations at this facility include:** Administration.

HIGHLINE COMMUNITY COLLEGE
P.O. Box 98000
Des Moines WA 98198-9800
206/878-3710
Contact: Human Resources Department
Description: A community college.

HIGHLINE SCHOOL DISTRICT
15675 Arbaum Boulevard SW
Seattle WA 98166
206/433-2281
Contact: Human Resources
Description: A 37-school district.

KENT SCHOOL DISTRICT
12033 SE 256th Street
Kent WA 98031
206/859-7209
Contact: Human Resources
Description: A 36-school district. **Common positions include:** Accountant/ Auditor; Budget Analyst; Buyer; Computer Programmer; Computer Systems Analyst; Construction Contractor and Manager; Counselor; Education Administrator; Electrician; Personnel/Labor Relations Specialist; Psychologist; Public Relations Specialist; Purchasing Agent and Manager; Registered Nurse; Statistician; Teacher. **Educational backgrounds include:** Teaching. **Benefits:** Dental Insurance; Disability Coverage; Life Insurance; Medical Insurance; Pension Plan. **Corporate headquarters location:** This Location. **Operations at this facility include:** Administration. **Number of employees at this location:** 2,500.

MARYSVILLE SCHOOL DISTRICT
4220 80th Street NE
Marysville WA 98270
206/653-0809
Contact: Human Resources
Description: A 14-school district.

MEAD SCHOOL DISTRICT
North 12508 Freya Street
Mead WA 99021
509/468-3007
Contact: Human Resources
Description: An 11-school district.

MERCER ISLAND SCHOOL DISTRICT
4160 86th Avenue SE
Mercer Island WA 98040
206/236-3318
Contact: Human Resources
Description: A six-school district.

RENTON SCHOOL DISTRICT
435 Main Avenue South
Renton WA 98055
206/235-2385
Contact: Human Resources
Description: A 25-school district.

RENTON TECHNICAL COLLEGE
3000 NE 4th Street
Renton WA 98056
206/235-2352
Contact: Human Resources Department
Description: A local technical college.

SEATTLE CENTRAL COMMUNITY COLLEGE
1701 Broadway
Seattle WA 98122
206/587-4155
Contact: Human Resources Department
Description: A community college. **Jobline:** 206/587-5454

SEATTLE SCHOOL DISTRICT
815 4th Avenue North
Seattle WA 98109
206/298-7377
Contact: Human Resources
Description: A school district. **Common positions include:** Teacher. **Educational backgrounds include:** Biology; Chemistry; Mathematics. **Benefits:** 401K; Dental Insurance; Disability Coverage; Legal Services; Medical Insurance; Pension Plan. **Corporate headquarters location:** This Location. **Number of employees at this location:** 5,500.

SEATTLE UNIVERSITY
Broadway and Madison
Seattle WA 98122-4460
206/296-6000
Contact: Human Resources Department
Description: A university.

SEDRO WOOLLEY SCHOOL DISTRICT 101
2079 Cook Road
Sedro Woolley WA 98284
206/856-0831
Contact: Human Resources
Description: Offices of the Sedro Woolley school system.

SHORELINE COMMUNITY COLLEGE
16101 Greenwood Avenue North
Seattle WA 98133
206/546-4621
Contact: Human Resources Department
Description: A community college.

SKAGIT VALLEY COLLEGE
2405 East College Way
Mt. Vernon WA 98273
206/428-1261
Contact: Human Resources Department
Description: A college.

SOUTH KITSAP SCHOOL DISTRICT
1962 Hoover Avenue SE
Port Orchard WA 98366
206/876-7306
Fax: 206/876-7675
Contact: Mrs. Sherrie Eggen, Executive Director for Personnel
Description: A school district. **Common positions include:** Education
Administrator; Librarian; Licensed Practical Nurse; Occupational Therapist;
Teacher. **Educational backgrounds include:** Teaching. **Benefits:** 401K; Dental
Insurance; Disability Coverage; Life Insurance; Medical Insurance; Pension
Plan; Savings Plan. **Corporate headquarters location:** This Location.
Operations at this facility include: Administration. **Number of employees at
this location:** 1,100.

SOUTH PUGET SOUND COMMUNITY COLLEGE
2011 Mottman Road SW
Olympia WA 98502-6218
Contact: Linda Bures, Job Developer
Description: A community college.

SPOKANE SCHOOL DISTRICT
Administrative Center
200 North Bernard Street
Spokane WA 99201
509/353-5336
Contact: Human Resources
Description: A 63-school school district. Other job hotline number: 509/353-
7639, certificated jobs.

TACOMA SCHOOL DISTRICT
601 South 8th Street
Tacoma WA 98405
206/596-1250
Contact: Human Resources
Description: A 71-school district.

TECHNICAL TRAINING INSTITUTES, INC.
5005 Pacific East #15
2033 Sixth Avenue
Fife WA 98424-2647
206/922-1123
Contact: Personnel Department
Description: Operates a vocational and technical school.

UNIVERSITY OF WASHINGTON
1320 NE Campus Parkway
Seattle WA 98105
206/543-2544
Contact: Staff Employment
Description: A university.

VANCOUVER SCHOOL DISTRICT
605 North Devine Road
Vancouver WA 98661
206/696-7127
Contact: Human Resources
Description: A 34 school district.

WASHINGTON STATE UNIVERSITY
French Administration Building
Pullman WA 99163
509/335-4521
Contact: Human Resources
Description: A state university.

WESTERN WASHINGTON UNIVERSITY
Personnel Department
Bellingham WA 98225-9021
206/650-3774
Contact: Personnel
Description: A university.

WHITMAN COLLEGE
345 Boyer Avenue
Walla Walla WA 99362
509/527-5172
Contact: Personnel Director
Description: A college.

YAKIMA SCHOOL DISTRICT
104 North 4th Avenue
Yakima WA 98901
509/575-3228
Contact: Human Resources
Description: A 27-school district.

Note: Because addresses and telephone numbers of smaller companies change rapidly, we recommend you call each company and verify the information below before mailing to employers. Mass mailings are not recommended.

Additional employers with over 250 employees:

JUNIOR COLLEGES AND TECHNICAL INSTITUTES

Spokane Community College
1810 North Greene Street, Spokane WA 99207-5320.
509/533-7000.

Spokane Falls Community College
3410 West Fort George Wright Drive, Spokane WA 99204-5204. 509/533-3500.

COLLEGES AND UNIVERSITIES

Gonzaga University
502 East Boone Avenue, Spokane WA 99258. 509/328-4220.

Whitworth College
300 West Hawthorne Road, Spokane WA 99251. 509/466-1000.

Additional employers with under 250 employees:

SCHOOLS AND SCHOOL DISTRICTS

Mead Senior High School
302 West Hastings Road, Spokane WA 99218-2545.
509/468-3050.

Wenatchee High School
1101 Millerdale Avenue, Wenatchee WA 98801-3299.
509/663-8117.

Annie Wright School
827 Tacoma Avenue N, Tacoma WA 98403-2899.
206/272-2216.

Lakeside School
14050 1st Avenue NE, Seattle WA 98125-3025.
206/368-3600.

AC Davis Senior High School
212 South 6th Avenue, Yakima WA 98902-3303.
509/575-3311.

Auburn Senior High School
800 4th Street NE, Auburn WA 98002-5018. 206/931-4883.

COLLEGES AND UNIVERSITIES

Cornish College Of The Arts
710 East Roy Street, Seattle WA 98102-4696. 206/323-1400.

Heritage College
3240 Fort Road, Toppenish WA 98948-9599. 509/865-2244.

Northwest College Assembly Of God
P.O. Box 579, Kirkland WA 98083-0579. 206/822-8266.

St. Martin's College
5300 Pacific Avenue SE, Olympia WA 98503-1297. 206/491-4700.

JUNIOR COLLEGES AND TECHNICAL INSTITUTES

Centia College
600 West Locust Street, Centralia WA 98531-4035. 206/736-9391.

Grays Harbor College
1620 Edward P Smith Drive, Aberdeen WA 98520-7599. 206/532-9020.

Lower Columbia College
P.O. Box 3010, Longview WA 98632. 206/577-2300.

Peninsula College
1502 East Lauridsen Boulevard, Port Angeles WA 98362-6698. 206/452-9277.

Tacoma Community College
5900 South 12th Street, Tacoma WA 98465-1950. 206/566-5000.

Walla Walla Community College
500 Tausick Way, Walla Walla WA 99362-9270. 509/522-2500.

Wenatchee Valley College
1300 5th Street, Wenatchee WA 98801-1799. 509/662-1651.

Whatcom Community College
237 West Kellogg Road, Bellingham WA 98226-8033. 206/676-2170.

Yakima Valley Community College
P.O. Box 1647, Yakima WA 98907-1647. 509/575-2350.

VOCATIONAL SCHOOLS

Lake Washington Technical College
11605 132nd Avenue NE, Kirkland WA 98034-8505. 206/828-5600.

For more information on career opportunities in educational services:

Associations

AMERICAN ASSOCIATION OF SCHOOL ADMINISTRATORS
1801 North Moore Street, Arlington VA 22209. 703/528-0700.

AMERICAN FEDERATION OF TEACHERS
555 New Jersey Avenue NW, Washington DC 20001. 202/879-4400.

COLLEGE AND UNIVERSITY PERSONNEL ASSOCIATION
1233 20th Street NW, Suite 301, Washington DC 20036. 202/429-0311. Membership required.

NATIONAL ASSOCIATION OF BIOLOGY TEACHERS
11250 Roger Bacon Drive, #19, Reston VA 22090. 703/471-1134.

NATIONAL ASSOCIATION OF COLLEGE AND UNIVERSITY BUSINESS OFFICERS
1 DuPont Circle, Suite 500, Washington DC 20036. 202/861-2500. Membership required.

NATIONAL ASSOCIATION OF COLLEGE ADMISSION COUNSELORS
1631 Prince Street, Alexandria VA 22314. 703/836-2222.

NATIONAL SCIENCE TEACHERS ASSOCIATION
8240-1840 Wilson Boulevard, Arlington VA 22201-3000. 703/243-7100.

Directories

WASHINGTON HIGHER EDUCATION ASSOCIATION DIRECTORY
Council for Advancement and Support of Education, 11 DuPont Circle NW, Suite 400, Washington DC 20036 202/328-5900.

Books

ACADEMIC LABOR MARKETS
Falmer Press, Taylor & Francis, Inc., 1900 Frost Road, Suite 101, Bristol PA 19007. 800/821-8312.

HOW TO GET A JOB IN EDUCATION
Bob Adams, Inc., 260 Center Street, Holbrook MA 02343. 617/787-8100.

ELECTRONIC/INDUSTRIAL ELECTRICAL EQUIPMENT

Shipments for the electrical component industry were expected to jump almost 9 percent in 1994, due to an increased demand for computers, communications equipment, and electronic automotive products. Semiconductors should lead the way, sporting an estimated 25 percent growth rate in 1994. Jobseekers should seek out companies that can anticipate which technologies and product variants will be among industry standards.

Electric lighting and wiring equipment shipments rose more than 4 percent in 1993, and were expected to climb 5 percent in 1994. Shipment growth will continue to be led by the rejuvenated market for residential and commercial construction. Electrical equipment shipment growth were also in the 4 percent range for 1994.

ALLIANT TECHNICAL SYSTEMS
6500 Harbor Heights Parkway
Muckilteo WA 98275
206/789-2000
Contact: Personnel Director
Description: A manufacturer of naval sonar and acoustic equipment for offshore oil and commercial marine applications. Nationally, the company is a high-technology firm doing business in four industry segments: Aerospace and Defense, Control Products, Control Systems, and Information Systems. **Corporate headquarters location:** Minneapolis MN. **Listed on:** New York Stock Exchange.

AVTECH CORPORATION
3400 Wallingford North
Seattle WA 98103
206/634-2544
Contact: Stan Hirooka, Personnel Director
Description: Manufactures a variety of electronics equipment products for a number of end uses.

BELL INDUSTRIES/ILLUMINATED DISPLAYS DIVISION
18225 Northeast 76th
Redmond WA 98052
206/885-4353
Contact: Human Resources Administrator
Description: Nationally, the company is primarily a distributor of electronic components and a manufacturer of uncoated aluminum memory discs and

other computer and electronic components. Also distributes building and construction, graphic arts and automotive products. **Common positions include:** Accountant/Auditor; Blue-Collar Worker Supervisor; Draftsperson; Industrial Engineer; Manufacturer's/Wholesaler's Sales Rep.; Marketing Specialist; Mechanical Engineer; Quality Control Supervisor; Technical Writer/Editor. **Educational backgrounds include:** Business Administration; Engineering; Finance; Marketing. **Benefits:** Dental Insurance; Disability Coverage; Life Insurance; Medical Insurance; Pension Plan; Profit Sharing; Savings Plan; Tuition Assistance. **Corporate headquarters location:** Los Angeles CA. **Operations at this facility include:** Manufacturing. **Listed on:** New York Stock Exchange.

BRANOM INSTRUMENT COMPANY
P.O. Box 80307
Seattle WA 98108-0307
206/762-6050
Contact: Personnel Department
Description: A wholesaler of electronic parts and equipment.

CARVER CORPORATION
P.O. Box 1237
Lynnwood WA 98046
206/775-1202
Contact: Personnel Department
Description: Manufactures audio components for consumer and industrial use. **Number of employees at this location:** 230.

COLUMBIA LIGHTING INC./LIGHTING PRODUCTS
Terminal Annex Box 2787
Spokane WA 99220
509/924-7000
Contact: Frank Lydon, Personnel Director
Description: A manufacturer of a variety of lighting equipment.

DATA IO CORPORATION
P.O. Box 97046
Redmond WA 98073
206/881-6444
Contact: Human Resources Department
Description: Produces semiconductors and related devices.

DATACOMM TECHNOLOGIES, INC.
11001 31st Place West
Everett WA 90204
206/355-0590
Contact: Personnel
Description: A manufacturer of high-technology support equipment, digital test equipment, and related products. **Common positions include:**

Accountant/Auditor; Administrator; Advertising Clerk; Blue-Collar Worker Supervisor; Buyer; Computer Programmer; Credit Manager; Customer Service Representative; Department Manager; Draftsperson; Electrical/Electronic Engineer; Financial Analyst; Manufacturer's/Wholesaler's Sales Rep.; Marketing Specialist; Mechanical Engineer; Operations/Production Manager; Personnel/Labor Relations Specialist; Purchasing Agent and Manager; Quality Control Supervisor; Systems Analyst. **Educational backgrounds include:** Accounting; Business Administration; Communications; Computer Science; Engineering; Finance; Marketing. **Benefits:** Dental Insurance; Disability Coverage; Life Insurance; Medical Insurance; Pension Plan; Profit Sharing; Tuition Assistance. **Corporate headquarters location:** This Location. **Operations at this facility include:** Administration; Manufacturing; Research and Development; Sales; Service.

EATON CORPORATION
720 80th Street Southwest
Everett WA 98203
206/353-0900
Contact: Human Resources Department
Description: A manufacturer of a wide variety of electronics equipment, including data processing systems and products and a line of communications equipment.

ELDEC CORPORATION
P.O. Box 100
Lynnwood WA 98046-0100
206/743-1313
Contact: Employment Department
Description: Custom designs precision electronic equipment.

ESTERLINE TECHNOLOGIES
10800 North East 8th Street, Suite 600
Bellevue WA 98004
206/453-6001
Contact: Personnel Department
Description: Manufactures printed circuit-board drilling machinery, and production machinery for the electronics and semiconductor industries.

JOHN FLUKE MANUFACTURING COMPANY, INC.
P.O. Box 9090
Everett WA 98206-9090
206/347-6100
Contact: Personnel Department
Description: A manufacturer of electronic instrumentation for test measurement and calibration.

HEWLETT-PACKARD COMPANY
15815 SE 37th Street
Bellevue WA 98006
206/643-4000
Contact: Human Resources Department
Description: Manufactures electronic measurement and computing products. **Common positions include:** Manufacturer's/Wholesaler's Sales Rep.; Personnel/Labor Relations Specialist; Secretary; Systems Analyst. **Educational backgrounds include:** Business Administration; Computer Science; Engineering; Marketing. **Benefits:** Dental Insurance; Disability Coverage; Employee Discounts; Life Insurance; Meal Discounts; Pension Plan; Profit Sharing; Savings Plan; Tuition Assistance. **Corporate headquarters location:** Palo Alto CA. **Operations at this facility include:** Sales; Service. **Listed on:** New York Stock Exchange. **Annual Revenues:** $21,000,000,000. **Number of employees at this location:** 225. **Number of employees nationwide:** 90,000.

HEWLETT-PACKARD/LAKE STEVENS INSTRUMENT DIVISION
8600 Soper Hill Road
Everett WA 98205-1298
Contact: Staffing Department
Description: Produces synthesizers and low-frequency spectrum and network analyzers for communications and electronics equipment; waveform generators and dynamics analyzers for electromechanical and mechanical systems. Parent company is engaged in the design and manufacture of measurement and computation products and systems used in business, industry, engineering, science, health care, and education. Principal products are integrated instrument and computer systems (including hardware and software), computer systems and peripheral products, and medical electronic equipment and systems. **Common positions include:** Electrical/Electronic Engineer; Financial Analyst; Software Engineer. **Educational backgrounds include:** Computer Science; Economics; Finance. **Corporate headquarters location:** Palo Alto CA. **Parent company:** Hewlett Packard. **Operations at this facility include:** Manufacturing; Research and Development.

HEWLETT-PACKARD/SPOKANE DIVISION
P.O. Box 2500
Spokane WA 99220-2500
509/921-4001
Contact: Personnel Department
Description: Produces RF (radio frequency) signal generators and synthesizers, RF measuring receivers and RF transceiver test equipment. Parent company is engaged in the design and manufacture of measurement and computation products and systems used in business, industry, engineering, science, health care, and education. Principal products are integrated instrument and computer systems (including hardware and software), computer systems and peripheral products, and medical electronic equipment and systems. **Parent company:** Hewlett Packard.

INTERPOINT CORPORATION

14833 NE 87th
Redmond WA 98052
206/882-3100
Contact: Barbie Runyon, Human Resources Administrator
Description: A manufacturer of electronic circuit equipment including microcircuits and ac/dc power converters. **Common positions include:** Draftsperson; Electrical/Electronic Engineer. **Educational backgrounds include:** Engineering. **Benefits:** Dental Insurance; Disability Coverage; Life Insurance; Medical Insurance; Profit Sharing; Tuition Assistance.

KORRY ELECTRONICS

901 Dexter Avenue North
Seattle WA 98109
206/281-1319
Fax: 206/281-1404
Contact: Marlene Winter, Director of Human Resources
Description: A manufacturer of lighted pushbutton switches, annunciators, panels, keyboards, and accessories. **Common positions include:** Accountant/ Auditor; Buyer; Cost Estimator; Customer Service Representative; Designer; Draftsperson; Economist/Market Research Analyst; Electrical/Electronic Engineer; Financial Analyst; Manufacturer's/Wholesaler's Sales Rep.; Mechanical Engineer; Personnel/Labor Relations Specialist; Purchasing Agent and Manager; Quality Control Supervisor; Technical Writer/Editor. **Educational backgrounds include:** Engineering. **Benefits:** 401K; Dental Insurance; Disability Coverage; Life Insurance; Medical Insurance; Pension Plan; Tuition Assistance. **Corporate headquarters location:** Bellevue WA. **Parent company:** Esterline Technologies. **Operations at this facility include:** Administration; Manufacturing; Research and Development; Sales; Service. **Listed on:** New York Stock Exchange. **Number of employees at this location:** 400.

PAINE CORPORATION

2401 South Bayview Street
Seattle WA 98144
206/329-8600
Contact: Personnel Department
Description: A company engaged in the manufacture of pressure-measuring instruments and thick film microcircuits.

STORM PRODUCTS

P.O. Box 387
Woodinville WA 98072
206/488-7400
Contact: Human Resources
Description: Manufactures electrical products.

Note: Because addresses and telephone numbers of smaller companies change rapidly, we recommend you call each company and verify the information below before mailing to employers. Mass mailings are not recommended.

Additional employers with over 250 employees:

TRANSFORMERS

Square D Company
7525 SE 24th Street,
Suite 320, Mercer
Island WA 98040-
2300. 206/232-9702.

ELECTRON TUBES

Pacific Circuits Inc.
17550 NE 67th Court,
Redmond WA 98052-
4986. 206/883-7575.

Westak Inc.
14815 NE 40th
Street, Redmond WA
98052-5327.
206/885-4194.

**SEMICONDUCTORS
AND RELATED
DEVICES**

**Matsushita
Semiconductor
Corporation**
1111 39th Avenue
SE, Puyallup WA
98374-2122.
206/841-6000.

SEH America Inc.
4111 NE 112th
Avenue, Vancouver
WA 98682-6799.
206/254-3030.

Sharp Microelectrics
5700 NW Pacific Rim
Boulevard, Camas WA
98607-9489.
206/834-8700.

**ELECTRONIC
COMPONENTS**

**AVX Vancouver
Corporation**
5701 East Fourth Plain
Boulevard, Vancouver
WA 98661-6857.
206/696-2840.

**Johnson Matthey
Electronics**
15128 East Euclid
Avenue, Spokane WA
99216-1801.
509/924-2200.

Telect Inc.
P.O. Box 665, Liberty
Lake WA 99019-
0665. 509/926-6000.

BATTERIES

**Standard Batteries Of
Seattle**
5200 4th Avenue
South, Seattle WA
98108-2215.
206/763-1244.

**ELECTRICAL
EQUIPMENT
WHOLESALE**

Grainger
6725 South Todd
Boulevard, Seattle WA
98188-4771.
206/251-5030.

**Siemens Electrical
Products**
1522 North
Washington Street,
Suite 201, Spokane
WA 99201-2454.
509/325-2582.

**ELECTRONIC PARTS
AND EQUIPMENT
WHOLESALE**

Kent Electronics
8469 154th Avenue
NE, Redmond WA
98052-3863.
206/883-7200.

Ratelco
1260 Mercer Street,
Seattle WA 98109-
5589. 206/624-7770.

Additional employers with under 250 employees:

SWITCHGEAR AND SWITCHBOARD APPARATUS

Cummins Inc.
811 SW Grady Way,
Renton WA 98055-
2944. 206/235-0808.

ELECTRON TUBES

Westak North
14815 NE 40th
Street, Redmond WA
98052-5327.
206/885-4194.

SEMICONDUCTORS AND RELATED DEVICES

Applied Microsystems Corporation
5020 148th Avenue
NE, Redmond WA
98052-5172.
206/882-2000.

ELECTRONIC COMPONENTS

Union Carbide Crystal Products
750 South 32nd
Street, Washougal WA
98671-2520.
206/835-8566.

ELECTRICAL EQUIPMENT FOR ENGINES

Tam Engineering Corporation
P.O. Box 11086,
Tacoma WA 98411-
0086. 206/383-1684.

MAGNETIC AND OPTICAL RECORDING MEDIA

Media Technologies
22027 17th Avenue
SE Suite 101, Bothell
WA 98021-7410.
206/483-8989.

ELECTRICAL APPARATUS WHOLESALE

Carlyle Inc.
17620 West Valley
Highway, Seattle WA
98188-5539.
206/251-0700.

Stusser Electric Company
660 South Andover
Street, Seattle WA
98108-5235.
206/624-8770.

T&T Flagging Inc.
3116 Wilton Lane
East, Tacoma WA
98424-2325.
206/922-4730.

Besco
6141 4th Avenue
South
Seattle WA 98108-
3216. 206/762-3800.

ELECTRONIC PARTS WHOLESALE

Alpha Technologies
3767 Alpha Way,
Bellingham WA
98226-8302.
206/647-2360.

Radar Electric Company
222 Symons Street,
Richland WA 99352-
3408. 509/943-8336.

Zetron Inc.
12335 134th Court
NE, Redmond WA
98052-2439.
206/820-6363.

Emerald Technology
19021 120th Avenue
NE, Bothell WA
98011-9505.
206/485-8200.

For more information on career opportunities in the electronic/industrial electrical equipment industry:

Associations

AMERICAN CERAMIC SOCIETY
735 Ceramic Place, Westerville OH
43081. 614/890-4700. 800/837-1804.
(Ceramics futures information)
Membership required.

ELECTROCHEMICAL SOCIETY
10 South Main Street, Pennington NJ
08534-2896. 609/737-1902

**ELECTRONIC INDUSTRIES
ASSOCIATION**
2001 Pennsylvania Avenue NW,
Washington DC 20006. 202/457-4900

**ELECTRONICS TECHNICIANS
ASSOCIATION**
602 North Jackson Street,
Greencastle IN 46135. 317/653-8262

**INSTITUTE OF ELECTRICAL AND
ELECTRONICS ENGINEERS (IEEE)**
345 East 47th Street, New York NY
10017. 212/705-7900

**INSTITUTE OF ELECTRICAL AND
ELECTRONICS ENGINEERS (IEEE)**
1828 Elm Street NW, Suite 1202,
Washington DC 20036-5104.
Professional activities line: 202/785-
0017. National information line:
202/785-2180.

**INTERNATIONAL BROTHERHOOD
OF ELECTRICAL WORKERS**
1125 15th Street NW, Washington DC
20005. 202/833-7000

**INTERNATIONAL SOCIETY OF
CERTIFIED ELECTRONICS
TECHNICIANS**
2708 West Berry Street, Fort Worth
TX 76109. 817/921-9101

**NATIONAL ELECTRICAL
MANUFACTURERS ASSOCIATION**
2101 L Street NW, Suite 300,
Washington DC 20037. 202/457-8400

**NATIONAL ELECTRONICS SALES
AND SERVICES ASSOCIATION**
2708 West Berry, Fort Worth TX
76109. 817/921-9061

**ROBOTICS INTERNATIONAL OF
THE SOCIETY OF
MANUFACTURING ENGINEERS**
P.O. Box 930, One SME Drive,
Dearborn MI 48121. 313/271-1500

ENVIRONMENTAL SERVICES

 *The environmental services industry is expected to continue growing, but according to industry observers, it will probably not have the "double-digit growth rate of the last decade." Amendments made to the Clean Air Act in 1990 will continue to drive domestic demand for environmental services, as clients try to meet tougher environmental standards. The continued closing of municipal landfills will generate growth in new technology in the waste treatment, recycling, and disposal markets. Internationally, the industry's greatest potential lies in Eastern Europe, Mexico, Latin America, the former Soviet Union, and Southeast Asia.*

DOWL ENGINEERS
8320 154th Avenue NE
Redmond WA 98052
206/869-2670
Contact: John Paulson, Office Manager
Description: Offers specialized environmental engineering services to a variety of clients in government and industry. Also provides civil engineering and surveying services to municipal and private development clients.

WASTE MANAGEMENT NORTHWEST INC.
P.O. Box 768
Bothell WA 98041
206/337-1197
Contact: Human Resources Department
Description: A water treatment company.

For more information on career opportunities in environmental services:

Associations

AIR AND WASTE MANAGEMENT ASSOCIATION
One Gateway Center, Third Floor, Pittsburgh PA 15222. 412/232-3444.

ASSOCIATION OF STATE & INTERSTATE WATER POLLUTION CONTROL ADMINISTRATORS
750 First Street NE, Suite 910, Washington DC 20002. 202/898-0905.

INSTITUTE OF CLEAN AIR COMPANIES
1707 L Street NW, Washington DC 20036. 202/457-0911

NATIONAL SOLID WASTE MANAGEMENT ASSOCIATION
1730 Rhode Island Avenue NW, Suite 1000, Washington DC 20036. 202/659-4613.

U.S. ENVIRONMENTAL PROTECTION ASSOCIATION
401 M Street SW, Washington DC 20460. 202/260-2090.

WATER ENVIRONMENT FEDERATION
601 Wythe Street, Alexandria VA 22314. 703/684-2400. Subscription to federation's jobs newsletter required for career information.

Magazines

JOURNAL OF AIR AND WASTE MANAGEMENT ASSOCIATION
One Gateway Center, Third Floor, Pittsburgh PA 15222. 412/232-3444

FABRICATED/PRIMARY METALS AND PRODUCTS

 *For steel manufacturers, the late '80s were a nightmare, with prices falling to ten-year lows. During 1992 and 1993, however, the industry began a modest recovery which should continue with an improving economy. A stronger economy will spur shipments of consumer goods and automobiles. Foreign companies will become more and more important; look for more joint ventures between the U.S. and overseas firms. Big Steel's toughest competition is now the increasing number of mini-mills that have spun off from large companies in an attempt to strike out on their own.*

Overall, employment prospects are weak, although metallurgical engineers are in demand.

ALASKAN COPPER WORKS
P.O. Box 3546
Seattle WA 98124-3546
206/623-5800
Contact: Ian Walker, Personnel Director
Description: A producer of fabricated pipe and other metals products, including heat exchangers and process equipment. **Common positions include:** Accountant/Auditor; Administrator; Blue-Collar Worker Supervisor; Buyer; Credit Manager; Draftsperson; Financial Analyst; Manufacturer's/Wholesaler's Sales Rep.; Personnel/Labor Relations Specialist; Purchasing Agent and Manager. **Educational backgrounds include:** Accounting; Business Administration; Engineering; Finance; Marketing. **Benefits:** Dental Insurance; Disability Coverage; Life Insurance; Medical Insurance; Profit Sharing. **Parent company:** Alaskan Copper Companies.

ATLAS FOUNDRY & MACHINERY COMPANY
3021 South Wilkeson
Tacoma WA 98409
206/475-4600
Contact: E. Russ Bodge, Personnel Director
Description: Produces a diversified range of steel and stainless steel castings for the construction, transportation, maritime, oil, nuclear, and other industries. The firm also has fabrication and machining capabilities in large, complex weldings and castings. **Common positions include:** Accountant/Auditor; Administrator; Blue-Collar Worker Supervisor; Buyer; Ceramics Engineer; Computer Programmer; Customer Service Representative; Department Manager; Metallurgical Engineer; Operations/Production

Manager; Personnel/Labor Relations Specialist; Purchasing Agent and Manager; Quality Control Supervisor. **Educational backgrounds include:** Engineering. **Benefits:** Dental Insurance; Disability Coverage; Life Insurance; Medical Insurance; Pension Plan; Tuition Assistance. **Corporate headquarters location:** This Location.

BIRMINGHAM STEEL CORPORATION
WEST SEATTLE DIVISION
2424 SW Andover
Seattle WA 98106
Contact: Human Resources
Description: A steel manufacturer.

CAPITAL INDUSTRIES INC.
P.O. Box 80983
Seattle WA 98108
206/762-8585
Contact: Personnel Department
Description: A company engaged in metal fabrication.

GM NAMEPLATE INC.
2040 15th Avenue West
Seattle WA 98119
206/284-2200
Contact: Personnel Department
Description: Involved in coating, engraving, allied services, paper coatings, and glazing.

INTALCO ALUMINUM CORPORATION
P.O. Box 937
Ferndale WA 98248
206/384-7061
Contact: Personnel Manager
Description: Primary aluminum manufacturing plant.

JORGENSEN FORGE CORPORATION
8531 East Marginal Way South
Seattle WA 98108
206/762-1100
Fax: 206/762-5414
Contact: Ron Altier, Vice-President, Administration
Description: A producer of forgings. The firm provides customers with melting, forging, heat treating, and machining of steel and aluminum forgings. **Common positions include:** Ceramics Engineer; Chemist; Cost Estimator; Electrician; Materials Engineer; Metallurgical Engineer. **Educational**

backgrounds include: Engineering. **Benefits:** 401K; Dental Insurance; Disability Coverage; Life Insurance; Medical Insurance; Profit Sharing; Tuition Assistance. **Corporate headquarters location:** This Location. **Operations at this facility include:** Administration; Manufacturing. **Listed on:** Privately held. **Number of employees at this location:** 200.

KAISER ALUMINUM & CHEMICAL CORPORATION
P.O. Box 15108
Spokane WA 99215
509/924-1500
Contact: Personnel Director
Description: A manufacturer of aluminum plate, sheet, and coil products for a variety of end uses. **Corporate headquarters location:** Oakland CA. **Number of employees nationwide:** 2,000.

REYNOLDS METALS COMPANY
P.O. Box 999
Longview WA 98632
206/425-2800
Contact: Human Resources
Description: A fabricated metals company.

VANALCO, INC.
P.O. Box 9805
Vancouver WA 98666
206/696-8661
Contact: Human Resources
Description: A fabricated metals company.

Note: Because addresses and telephone numbers of smaller companies change rapidly, we recommend you call each company and verify the information below before mailing to employers. Mass mailings are not recommended.

Additional employers with over 250 employees:

FABRICATED METAL PRODUCTS

Salmon Bay Steel Corporation
P.O. Box 16995,
Seattle WA 98116-0995. 206/933-2222.

NONFERROUS METALS

Northwest Alloys Inc.
P.O. Box 115, Addy
WA 99101-0115
509/935-3300.

ALUMINUM PRODUCTS

Breezeline Aluminum
P.O. Box 25061,
Seattle WA 98125-1961. 206/527-4532.

NONFERROUS WIRE

Storm Products
P.O. Box 387,
Woodinville WA
98072-0387.
206/488-7400.

METAL CONTAINERS

Crown Cork & Seal
P.O. Box 757, Walla
Walla WA 99362-
0243. 509/525-3440.

Crown Cork & Seal
1202 Fones Road SE,
Olympia WA 98501-
2716. 206/491-4900.

**WHOLESALE METALS
SERVICE CENTERS
AND OFFICES**

**Alcan Aluminum
Corporation Metal**
P.O. Box 4006,
Spokane WA 99202-
0006. 509/534-0586.

**Columbia Aluminum
Corporation**
8000 NE Parkway
Drive, Suite 200,
Vancouver WA
98662-6737.
206/896-8425.

WIRE PRODUCTS

**Davis Wire
Corporation**
19411 80th Avenue
South, Kent WA
98032-1134.
206/872-8910.

Additional employers with under 250 employees:

**ELECTRO-
METALLURGICAL
PRODUCTS**

SMI Group
P.O. Box 68, Rock
Island WA 98850-
0068. 509/884-7171.

**STEEL WIREDRAWING
AND NAILS**

Cablecraft Division
4401 South Orchard
Street, Tacoma WA
98466-6619.
206/475-1080.

STEEL FOUNDRIES

Spokane Industries
P.O. Box 3305,
Spokane WA 99220-
3305. 509/924-0440.

**MISCELLANEOUS
STRUCTURAL METAL
WORK**

**Jesse Engineering
Company**
5225 7th Street East,
Tacoma WA 98424-
2708. 206/922-7433.

**IRON AND STEEL
FORGINGS**

**The Gear Works
Seattle**
500 South Portland
Street, Seattle WA
98108-4329.
206/762-3333.

**ELECTROPLATING
AND POLISHING**

Asko Processing
434 North35th Street,
Seattle WA 98103-
8689. 206/634-2080.

**Hytek Finishes
Company**
8127 South 216th
Street, Kent WA
98032-1996.
206/872-7160.

Production Plating
4412 Russell Road,
Suite A, Mukilteo WA
98275-5498.
206/743-3302.

TC Systems
1028 SW Marine View
Circle, Seattle WA
98166-3834.
206/284-9818.

TC Systems
1028 West Marine
View Drive, Building
B, Everett WA 98201-
1579. 206/258-4055.

**FABRICATED METAL
PRODUCTS**

Brudi
26709 NW 19th
Avenue, Ridgefield
WA 98642-9348.
206/887-4666.

METALS SERVICES

**Graham Steel
Corporation**
13210 NE 124th
Street, Kirkland WA
98034-8004.
206/823-5656.

**Thompson Metal
Fabricators**
3000 SE Hidden Way
Building, Vancouver
WA 98661-8016.
206/696-0811.

**METAL DOORS AND
FRAMES**

Milgard Manufacturing
1010 54th Avenue E,
Tacoma WA 98424-
2793. 206/922-6030.

**Pacific Products &
Services Company**
4790 1st Avenue
South, Seattle WA
98134-2304.
206/764-3373.

**FABRICATED PLATE
WORK**

Capital Industries
P.O. Box 80983,
Seattle WA 98108-
0983. 206/762-8585.

Omega Environmental
19125 North Creek
Parkway, Bothell WA
98011-8000.
206/487-6577.

PSF Industries Inc.
65 South Horton
Street, Seattle WA
98134-1824.
206/622-1252.

SHEET METAL WORK

Accra-Fab Inc.
P.O. Box 11895,
Spokane WA 99211-
1895. 509/534-1717.

Apollo Sheet Metal
P.O. Box 7287,
Kennewick WA
99336-0617.
509/586-1104.

**Beadex Manufacturing
Company**
401 C Street NW,
Auburn WA 98001-
3908. 206/931-6600.

Flohr Metal Fabricators
P.O. Box 70469,
Seattle WA 98107-
0469. 206/633-2222.

**ARCHITECTURAL
AND ORNAMENTAL
METAL WORK**

**Ecolite Manufacturing
Company**
P.O. Box 11366,
Spokane WA 99211-
1366. 509/922-8888.

Utility Vault Company
2808 A Street SE,
Auburn WA 98002-
7501. 206/839-3500.

For more information on career opportunities in the fabricated/primary metals and products industries:

Associations

AMERICAN FOUNDRYMEN'S SOCIETY
505 State Street, Des Plaines IL 60016-708/824-0181.

AMERICAN SOCIETY FOR METALS
9639 Kinsman Road, Materials Park OH 44073-0002. 216/338-5151.

AMERICAN WELDING SOCIETY
P.O. Box 351040, 550 LeJeune Road NW, Miami FL 33126. 305/443-9353.

Directories

DIRECTORY OF STEEL FOUNDRIES IN THE UNITED STATES, CANADA, AND MEXICO
Steel Founder's Society of America, 455 State Street, Des Plaines IL 60016. 708/299-9160.

Magazines

AMERICAN METAL MARKET
Capital Cities ABC, 825 7th Avenue, New York NY 10019. 212/887-8580.

IRON AGE
191 South Gary, Carol Stream IL 60188. 708/462-2285.

IRON & STEEL ENGINEER
Association of Iron and Steel Engineers, Three Gateway Center, Suite 2350, Pittsburgh PA 15222. 412/281-6323.

MODERN METALS
625 North Michigan Avenue, Suite 2500, Chicago IL 60611. 312/654-2300.

FINANCIAL SERVICES

 *Since the 1987 stock market crash, one of the few hot financial products has been mutual funds. Jobseekers should note that while the phenomenal growth of mutual fund investing was expected to slow in 1994, demographics bode well for the long-term prospects of the industry. Expect to see steady, but slower growth. Investment managers and related mutual fund service firms should reap the benefits.*

Brokerage houses posted their third straight year of record profits in 1993, and the securities industry was expected to continue at high levels in '94. According to Fortune *magazine, low interest rates boosted the securities industry, but on three occasions during the spring of 1994 the Fed raised interest rates in an attempt to ward off runaway inflation. Despite the large amount of trading, brokerage houses are continuing to shrink their staffs to keep a tight reign on costs. Uncertainty over health care reform and executive compensation have created a volatile trading environment.*

AMERICAN GENERAL
10740 Meridian Avenue North, Suite 105
Seattle WA 98133
206/362-4566
Contact: Manager
Description: Provides a broad range of financial services to area customers. Parent company is a national financial services company with operations in consumer banking, correspondent banking, and investment services. **Corporate headquarters location:** New York NY. **Parent company:** Manufacturers Hanover Corporation.

BENAROYA COMPANY
1001 4th Avenue, Suite 4700
Seattle WA 98154
206/343-4750
Contact: Personnel Department
Description: A securities brokerage firm.

INTERPACIFIC INVESTORS SERVICES
600 University Street, #2310
Seattle WA 98101
206/623-2784
Fax: 206/623-8553
Contact: Allyn D. Close, President
Description: A regional securities broker/dealer, specializing in conservative investments such as corporate and municipal bonds, mutual funds, stocks and life insurance. The company has offices from Hawaii to Georgia, but their primary locations are on the West Coast. **Common positions include:** Branch Manager; Customer Service Representative. **Benefits:** Dental Insurance; Medical Insurance.

NATIONAL SECURITIES CORPORATION
1001 Fourth Avenue, Suite 2200
Seattle WA 98154
206/622-7200
Contact: Human Resources
Description: A security brokerage.

OLYMPIC CAPITAL MANAGEMENT
1301 5th Avenue, Suite 3320
Seattle WA 98101
206/447-9399
Contact: Personnel Department
Description: An investment advisory company.

RAGEN MacKENZIE
999 Third Avenue, Suite 4300
Seattle WA 98104
206/343-5000
Contact: Personnel Department
Description: A company engaged in investment banking.

SEAFIRST BANK CORPORATION
800 Fifth Avenue, 33rd Floor
P.O. Box 3977
Seattle WA 98124
Contact: Employment Department
Description: Mailed inquiries only. A financial services firm; engaged in such activities as: trust, mortgage, corporate cash management, securities, wholesale, and retail lending. **Common positions include:** Accountant/ Auditor; Bank Officer/Manager; Branch Manager; Computer Programmer; Credit Manager; Department Manager; Financial Analyst; Marketing Specialist; Operations/Production Manager; Systems Analyst. **Educational backgrounds include:** Accounting; Business Administration; Computer Science; Economics; Finance; Liberal Arts; Marketing. **Benefits:** Dental Insurance; Disability Coverage; Employee Discounts; Legal Services; Life

Insurance; Medical Insurance; Pension Plan; Tuition Assistance. **Parent company:** BankAmerica Corporation. **Number of employees nationwide:** 7,000.

SEATTLE NORTHWEST SECURITY CORPORATION
1420 5th Avenue, Suite 4300
Seattle WA 98101
206/628-2882
Contact: Personnel Department
Description: A security brokerage and dealership company.

SHEARSON LEHMAN HUTTON AMERICAN EXPRESS INC.
999 3rd Avenue, Suite 3800
Seattle WA 98104
206/344-3500
Contact: Personnel Department
Description: An investment banker.

WASHINGTON MUTUAL
1201 3rd Avenue
Seattle WA 98101-3009
206/461-2000
Contact: Personnel Director
Description: Offers a wide variety of financial services.

For more information on career opportunities in financial services:

Associations

FINANCIAL EXECUTIVES INSTITUTE
P.O. Box 1938, Morristown NJ 07962-1938
201/898-4600. Fee and membership required.

INSTITUTE OF FINANCIAL EDUCATION
111 East Wacker Drive, Chicago IL 60601. 312/946-8800.

NATIONAL ASSOCIATION OF BUSINESS ECONOMISTS
1801 East 9th Street, Cleveland OH 44114. 216/241-6223.

NATIONAL ASSOCIATION OF CREDIT MANAGEMENT
8815 Centre Park Drive, Suite 200, Columbia MD 21045-2158.
410/740-5560.

NATIONAL ASSOCIATION OF REAL ESTATE INVESTMENT TRUSTS
1129 20th Street NW, Suite 305, Washington DC 20036
202/785-8717.

PUBLIC SECURITIES ASSOCIATION
40 Broad Street, 12th Floor, New York NY 10004. 212/809-7000.

SECURITIES INDUSTRY ASSOCIATION
120 Broadway, New York NY 10271. 212/608-1500.

TREASURY MANAGEMENT ASSOCIATION
7315 Wisconsin Avenue, Suite 1250-W, Bethesda MD 20814. 301/907-2862.

Directories

DIRECTORY OF AMERICAN FINANCIAL INSTITUTIONS
Thomson Business Publications, 6195 Crooked Creek Road, Norcross GA 30092. 404/448-1011.

MOODY'S BANK AND FINANCE MANUAL
Moody's Investor Service, 99 Church Street, New York NY 10007. 212/553-0300.

TEXAS BUSINESS DIRECTORY
American Business Directories, 5711 South 86th Circle, P.O. Box 27347, Omaha NE 68127. 402/593-4600.

Magazines

BARRON'S: NATIONAL BUSINESS AND FINANCIAL WEEKLY
Dow Jones & Co., 200 Liberty Street, New York NY 10281. 212/416-2700.

FINANCIAL PLANNING
40 West 57th Street, 11th Floor, New York NY 1001. 212/765-5311.

FINANCIAL WORLD
Financial World Partners, 1328 Broadway, 3rd Floor, New York NY 10001. 212/594-5030.

FUTURES: THE MAGAZINE OF COMMODITIES AND OPTIONS
250 South Wacker Drive, Suite 1150, Chicago IL 60606. 312/977-0999.

INSTITUTIONAL INVESTOR
488 Madison Avenue, 12th Floor, New York NY 10022. 212/303-3300.

FOOD AND BEVERAGES/AGRICULTURE

 *While the food and beverage industry makes the nation's largest manufacturing sector, the processed food and beverage industry is experiencing sluggish growth. But improvements are expected to snowball as the effects of NAFTA and the as yet-unratified GATT agreement take hold and boost international trade. As an example, the U.S. Commerce Department claims NAFTA provides at least three advantages to the American processed food and beverage industry sector. NAFTA is expected to: reduce mutual tariff restrictions over 15 years; abolish all Mexican import licenses; and require the mutual recognition of distinctive products, like bourbon and Tennessee whiskey. For example, only bourbon distilled in the U.S. would be sold in Canada and Mexico.*

ACME POULTRY COMPANY INC.
P.O. Box 820
Renton WA 98057-0820
206/235-1940
Contact: Bob Boprey, Sales Manager
Description: A processor of poultry and related food products.

AGRINORTHWEST
P.O. Box 2308
Tri-Cities WA 99302
509/734-6461
Fax: 509/735-6471
Contact: Diane Kummer, Manager-Human Resources/Benefits
Description: One of the largest diversified agricultural operations in the western U.S., Agrinorthwest is engaged in the production of a variety of food crops, primarily potatoes, grain corn, and apples. Total number of employees varies from 200 to 1,000. **Listed on:** American Stock Exchange. **Number of employees nationwide:** 1,500.

AMERICAN FINE FOODS, INC.
P.O. Box 458
Walla Walla WA 99362-0013
509/525-8390
Contact: Personnel Department
Description: Produces canned green peas, carrots, corn, asparagus, green beans, and spinach. **Number of employees nationwide:** 1,500.

ASSOCIATED GROCERS, INC.
P.O. Box 3763
Seattle WA 98124
206/767-8788
Contact: Human Resources
Description: Provides general merchandise and grocery products to over 300 independently owned retail markets in a number of western states. Also offers a variety of related services, including retail promotion. **Common positions include:** Accountant/Auditor; Administrator; Buyer; Claim Representative; Commercial Artist; Computer Programmer; Credit Manager; Customer Service Representative; Department Manager; Editor; Electrical/Electronic Engineer; Financial Analyst; General Manager; Insurance Agent/Broker; Marketing Specialist; Mechanical Engineer; Operations/Production Manager; Personnel/Labor Relations Specialist; Reporter; Systems Analyst; Transportation/Traffic Specialist. **Educational backgrounds include:** Accounting; Business Administration; Communications; Computer Science; Finance; Marketing. **Benefits:** Dental Insurance; Disability Coverage; Life Insurance; Medical Insurance; On-Site Gym; Pension Plan; Tuition Assistance. **Other U.S. locations:** Kent WA. **Number of employees nationwide:** 1,400.

CONTINENTAL BAKING COMPANY
P.O. Box 3226
Seattle WA 98114
206/322-4242
Contact: Personnel Director
Description: A facility operating as part of a national wholesale bakery operation, manufacturing and distributing a line of high-quality bread and cake products. Parent company is a producer of consumer grocery products, livestock and pet food products, and other goods and services. **Common positions include:** Manufacturer's/Wholesaler's Sales Rep.; Safety Specialist. **Educational backgrounds include:** Business Administration. **Benefits:** Dental Insurance; Disability Coverage; Life Insurance; Medical Insurance; Pension Plan; Profit Sharing; Savings Plan; Tuition Assistance. **Corporate headquarters location:** St. Louis MO. **Parent company:** Ralston Purina Company. **Operations at this facility include:** Manufacturing.

DARIGOLD INC.
P.O. Box 79007
Seattle WA 98119
Contact: Thomas D. Lee, Human Resources Supervisor
Description: A dairy company specializing in the manufacturing, marketing, sales, and distribution of dairy products. **Common positions include:** Accountant/Auditor; Administrative Worker/Clerk, Blue-Collar Worker Supervisor; Branch Manager; Computer Programmer; Customer Service Representative; Department Manager; Financial Analyst; Food Scientist/Technologist; Manufacturer's/Wholesaler's Sales Rep.; Operations/Production Manager; Production Worker; Quality Control Supervisor; Systems Analyst;

Truck Driver. **Educational backgrounds include:** Accounting; Biology; Computer Science; Finance; High School Diploma; Liberal Arts; Marketing. **Benefits:** Dental Insurance; Disability Coverage; Life Insurance; Medical Insurance; Pension Plan; Savings Plan; Tuition Assistance. **Corporate headquarters location:** This Location. **Other U.S. locations:** Los Angeles CA; San Jose CA; Boise ID; Caldwell ID; Eugene OR; Medford OR; Portland OR; Chehalis WA; Issaquah WA; Lynden WA; Seattle WA; Spokane WA; Sunnyside WA; Yakima WA. **Operations at this facility include:** Administration; Research and Development. **Number of employees at this location:** 1,800.

DEL MONTE CORPORATION
P.O. Box 1528
Yakima WA 98907-1528
509/575-6580
Contact: Connie Rines, Personnel Director
Description: A national processor and distributor of foods, engaged in processed foods, fresh fruit, and refrigerated transport operations; trucking; and institutional foods services. This facility is engaged in the processing of canned fruits. **Corporate headquarters location:** San Francisco CA. **Listed on:** New York Stock Exchange.

FOOD SERVICES OF AMERICA
18430 East Valley Highway
Kent WA 98032
206/251-9100
Contact: Human Resources
Description: A food service company specializing in the distribution of fruit, fresh seafood, canned and frozen goods, fresh meat, supply and equipment, and disposables.

GAI'S SEATTLE FRENCH BAKING COMPANY
P.O. Box 24327
Seattle WA 98124
206/322-0931
Contact: Human Resources
Description: A baking company.

GENERAL BREWING CORPORATION
P.O. Box 4556
Vancouver WA 98662
206/260-9500
Contact: Personnel Department
Description: Brewing company for Lucky Lager, Lucky Draft, Fisher, and Regal Beers.

GREEN GIANT COMPANY/DAYTON PLANT

711 East Main
Dayton WA 99328
509/382-2511
Contact: Duane Dunlap, Personnel Director
Description: A producer of canned food products, including asparagus. **Corporate headquarters location:** Minneapolis MN. **Parent company:** Pillsbury Company.

ICICLE SEAFOODS INC.

P.O. Box 79003
Seattle WA 98119
206/282-0988
Contact: Personnel Department
Description: A seafood company engaged in the manufacture of canned and frozen fish, shellfish, and shrimp-based products.

LAMB-WESTON, INC.

P.O. Box C 1900
Tri-Cities WA 99302
509/735-4651
Contact: Personnel Administrator
Description: A processor of a broad line of nationally distributed frozen potato products, including french fries and potato wedges. **Common positions include:** Accountant/Auditor; Biological Scientist/Biochemist; Chemical Engineer; Computer Programmer; Credit Manager; Customer Service Representative; Department Manager; Food Scientist/Technologist; Industrial Engineer; Manufacturer's/Wholesaler's Sales Rep.; Marketing Specialist; Mechanical Engineer; Operations/Production Manager; Quality Control Supervisor; Transportation/Traffic Specialist. **Educational backgrounds include:** Accounting; Business Administration; Chemistry; Economics; Engineering; Finance; Marketing. **Benefits:** Dental Insurance; Disability Coverage; Employee Discounts; Life Insurance; Medical Insurance; Pension Plan; Profit Sharing; Relocation Assist.; Savings Plan; Tuition Assistance. **Corporate headquarters location:** This Location. **Parent company:** AMFAC, Inc. **Operations at this facility include:** Administration; Research and Development; Sales; Service. **Listed on:** American Stock Exchange; New York Stock Exchange.

LANGENDORF BAKING COMPANY OF SEATTLE INC.

P.O. Box 3664, 2901 6th Avenue South
Seattle WA 98124
206/682-2244
Contact: Ms. Lee Norton, Office Manager
Description: A producer of bread, pastry, and other bakery products. **Number of employees nationwide:** 340.

MARRIOTT CONCESSIONS
University of Washington, GB-19
Seattle WA 98195
206/543-8880
Contact: Human Resources Department
Description: A food service management company.

McCAIN FOODS
P.O. Box 607
Othello WA 99344
509/488-9611
Contact: Personnel
Description: A processor of prepared potato products, including potato rounds and french fries. **Number of employees nationwide:** 500.

NALLEY'S FINE FOODS
P.O. Box 11046
Tacoma WA 98411-0046
Contact: Personnel
Description: A food manufacturing company.

NATIONAL FROZEN FOODS CORPORATION
P.O. Box 479
Chehalis WA 98532
206/748-4403
Contact: Human Resources
Description: A frozen fruits and vegetables company.

OCEAN BEAUTY SEAFOODS, INC.
P.O. Box 70739
Seattle WA 98107
Contact: Personnel
Description: Involved in the production and sale of seafood products.

THE ODOM CORPORATION
26 South Hanford
Seattle WA 98134
206/623-3256
Contact: Personnel Department
Description: A holding company for the food services business. **Number of employees nationwide:** 497.

PABST BREWING COMPANY
P.O. Box 947
Olympia WA 98507
206/754-5000
Contact: Alice Riley, Personnel Director
Description: Produces a line of widely-distributed beers and malt beverages including Pabst Blue Ribbon, Pabst Light, and Pabst Extra Light low alcohol.

PACIFIC FOODS
21612 88th Avenue South
Kent WA 98031
206/395-9400
Contact: Personnel Department
Description: A prime manufacturing company dealing with mapleine, raw and salted nuts, spices, extracts and seasoning mixes.

PENWEST, LTD.
777 108th Avenue NE, Suite 2390
Bellevue WA 98004
206/462-6000
Contact: Personnel Department
Description: A holding company for a food and flavor ingredients and specialty carbohydrate products company. **Number of employees nationwide:** 500.

PEPSI COLA COMPANY
2300 26th Avenue South
Seattle WA 98144
206/323-2932
Contact: David Sacco, Vice President, Human Resources
Description: A soft drink bottler. **Number of employees at this location:** 1,300.

PETER PAN SEAFOODS
2200 6th Avenue, Suite 1000
Seattle WA 98121
206/728-6000
Contact: Cathy Wingert, Corporate Secretary
Description: Processes a variety of canned, fresh, and frozen seafoods.

RAINIER BREWING COMPANY
P.O. Box 24828
Seattle WA 98124
206/622-2600
Contact: Personnel
Description: Produces a widely-distributed line of beers and ales.

SNOKIST GROWERS
P.O. Box 1587
Yakima WA 98907
509/453-5631
Contact: Personnel
Description: A fruit processor, with operations in plums, apples, cherries, and other items. **Number of employees at this location:** 400.

STADELMAN FRUIT INC.
P.O. Box 1323
Yakima WA 98907
509/452-8571
Contact: Larry Lembeck, Personnel Director
Description: A fruit packer and wholesaler.

SYSCO FOOD SERVICE OF SEATTLE
P.O. Box 97054
Kent WA 98064
206/622-2772
Contact: Human Resources Department
Description: A food service company.

P.J. TAGGARES COMPANY
850 North South Broadway
Othello WA 99344
509/488-3356
Contact: Personnel
Description: A potato processor.

TREE TOP, INC.
220 East 2nd Avenue, P.O. Box 248
Selah WA 98942
509/697-7251
Contact: Personnel Department
Description: Producer of the following drinks: Tree Top Brand Apple Juice & Cider, frozen Apple Juice Concentrate, Bulk Pear concentrate, Apple & Concord Grape Juice Concentrate.

TRIDENT SEAFOOD
5303 Shilshole Avenue NW
Seattle WA 98107
206/783-3818
Contact: Personnel Department
Description: A company engaged in seafood canning.

TWIN CITY FOODS INC.
P.O. Box 699
Stanwood WA 98292
206/629-2111
Contact: Don Heitman, Corporate Personnel Manager
Description: A processor of frozen vegetable products.

UNISEA
P.O. Box 97019
15400 N.E. 90th Street
Redmond WA 98073-9719
206/881-8181
Contact: Personnel
Description: A processor of seafood and related fishery items.

VITA-MILK DAIRY INC.
427 North East 72nd
Seattle WA 98115
206/524-7070
Contact: Personnel Department
Description: A manufacturer of dairy products.

WARDS COVE PACKING COMPANY INC.
P.O. Box C-5030
Seattle WA 98105
206/323-3200
Contact: Personnel Department
Description: Operates salmon canneries and a general retail business.

WEST COAST GROCERY
A DIVISION OF SUPERVALU INC.
1525 East D Street
Tacoma WA 98401
206/593-3200.
Fax: 206/593-3288
Contact: Human Resources Department
Description: Distributes dry groceries, frozen food, general merchandise, fruit produce, and meat (wholesale). **Common positions include:** Accountant/ Auditor; Buyer; Secretary; Transportation/Traffic Specialist; Truck Driver. **Educational backgrounds include:** Business Administration; Marketing. **Benefits:** Life Insurance; Medical Insurance; Pension Plan; Profit Sharing; Tuition Assistance. **Special Programs:** Internships; Training Programs. **Corporate headquarters location:** Eden Prairie MN. **Parent company:** Supervalu Inc. **Operations at this facility include:** Divisional Headquarters. **Listed on:** New York Stock Exchange. **Number of employees at this location:** 935.

Note: Because addresses and telephone numbers of smaller companies change rapidly, we recommend you call each company and verify the information below before mailing to employers. Mass mailings are not recommended.

Additional employers with over 250 employees:

FOODS WHOLESALE

Tyson Seafood Group
P.O. Box 79021,
Seattle WA 98119-
7921. 206/282-3445.

Draper Valley Farms
P.O. Box 838, Mount
Vernon WA 98273-
0838. 206/424-7947.

Royal Seafoods Inc.
P.O. Box 19032,
Seattle WA 98109-
1032. 206/285-8900.

IBP Inc.
P.O. Box 4329, Pasco
WA 99302-4329.
509/547-7545.

**Washington Fruit &
Produce Company**
401 North 1st
Avenue, Yakima WA
98902-2125.
509/457-6177.

**Entenmann Oroweat
Food**
1604 North 34th
Street, Seattle WA
98103-9002.
206/634-2700.

**Independent Food
Processing**
P.O. Box 357,
Sunnyside WA 98944-
0357. 509/837-3806.

MEAT

Washington Beef Inc.
P.O. Box 9344,
Yakima WA 98909-
0344. 509/248-3350.

**Washington Beef
Slaughter**
42 Fort Road,
Toppenish WA 98948-
9782. 509/865-2121.

**Washington Beef
Warehouse**
P.O. Box 128,
Ellensburg WA 98926-
0128. 509/248-9394.

**Oberto Sausage
Company**
P.O. Box 429, Kent
WA 98035-0429.
206/623-3470.

Pederson Fryer Farms
2901 72nd Street
East, Tacoma WA
98404-4199.
206/537-0243.

DAIRY PRODUCTS

**Rosauers Ice Cream
Plant**
Spokane Industrial
Park, Building 1,
Spokane WA 99216.
509/924-2135.

DAIRY FOODS

Basic American Foods
P.O. Box 1519, Moses
Lake WA 98837-
0234. 509/765-8601.

Pillsbury/Green Giant
711 East Main Street,
Dayton WA 99328-
1443. 509/382-2511.

FROZEN FOODS

**Nestle Brand
Foodservice**
14124 Wheeler Road
NE, Moses Lake WA
98837-9119.
509/765-3443.

**Ocean Spray
Cranberries Inc.**
1480 State Route
105, Aberdeen WA
98520-9524.
206/648-2201.

Stokely USA
P.O. Box 400,
Grandview WA
98930-0400.
509/882-3322.

Stokely USA
P.O. Box 818, Walla
Walla WA 99362-
0256. 509/525-7890.

Universal Frozen Food Company
P.O. Box 2324, Pasco WA 99302-2324.
509/547-8851.

JR Simplot Company-Food Division
222 Columbia Way, Quincy WA 98848.
509/787-4521.

Seafreeze Cold Storage
206 SW Michigan Street, Seattle WA 98106-1908.
206/767-7350.

FLOUR AND GRAIN MILL PRODUCTS

Centennial Mills/Mix Division
1131 East Sprague Avenue, Spokane WA 99202. 509/535-2995.

BAKERY PRODUCTS

Snyder's Bakery Inc.
16 North 3rd Avenue, Yakima WA 98902-2628. 509/453-8223.

SEAFOOD

Dutch Harbor Seafoods Ltd.
P.O. Box 97019, Redmond WA 98073-9719. 206/881-8181.

All Alaskan Seafoods
130 Nickerson Street, Suite 307, Seattle WA 98109-1658.
206/285-8200.

Bornstein Seafoods
P.O. Box 188, Bellingham WA 98227-0188.
206/734-7990.

Coast Seafoods
P.O. Box 166, South Bend WA 98586-0166. 206/875-5557.

Glacier Fish Company
1200 Westlake Avenue North, Suite 900, Seattle WA 98109-3530.
206/298-1200.

Oceantrawl Inc.
2025 1st Avenue, Suite 1200, Seattle WA 98121-2148.
206/448-6770.

COFFEE

Farmer Brothers Coffee Company
8660 Willows Road NE, Redmond WA 98052-3411.
206/881-7030.

CHIPS AND SNACKS

Frito-Lay Inc.
4808 Fruit Valley Road, Vancouver WA 98660-1242.
206/694-8478.

Additional employers with under 250 employees:

VEGETABLES AND MELONS

Beebe Orchard Company
McNeil Canyon Road, Chelan WA 98816.
509/682-2526.

Haas Fruit Company
711 Russell Lane, Yakima WA 98903-3728. 509/248-6870.

Snokist Growers
802 2nd, Naches WA 98937. 509/653-2242.

Sun River Fruit
Railroad & Elm Streets, Grandview WA 98930. 509/882-1011.

Wells & Wade Fruit Sales
201 South Union Avenue, East Wenatchee WA 98802-9137.
509/886-0547.

Zirkle Fruit Company
352 Harrison Road, Selah WA 98942-9505. 509/697-5656.

FRUITS

Bardin Farms Corporation
P.O. Box 223, Monitor
WA 98836-0223.
509/782-3511.

CATTLE FEEDLOTS

Van De Graaf Ranches
Bishop Road,
Sunnyside WA 98944.
509/837-6195.

POULTRY HATCHERIES

H&N International
3825 154th Avenue
NE, Redmond WA
98052-5300.
206/885-1414.

ANIMAL SPECIALTY SERVICES

Dandar Farm
903 B Street,
Centralia WA 98531-
4919. 206/736-9935.

MEAT PACKING PLANTS

Longhorn Barbecue Production
10420 East
Montgomery Drive,
Spokane WA 99206-
4279. 509/922-0702.

Superior Farms
P.O. Box 277,
Ellensburg WA 98926-
0277. 509/925-1495.

CREAMERY BUTTER

Dairygold Inc.
P.O. Box 1308,
Issaquah WA 98027-
1308. 206/392-6463.

MILK

Smith Bros Farms
27441 68th Avenue
South, Kent WA
98032-7262.
206/852-1000.

CANNED FRUITS AND VEGETABLES

Hi-Country Foods Corporation
P.O. Box 338, Selah
WA 98942-0338.
509/697-7292.

Northwest Packing Company
P.O. Box 30,
Vancouver WA
98666-0030.
206/696-4356.

Welch Foods Inc.
P.O. Box 6067,
Kennewick WA
99336-0067.
509/582-2131.

FROZEN FRUITS, JUICES AND VEGETABLES

Bellingham Frozen Foods
P.O. Box 1016,
Bellingham WA
98227-1016.
206/734-4040.

Carriage House Fruit
P.O. Box 33, Lynden
WA 98264-0033.
206/354-5627.

Columbia Foods Inc.
P.O. Box 605, Quincy
WA 98848-0605.
509/787-1585.

FLOUR

Centennial Mills
P.O. Box 2545,
Spokane WA 99220-
2545. 509/534-2636.

Fisher Mills Inc.
3235 16th Avenue
SW, Seattle WA
98134-1023.
206/622-4430.

PREPARED FLOUR MIXES AND DOUGHS

Lucks Company Inc.
P.O. Box 24266,
Seattle WA 98124-
0266. 206/622-4608.

FEEDS AND FEED INGREDIENTS

National Feed
1921 North Park
Road, Spokane WA
99212-1268.
509/922-2621.

CANE SUGAR

Columbia River Sugar Company
13184 Wheeler Road
NE Suite 1, Moses
Lake WA 98837-
9152. 509/766-1933.

MALT BEVERAGES

Coors Brewing Company
301 116th Avenue SE Suite 550, Bellevue WA 98004-6401. 206/453-0090.

Onalaska Brewing Company
248 Burchett Road, Onalaska WA 98570-9405. 206/978-4253.

The Stroh Brewery Company
12826 SE 40th Lane, Bellevue WA 98006-5266. 206/746-2121.

MALT

Great Western Malting Company
P.O. Box 1529, Vancouver WA 98668-1529. 206/693-3661.

Great Western Malting Company
1215 East Wheeler Road, Moses Lake WA 98837-1859. 509/766-9453.

WINES AND BRANDY

Columbia Crest Winery
P.O. Box 231, Paterson WA 99345-0231. 509/875-2061.

SOFT DRINKS

Northwest Beverages
8462 South 190th Street, Kent WA 98031-1200. 206/251-0800.

FLAVORING EXTRACTS AND SYRUPS

Callisons Inc.
P.O. Box 120, Chehalis WA 98532-0120. 206/748-3315.

CANNED AND CURED FISH AND SEAFOOD

Kodiak Salmon Packers
20520 Brown Road, Monroe WA 98272-8733. 206/486-9872.

Wiegardt Brothers
P.O. Box 309, Ocean Park WA 98640-0309. 206/665-4111.

FRESH OR FROZEN FISH AND SEAFOOD

Coast Seafoods
P.O. Box 327, Quilcene WA 98376-0327. 206/765-3474.

Commercial Cold Storage
P.O. Box 1167, Mount Vernon WA 98273-1167. 206/336-0025.

Frank B. Peterson Company
88 East Hamlin Street, Seattle WA 98102-3144. 206/323-3200.

Royal Aleutian Seafoods
701 Dexter Avenue North Suite 403, Seattle WA 98109-4343. 206/283-6605.

Sea K Fish Company
P.O. Box 2040, Blaine WA 98231-2040. 206/332-5121.

Washington Crab Producers Inc.
P.O. Box 1488, Westport WA 98595-1488. 206/268-9161.

Yak Inc.
180 Nickerson Street, Seattle WA 98109-1631. 206/286-1303.

PASTA

Golden Grain Company
4100 4th Avenue South, Seattle WA 98134-2310. 206/623-2038.

Merlinos Macaroni Company Inc.
8247 South 194th Street, Kent WA 98032-1124. 206/872-7155.

FOOD PREPARATIONS

**American Foods
Corporation**
115 West I Street,
Yakima WA 98902-
1431. 509/248-4155.

El Ranchito Foods
P.O. Box 717, Zillah
WA 98953-0717.
509/829-5880.

CONFECTIONERY
WHOLESALE

Brown & Haley
1940 East 11th
Street, Tacoma WA
98421-3301.
206/593-3000.

CIGARETTES

**Brown & Williamson
Tobacco Corporation**
N524 North Mullan
Road, Spokane WA
99206-3853.
509/928-1144.

**Lorillard Tobacco
Company**
14828 NE 31st Circle
Building B-0,
Redmond WA 98052-
5321. 206/882-3531.

Philip Morris USA
110 110th Avenue NE
Suite 311, Bellevue
WA 98004-5840.
206/453-1459.

PACKAGED FROZEN
FOODS WHOLESALE

Queen Fisheries Inc.
4005 20th Avenue
West Suite 116,
Seattle WA 98199-
1290. 206/284-7571.

Valley Packers Inc.
P.O. Box 1226,
Puyallup WA 98371-
0196. 206/845-8886.

BEER AND ALE
WHOLESALE

Miller Brands Inc.
6030 South 196th
Street, Kent WA
98032-2188.
206/872-2600.

POULTRY
WHOLESALE

**National Food
Corporation**
16740 Aurora Avenue
North, Seattle WA
98133-5311.
206/546-6533.

FRESH FRUITS AND
VEGETABLES
WHOLESALE

**Peirone Produce
Company**
E524 East Trent
Avenue, Spokane WA
99202-1638.
509/838-3515.

Tat-On Inc.
418 South Alder
Street, Moses Lake
WA 98837-1756.
509/765-2920.

Trout Inc.
P.O. Box 669, Chelan
WA 98816-0669.
509/682-2591.

WINE AND DISTILLED
ALCOHOLIC
BEVERAGES
WHOLESALE

Sid Eland Inc.
555 Monster Road
SW, Renton WA
98055-2937.
206/255-5511.

For more information on career opportunities in the food and beverage, and agriculture industries:

Associations

AMERICAN ASSOCIATION OF CEREAL CHEMISTS
3340 Pilot Knob Road, Street. Paul MN 55121. 612/454-7250.

AMERICAN FROZEN FOOD INSTITUTE
1764 Old Meadow Lane, McLean VA 22102. 703/821-0770.

AMERICAN SOCIETY OF AGRICULTURAL ENGINEERS
2950 Niles Road, Street. Joseph MI 49085. 616/429-0300.

AMERICAN SOCIETY OF BREWING CHEMISTS
3340 Pilot Knob Road, St. Paul MN 55121. 612/454-7250.

DAIRY AND FOOD INDUSTRIES SUPPLY ASSOCIATION
6245 Executive Boulevard, Rockville MD 20852. 301/984-1444.

MASTER BREWERS ASSOCIATION OF THE AMERICAS
2421 North Mayfair, Suite 310, Wauwatosa, WI 53226. 414/774-8558.

NATIONAL AGRICULTURAL CHEMICALS ASSOCIATION
1156 15th Street NW, Suite 900, Washington DC 20005. 202/296-1585.

NATIONAL BEER WHOLESALERS' ASSOCIATION
1100 South Washington Street, Alexandria VA 22314. 703/683-4300.

NATIONAL DAIRY COUNCIL
10255 West Higgins Road, Suite 900, Rosemont IL 60018. 708/803-2000.

NATIONAL FOOD PROCESSORS ASSOCIATION
1401 New York Avenue NW, Suite 400, Washington DC 20005. 202/639-5900.

NATIONAL SOFT DRINK ASSOCIATION
1101 16th Street NW, Washington DC 20036. 202/463-6732.

Directories

FOOD ENGINEERING'S DIRECTORY OF U.S. FOOD PLANTS
Chilton Book Co., Chilton Way, Radnor PA 19089. 800/695-1214.

THOMAS FOOD INDUSTRY REGISTER
Thomas Publishing Co., Five Penn Plaza, New York NY 10001. 212/695-0500.

Magazines

BEVERAGE WORLD
150 Great Neck Road, Great Neck NY 11021. 516/829-9210.

FOOD PROCESSING
301 East Erie Street, Chicago IL
60611. 312/644-2020.

FROZEN FOOD AGE
Maclean Hunter Media, #4
Stamford Forum, Stamford CT
06901. 203/325-3500.

PREPARED FOODS
Gorman Publishing Company, 8750
West Bryn Mawr, Chicago IL
60631. 312/693-3200.

GOVERNMENT

The Federal Government is the nation's largest single employer, and one of the most stable. More than 300,000 people are hired each year to work a variety of government jobs, and there is usually little change in the level of employment. The concentration of jobs is changing, however. The Department of Defense currently generates over half of all federal jobs, but both its staff and budget are being reduced due to the end of the Cold war. Other departments may suffer some job loss as a result of Vice President Al Gore's plan to "reinvent government," which was announced in September 1993, but overall, government jobs remain some of the most stable in the country. Two occupations with especially good prospects: nurses and engineers.

State: According to the state's Bureau of Labor Statistics, government employment will continue to be tight in Washington. In addition to a lean budget, the governor has set a goal of reducing state government employment by ten percent by re-election. Both factors are forcing government agencies to cut back, and be "careful" when filling vacancies.

ARMY CORPS OF ENGINEERS/WALLA WALLA
DISTRICT DEPARTMENT OF THE ARMY
602 City County Airport
Walla Walla WA 99362-9265
509/522-6427
Contact: Mr. Robert L. Alley, Chief of Recruitment/Placement
Description: A federal government agency engaged in water resource engineering.

AUBURN, CITY OF
City Hall, 25 West Main Street
Auburn WA 98001
206/931-3040
Contact: Human Resources
Description: Provides municipal services.

AUBURN FIRE DEPARTMENT
1101 D Street NE
Auburn WA 98002
206/931-3060
Contact: Personnel
Description: Auburn's fire department.

AUBURN POLICE DEPARTMENT
15 North Division
Auburn WA 98001
206/931-3080
Contact: Personnel
Description: Auburn's police department.

BREMERTON FIRE DEPARTMENT
817 Pacific
Bremerton WA 98310
206/478-5380
Contact: Personnel
Description: Bremerton's fire department.

BREMERTON POLICE DEPARTMENT
239 4th Street
Bremerton WA 98310
206/478-5220
Contact: Personnel
Description: Bremerton's police department.

CLARK COUNTY
1013 Franklin Street
Vancouver WA 98660
206/699-2456
Contact: Human Resources
Description: Provides county government services.

EIGHTH U.S. ARMY CIVILIAN RECRUITING OFFICE
P.O. Box 34102
Seattle WA 98124-1102
206/764-3821
Contact: James A. Fenis, Chief/EUSA CRO
Description: Recruits civilians as support staff for the Eighth U.S. Army in Korea. Professional, administrative, and technical positions. **Number of employees at this location:** 3,200.

EMPLOYMENT SECURITY DEPARTMENT
840 North Broadway
Everett WA 98201
206/339-4900
Contact: Georgia van Amerongen, Operations Manager
Description: A branch of the state's job service center.

EVERETT, CITY OF
3002 Wetmore Avenue
Everett WA 98201
206/259-8767
Contact: Human Resources
Description: Provides municipal services.

EVERETT FIRE DEPARTMENT
2811 Oaks Avenue
Everett WA 98201
206/259-8709
Contact: Personnel
Description: Everett's fire department.

EVERETT POLICE DEPARTMENT
3002 Wetmore Avenue
Everett WA 98201
206/259-0400
Contact: Personnel
Description: Everett's police department.

FAIRCHILD AIR FORCE BASE
92nd MSSQ/MSCS
West 220 Bong Street
Fairchild AFB WA 99011-8524
509/247-2453
Contact: Human Resources
Description: A U.S. Air Force base.

FEDERAL WAY, CITY OF
33530 1st Way South
Federal Way WA 98003
206/661-4083
Contact: Human Resources
Description: Provides municipal services.

KENT, CITY OF
220 4th Avenue
Kent WA 98032
206/859-3328
Contact: Human Resources
Description: Provides municipal services.

KENT CIVIL SERVICE COMMISSION, CITY OF
220 4th Avenue South
Kent WA 98032
206/859-3328
Contact: Human Resources
Description: Administers exams for government occupations such as police, correctional, and firefighting positions.

KING COUNTY
King County Administration Building
500 4th Avenue, Room 450
Seattle WA 98104
206/296-7340
Contact: Human Resources
Description: Provides county government services.

KING COUNTY METROPOLITAN SERVICES
Exchange Building
821 2nd Avenue, 4th Floor
Seattle WA 98104
206/684-2100
Contact: Human Resources
Description: Provides transit authority and water treatment.

KITSAP COUNTY
614 Division Street
Port Orchard WA 98366
206/876-7185
Contact: Human Resources
Description: Provides county government services.

LACEY, CITY OF
420 College Street SE
Lacey WA 98503
206/491-3214
Contact: Human Resources
Description: Provides municipal services.

MERCER ISLAND, CITY OF
9611 SE 36th Street
Mercer Island WA 98040-3732
206/236-5300.
Fax: 206/236-3651
Contact: Lindsay Andreotti, Employee Services Administrator
Description: Provides municipal services to over 21,000 residents in a suburb of Seattle. **Common positions include:** Accountant/Auditor; Attorney; Blue-Collar Worker Supervisor; Budget Analyst; Civil Engineer; Computer Systems Analyst; Construction and Building Inspector; Counselor; Draftsperson;

Financial Analyst; Human Service Worker; Personnel/Labor Relations Specialist; Structural Engineer. **Educational backgrounds include:** Accounting; Business Administration; Finance; Public Administration. **Benefits:** 401K; Dental Insurance; Disability Coverage; Life Insurance; Medical Insurance; Pension Plan; Tuition Assistance. **Corporate headquarters location:** This Location. **Operations at this facility include:** Administration. **Number of employees at this location:** 156.

OLYMPIA, CITY OF
900 Plum Street SE
Olympia WA 98501
206/753-8442
Contact: Human Resources
Description: Provides municipal services.

PIERCE COUNTY
615 South 9th Street, Suite 200
Tacoma WA 98405
206/591-7480
Contact: Human Resources
Description: Provides county government services.

RENTON, CITY OF
City Hall, 200 Mill Avenue South
Renton WA 98055
206/235-2556
Contact: Human Resources
Description: Provides municipal services.

RENTON CITY POLICE DEPARTMENT
200 Mill Avenue South
Renton WA 98055
206/235-2600
Contact: Personnel
Description: Renton's police department.

RENTON FIRE DEPARTMENT
211 Mill Avenue South
Renton WA 98055
206/235-2643
Contact: Personnel
Description: Renton's fire department.

RICHLAND, CITY OF
505 Swift Boulevard
Richland WA 99352
509/943-7391
Contact: Human Resources
Description: Provides municipal services.

SEATAC, CITY OF
17900 International Boulevard, Suite 401
SeaTac WA 98188
206/241-1594
Fax: 206/241-3999
Contact: Gretel Sloan, Human Resources Director
Description: Provides municipal services. **Common positions include:** Attorney; Budget Analyst; Buyer; Civil Engineer; Computer Programmer; Computer Systems Analyst; Personnel/Labor Relations Specialist. **Educational backgrounds include:** Accounting; Business Administration; Engineering; Finance. **Benefits:** Dental Insurance; Disability Coverage; Life Insurance; Medical Insurance; Pension Plan. **Special Programs:** Internships. **Corporate headquarters location:** This Location. **Operations at this facility include:** Administration. **Number of employees at this location:** 140.

SEATTLE, CITY OF
Dexter Horton Building
710 2nd Avenue, 12th Floor
Seattle WA 98104
206/684-7952
Contact: Human Resources
Description: Provides municipal services.

SEATTLE, CITY OF
STREET ENGINEERING DEPARTMENT
600 4th Avenue
Seattle WA 98104
206/684-5083
Contact: Human Resources
Description: Seattle's street maintenance and repair division.

SEATTLE FIRE DEPARTMENT
301 2nd Avenue South
Seattle WA 98104
206/386-1470
Contact: Personnel
Description: Seattle's fire department.

SEATTLE POLICE DEPARTMENT
610 3rd Avenue
Seattle WA 98104
206/625-5011
Contact: Personnel
Description: Seattle's police department.

SNOHOMISH COUNTY
Administration Building, 1st Floor
3000 Rockefeller Avenue, Mail Stop 503
Everett WA 98201
206/386-3411
Contact: Human Resources
Description: Provides county government services.

SNOQUALMIE POLICE DEPARTMENT
P.O. Box 337
Snoqualmie WA 98065
206/888-3333
Contact: Personnel
Description: Snoqualmie's police department.

SPOKANE, CITY OF
City Hall, 808 West Spokane Falls Boulevard
Spokane WA 99201
509/625-6363
Contact: Human Resources
Description: Manages parks, libraries, and public works, and provides services such as police and fire protection for the city of Spokane.

TACOMA, CITY OF
747 Market Street, Suite 1336
Tacoma WA 98402-3764
206/591-5400
Fax: 206/591-5793
Contact: J.C. Gilbertson, Human Resources Director
Description: City providing a broad range of municipal services plus generation/distribution of electrical power. Council-manager form of government. **Common positions include:** Accountant/Auditor; Adjuster; Administrative Services Manager; Attorney; Automotive Mechanic/Body Repairer; Budget Analyst; Buyer; Chemist; Civil Engineer; Clerical Supervisor; Computer Programmer; Computer Systems Analyst; Construction and Building Inspector; Electrical/Electronic Engineer; Electrician; Emergency Medical Technician; Financial Analyst; Landscape Architect; Management Analyst/Consultant; Mechanical Engineer; Paralegal; Personnel/Labor Relations Specialist; Property and Real Estate Manager; Purchasing Agent and Manager; Surveyor; Urban/Regional Planner. **Educational backgrounds include:** Accounting; Business Administration; Communications; Computer

Science; Economics; Finance; Liberal Arts. **Benefits:** Dental Insurance; Disability Coverage; Life Insurance; Medical Insurance; Pension Plan; Tuition Assistance. **Special Programs:** Internships. **Corporate headquarters location:** This Location. **Operations at this facility include:** Administration. **Number of employees nationwide:** 3,000.

TACOMA FIRE DEPARTMENT
901 South Fawcett
Tacoma WA 98402
206/591-5737
Contact: Personnel
Description: Tacoma's fire department.

THURSTON COUNTY
921 Lakeridge Drive SW
Building 4, Room 202
Olympia WA 98502
206/786-5498
Contact: Human Resources
Description: Provides county services.

UNITED STATES DEPARTMENT OF THE ARMY
CORPS OF ENGINEERS
District Office
4735 East Marginal Way
Seattle WA 98134
206/764-3742
Contact: Human Resources
Description: Organizes, trains and equips forces to defend the security of the United States.

UNITED STATES DEPARTMENT OF COMMERCE
Western Administrative Support Center
7600 Sand Point Way NE
Seattle WA 98115
206/526-6053
Contact: Human Resources
Description: Studies, monitors, and predicts conditions in the oceans, atmosphere, and space.

UNITED STATES DEPARTMENT OF ENERGY
BONNEVILE POWER ADMINISTRATION
Puget Sound Area Office
201 Queen Anne Avenue
Seattle WA 98109
206/553-6053
Contact: Human Resources
Description: Markets electric power and energy from federal hydroelectric projects in the Pacific Northwest.

UNITED STATES DEPARTMENT OF ENERGY
RICHLAND FIELD OFFICE
825 Jadwin Avenue, P.O. Box 550
Richland WA 99352
509/376-7395
Contact: Human Resources
Description: Coordinates and administers the energy functions of the federal government.

UNITED STATES DEPARTMENT OF HEALTH AND HUMAN SERVICES
REGION X
Regional Personnel Office
RX-05, 2201 6th Avenue
Seattle WA 98121
206/615-2033
Fax: 206/615-2076
Contact: Human Resources
Description: Provides health programs and services to the nation. **Common positions include:** Claim Representative; Customer Service Representative; Management Analyst/Consultant. **Benefits:** 401K; Life Insurance; Medical Insurance; Pension Plan. **Corporate headquarters location:** Washington DC. **Operations at this facility include:** Regional Headquarters; Service.

UNITED STATES DEPARTMENT OF THE INTERIOR
National Park Service
600 East Park
Port Angeles WA 98362
206/452-0330
Contact: Human Resources
Description: Manages the Olympia State Park.

UNITED STATES DEPARTMENT OF THE INTERIOR
Pacific Northwest Regional Office
83 South King Street
Seattle WA 98104
206/220-4053
Contact: Human Resources
Description: Manages most of the U.S.'s nationally owned public lands and natural resources.

UNITED STATES DEPARTMENT OF TRANSPORTATION
FEDERAL AVIATION ADMINISTRATION
Northwest Mountain Regional Headquarters
1601 Lind Avenue SW
Renton WA 98055
206/227-1727
Contact: Human Resources
Description: Regulates the manufacture, operation, and maintenance of aircraft; certifies pilots and airports.

UNITED STATES DEPARTMENT OF THE TREASURY
INTERNAL REVENUE SERVICE
Seattle District, 915 2nd Avenue
Seattle WA 98104
206/220-5725
Contact: Human Resources
Description: Provides taxpayer assistance, personnel examinations, and other services.

VANCOUVER, CITY OF
1313 Main Street, P.O. Box 1995
Vancouver WA 98668
206/696-8142
Contact: Human Resources
Description: Provides municipal services.

WASHINGTON STATE
600 Franklin Street SE
Olympia WA 98501
206/753-5368
Contact: Human Resources
Description: Provides state government services. For the Seattle area, the job hotline is 206/464-7378; for the Spokane area, the job hotline is 509/456-2889.

WASHINGTON STATE APPLE COMMISSION
P.O. Box 18
Wenatchee WA 98807
509/663-9600
Contact: Personnel Department
Description: A commission engaged in the promotion of Washington's apple industry.

WASHINGTON STATE DAIRY PRODUCTS COMMISION
4201 198th Street SW, Suite 101
Lynnwood WA 98036
206/545-6763
Contact: Personnel Department
Description: Engaged in the promotion of Washington's milk and dairy products.

WASHINGTON STATE DEPARTMENT OF REVENUE
415 General Administration Building
Mail Stop AX-02
Olympia WA 98504
206/753-5527
Contact: James L. Flynn, Personnel Manager
Description: The Department administers state tax laws; acts as revenue advisor to the Governor, the Legislature, and other state and local agencies; and oversees the administration of property tax laws. **Common positions include:** Accountant/Auditor; Adjuster. **Educational backgrounds include:** Accounting; Business Administration; Computer Science. **Benefits:** Daycare Assistance; Dental Insurance; Disability Coverage; Life Insurance; Medical Insurance; Pension Plan; Tuition Assistance. **Corporate headquarters location:** This Location. **Number of employees at this location:** 840.

STATE OF WASHINGTON
DEPARTMENT OF PERSONNEL
P.O. Box 47500
Olympia WA 98504-7500
206/753-5393
Contact: Human Resources Department
Description: Engaged in the recruitment and examination of candidates for the purpose of establishing a register of qualified personnel for all state agencies and all job classifications. **Number of employees at this location:** 50,000.

WASHINGTON STATE POTATO COMMISSION
108 Interlake Road
Moses Lake WA 98837
509/765-8845
Contact: Personnel Department
Description: Division in charge of regulating Washington's potato industry.

WHATCOM COUNTY
316 Lottie Street
Bellingham WA 98225
206/676-6802
Contact: Human Resources
Description: Provides county government services.

YAKIMA, CITY OF
129 North 2nd Street
Yakima WA 98901
509/575-6090
Contact: Human Resources
Description: Provides municipal services.

For more information about career opportunities in the government:

Directories

ACCESS..FCO ONLINE
Federal Research Service, Inc., P.O.
Box 1059, 243 Church Street, Vienna
VA 22183-1059. 703/281-0200.
This is the on-line service of the
Federal Career Opportunities
publication.

HEALTH CARE: SERVICE, EQUIPMENT AND PRODUCTS

Employment in the health care industry has gone up steadily during the past few years, with an average annual growth rate of 8 percent -- and that doesn't include medical equipment manufacturers, where business is also booming. Health care expenditures are now rising to over $800 billion a year. While health reform stalled in Congress during 1994, other reform bills are expected to be presented in 1995. Many reforms are already underway within the industry. Best bets for jobseekers: HMOs. Also, check out nursing homes and home health care companies. Hospitals, already under tight restraints, will find things getting even tighter.

ADVANCED TECHNOLOGY LABORATORIES INC.
P.O. Box 3003
Bothell WA 98041-3003
206/487-7416
Contact: Personnel Manager
Description: Engaged in the production and manufacture of a variety of electronic diagnostic equipment for use in healthcare. Products include scanners and ultra-sound systems.

AFFILIATED HEALTH SERVICES
UNITED GENERAL HOSPITAL
P.O. Box 1376
Mount Vernon WA 98273-1376
206/428-2174
Fax: 206/428-2482
Contact: Human Resources Department
Description: A hospital. **Common positions include:** Accountant/Auditor; Claim Representative; Customer Service Representative; Dietician/ Nutritionist; Electrical/Electronic Engineer; Emergency Medical Technician; Industrial Engineer; Librarian; Licensed Practical Nurse; Medical Record Technician; Nuclear Medicine Technologist; Occupational Therapist; Personnel/Labor Relations Specialist; Pharmacist; Physical Therapist; Radiologic Technologist; Recreational Therapist; Registered Nurse; Respiratory Therapist; Social Worker; Structural Engineer; Surgical Technician. **Educational backgrounds include:** Accounting; Business

Administration; Commercial Art; Engineering. **Benefits:** Dental Insurance; Employee Discounts; Life Insurance; Medical Insurance; Pension Plan; Tuition Assistance. **Corporate headquarters location:** This Location. **Operations at this facility include:** Administration. **Number of employees at this location:** 500.

BALLARD COMMUNITY HOSPITAL
P.O. Box 70707
Seattle WA 98107-1507
206/782-2700
Contact: Human Resources Department
Description: A hospital.

CHILDREN'S HOSPITAL AND MEDICAL CENTER
4800 Sand Point Way NE
Seattle WA 98105
206/526-2111
Contact: Human Resources Department
Description: A tertiary, pediatric hospital and medical center. **Common positions include:** Accountant/Auditor; Administrator; Biological Scientist/Biochemist; Chemist; Claim Representative; Dietician/Nutritionist; Food Scientist/Technologist; Personnel/Labor Relations Specialist; Registered Nurse. **Educational backgrounds include:** Accounting; Biology; Business Administration; Chemistry; Communications; Computer Science; Finance; Liberal Arts; Mathematics; Physics. **Benefits:** Dental Insurance; Disability Coverage; Employee Discounts; Life Insurance; Medical Insurance; Pension Plan; Savings Plan. **Corporate headquarters location:** This Location. **Operations at this facility include:** Service. **Number of employees at this location:** 2,400.

EVERETT CLINIC
P.O. Box 5127
Everett WA 98206
206/259-0966
Contact: Human Resources Department
Description: A medical clinic.

EVERGREEN HOSPITAL MEDICAL CENTER
12040 NE 128th Street
Kirkland WA 98034
206/899-2501
Fax: 206/899-2510
Contact: Tracy Monteau, Personnel Assistant
Description: A medical center containing: an acute care hospital, a surgery center, a hospice center, a head injury rehabilitation center, a telemarketing center, and a home health department. **Common positions include:** Computer Programmer; Computer Systems Analyst; Dietician/Nutritionist; Emergency Medical Technician; Financial Analyst; Health Services Manager; Medical

Record Technician; Nuclear Medicine Technologist; Occupational Therapist; Pharmacist; Physical Therapist; Radiologic Technologist; Recreational Therapist; Registered Nurse; Respiratory Therapist; Restaurant/Food Service Manager; Social Worker; Speech-Language Pathologist; Surgical Technician. **Educational backgrounds include:** Nursing. **Benefits:** 401K; Dental Insurance; Disability Coverage; Employee Discounts; Life Insurance; Matching Gift; Medical Insurance; Pension Plan. **Corporate headquarters location:** This Location. **Operations at this facility include:** Administration. **Number of employees at this location:** 1,500.

GENERAL HOSPITAL MEDICAL CENTER
P.O. Box 1147
Everett WA 98206
206/261-2000
Contact: Human Resources Department
Description: A hospital.

GROUP HEALTH HOSPITAL
2700 152nd Avenue NE
Redmond WA 98052
206/883-5151
Contact: Human Resources Department
Description: A hospital.

HARBORVIEW MEDICAL CENTER
325 9th Avenue
Seattle WA 98104
206/223-3000
Contact: Human Resources Department
Description: A hospital.

HILLHAVEN CORPORATION
P.O. Box 2264
Tacoma WA 98401
206/572-4901
Contact: Human Resources
Description: A nursing-care facility.

HOLY FAMILY HOSPITAL
5633 North Lidgerwood Street
Spokane WA 99207
509/482-2111
Fax: 509/482-2178
Contact: Mr. Alan Hill, Human Resources Director
Description: Holy Family Hospital is a growing health care facility. **Common positions include:** Accountant/Auditor; Computer Systems Analyst; EEG Technologist; EKG Technician; Licensed Practical Nurse; Medical Record Technician; Occupational Therapist; Pharmacist; Physical Therapist;

Radiologic Technologist; Registered Nurse; Respiratory Therapist; Social Worker; Speech-Language Pathologist; Surgical Technician. **Benefits:** Dental Insurance; Life Insurance; Medical Insurance; Pension Plan; Savings Plan; Tuition Assistance.

IMRE CORPORATION
401 Queen Anne Avenue North
Seattle WA 98109
206/298-9400
Contact: Sonja Nutley, Office Manager
Description: A medical products company engaged in the field of immunoadsorption. **Benefits:** 401K; Dental Insurance; Disability Coverage; Life Insurance; Medical Insurance. **Operations at this facility include:** Administration; Manufacturing; Research and Development; Service. **Number of employees at this location:** 39. **Number of employees nationwide:** 62.

INTERIM HEALTHCARE OF SEATTLE INC.
2033 6th Avenue, Suite 310
Seattle WA 98121
206/443-7665
Fax: 206/443-1611
Contact: Human Resources Department
Description: A home health agency. Medicare certified and JACHO accredited. **Common positions include:** Licensed Practical Nurse; Occupational Therapist; Physical Therapist; Registered Nurse; Social Worker. **Corporate headquarters location:** This Location. **Other U.S. locations:** Tacoma WA; Port Angeles WA.

VIRGINIA MASON MEDICAL CENTER
P.O. Box 900
Seattle WA 98111
206/223-6600
Contact: Human Resources, Department G
Description: A medical center. Call jobline for weekly listings. **Common positions include:** Health Services Worker; Registered Nurse. **Educational backgrounds include:** Health Care; Nursing. **Benefits:** Daycare Assistance; Dental Insurance; Disability Coverage; Life Insurance; Medical Insurance; Pension Plan; Transportation Pass; Tuition Assistance. **Special Programs:** Internships; Training Programs.

NORTHWEST HOSPITAL
1550 North 115th Street
Seattle WA 98133
206/364-0500
Contact: Human Resources Department
Description: A hospital.

OVERLAKE HOSPITAL MEDICAL CENTER
1035 116th Avenue NE
Bellevue WA 98004
206/688-5201
Contact: Human Resources Department
Description: A hospital. **Common positions include:** Registered Nurse.
Number of employees at this location: 1,700.

PACIFIC MEDICAL CENTER
1200 12th Avenue South
Seattle WA 98144
206/326-4000
Contact: Human Resources Department
Description: Manufactures contact lenses.

PHYSIO-CONTROL CORPORATION
P.O. Box 97006
Redmond WA 98073-9706
206/867-4000
Contact: Human Resources Department
Description: Manufacturers, sells, and services defribillators/monitors/pacemakers. Has sales and service offices in multiple locations. **Common positions include:** Accountant/Auditor; Administrative Services Manager; Attorney; Biomedical Engineer; Budget Analyst; Buyer; Chemical Engineer; Chemist; Computer Operator; Computer Programmer; Computer Systems Analyst; Credit Clerk and Authorizer; Customer Service Representative; Department Manager; Draftsperson; Electrical/Electronic Engineer; Employment Interviewer; Financial Manager; Graphic Artist; Industrial Engineer; Industrial Manager; Inspector/Tester/Grader; Librarian; Licensed Practical Nurse; Manufacturer's/Wholesaler's Sales Rep.; Marketing Research Analyst; Marketing/Advertising/PR Manager; Mechanical Engineer; Paralegal; Payroll Clerk; Personnel/Labor Relations Specialist; Precision Assembler; Purchasing Agent and Manager; Quality Control Supervisor; Receptionist; Secretary; Software Engineer; Systems Analyst; Technical Writer/Editor. **Educational backgrounds include:** Accounting; Business Administration; Chemistry; Computer Science; Engineering; Finance; Marketing. **Benefits:** Dental Insurance; Disability Coverage; Life Insurance; Medical Insurance; Pension Plan; Profit Sharing; Savings Plan; Tuition Assistance. **Corporate headquarters location:** This Location. **Operations at this facility include:** Administration; Manufacturing; Research and Development; Sales; Service.

PROVIDENCE HOSPITAL
P.O. Box 1067
Everett WA 98206
206/258-7563
Contact: Human Resources Department
Description: A hospital.

QUINTON INSTRUMENT COMPANY
2121 Terry Avenue
Seattle WA 98121-2791
206/223-7373
Contact: Industrial Relations Department
Description: Manufactures electronic medical instruments.

SIEMENS MEDICAL SYSTEMS, INC.
ULTRASOUND GROUP
P.O. Box 7002
Issaquah WA 98027
206/392-9180
Contact: Human Resources
Description: Manufactures surgical medical products.

SPACELABS, INC.
15220 NE 40th Street
Redmond WA 98052
206/882-3700
Contact: Human Resources
Description: A manufacturer of patient-monitoring equipment, clinical information systems, ambulatory-monitoring products, and monitoring supplies. Number of employees nationwide: 1,600. **Common positions include:** Accountant/Auditor; Biomedical Engineer; Buyer; Computer Operator; Computer Programmer; Computer Systems Analyst; Customer Service Representative; Dispatcher; EKG Technician; Electrical/Electronic Engineer; Marketing Research Analyst; Mechanical Engineer; Order Clerk; Payroll Clerk; Personnel/Labor Relations Specialist; Precision Assembler; Purchasing Agent and Manager; Receptionist; Secretary; Software Engineer; Stock Clerk. **Educational backgrounds include:** Accounting; Business Administration; Computer Science; Engineering; Finance; Marketing. **Benefits:** Dental Insurance; Disability Coverage; Life Insurance; Medical Insurance; Pension Plan; Savings Plan; Tuition Assistance. **Corporate headquarters location:** This Location. **Other U.S. locations:** Chatsworth CA; Hillsboro OR. **Operations at this facility include:** Administration; Research and Development. **Listed on:** NASDAQ. **Number of employees at this location:** 500. **Number of employees nationwide:** 1,600.

STEVENS MEMORIAL HOSPITAL
21601 76th Avenue West
Edmonds WA 98026
206/640-4000
Contact: Human Resources Department
Description: A hospital.

SWEDISH HOSPITAL MEDICAL CENTER
P.O. Box 14999
Seattle WA 98114-0999
206/386-6000
Contact: Human Resources Department
Description: A medical center.

SYNAPTIC MEDICAL
2720 3rd Avenue
Seattle WA 98121
206/728-8206
Contact: Steve Doucette, Executive Producer
Description: Synaptic Medical specializes in the production of healthcare films and videos. *Note:* Only highly-qualified applicants for media/medical sales representative positions or production coordinator positions will be considered. **Common positions include:** Writer/Producer/Director. **Educational backgrounds include:** Art/Design; Communications; M.D./Medicine; Marketing. **Parent company:** Bonneville, Inc.

UNIVERSITY OF WASHINGTON MEDICAL CENTER
1959 NE Pacific Street
Seattle WA 98195
206/548-4040
Contact: Human Resources Department
Description: A medical center.

VETERANS ADMINISTRATION MEDICAL CENTER
1660 South Columbian Way
Seattle WA 98108
206/764-2135
Contact: Rob Davies, Chief of Staffing
Description: A 488-bed critical care hospital affiliated with the University of Washington. **Number of employees at this location:** 1,800.

Note: Because addresses and telephone numbers of smaller companies change rapidly, we recommend you call each company and verify the information below before mailing to employers. Mass mailings are not recommended.

Additional employers with over 250 employees:

MEDICAL EQUIPMENT

Picker International
11715 North Creek Parkway South, Suite 110, Bothell WA 98011. 206/481-3171.

DOCTORS' OFFICES & CLINICS

St. Joseph Hospital
2901 Squalicum Parkway, Bellingham WA 98225-1898. 206/734-5400.

NURSING AND PERSONAL CARE FACILITIES

Grays Harbor Convalescence Center
920 Anderson Drive, Aberdeen WA 98520-1007. 206/532-5122.

HOSPITALS AND MEDICAL CENTERS

Capital Medical Center
3900 Capitol Mall Drive SW, Olympia WA 98502-5026. 206/754-5858.

Deaconess Medical Center Spokane
P.O. Box 248, Spokane WA 99210-0248. 509/458-5800.

Empire Health Centers Group
P.O. Box 248, Spokane WA 99210-0248. 509/458-7960.

Ferry County Memorial Hospital
P.O. Box 365, Republic WA 99166-0365. 509/775-3998.

Health and Hospital Services
15325 SE 30th Place, #300, Bellevue WA 98007-6538. 206/454-8068.

Mark Reed Hospital
P.O. Box 28, McCleary WA 98557-0028. 206/495-3244.

Multicare Health System
P.O. Box 5299, Tacoma WA 98415-0299. 206/552-1251.

Naval Hospital
Boone Road, Bremerton WA 98312. 206/479-9344.

Okanogan Douglas County Hospital
P.O. Box 577, Brewster WA 98812-0577. 509/689-2517.

Olympic Memorial Hospital
939 Caroline Street, Port Angeles WA 98362-3997. 206/457-8513.

State Penitentiary Hospital
P.O. Box 520, Walla Walla WA 99362-0520. 509/525-3610.

Deaconess Rehabilitation Institute
P.O. Box 288, Spokane WA 99210-0288. 509/838-4771.

Allenmore Hospital
P.O. Box 11414, Tacoma WA 98411-0414. 206/572-2323.

CPC Fairfax Hospital
10200 NE 132nd Street, Kirkland WA 98034-2899. 206/821-2000.

Olympic Mental Health
10710 Mukilteo Speedway, Mukilteo WA 98275-5021. 206/290-9745.

Mountainview Hospital Spokane
P.O. Box 598, Spokane WA 99210-0598. 509/624-3226.

Schick Shadel Hospital
P.O. Box 48149,
Seattle WA 98148-
0149. 206/244-8100.

**Fred Hutchinson
Cancer Research**
1124 Columbia Street,
Seattle WA 98104-
2092. 206/667-5000.

Samaritan Hospital
801 East Wheeler
Road, Moses Lake WA
98837-1899.
509/765-5606.

**Southwest
Washington Medical
Center**
P.O. Box 1600,
Vancouver WA
98668-1600.
206/256-2000.

**HEALTH AND ALLIED
SERVICES**

Naval Hospital
3475 North Saratoga
Street
OakHarbor WA
98278-8800.
206/257-9500.

**Our Lady Of Lourdes
Health Center**
P.O. Box 2568, Pasco
WA 99302-2568.
509/547-7704.

**Auburn General
Hospital**
20 2nd Street, NE,
Auburn WA 98002-
4900. 206/833-7711.

**SPECIALTY
OUTPATIENT
FACILITIES**

Eastern State Hospital
P.O. Box A, Medical
Lake WA 99022-
0045. 509/299-4351.

Kadlec Medical Center
888 Swift Boulevard,
Richland WA 99352-
3542. 509/946-4611.

Additional employers with under 250 employees:

**GENERAL MEDICAL
AND SURGICAL
HOSPITALS**

Mid-Valley Hospital
P.O. Box 793, Omak
WA 98841-0793.
509/826-1760.

**Snohomish County
Public Hospital**
P.O. Box 370,
Arlington WA 98223-
0370. 206/435-2133.

**SKILLED NURSING
FACILITIES**

**Lincoln County
Hospital**
P.O. Box 68,
Davenport WA 99122-
0068. 509/725-7101.

**Rosary Manor Nursing
Home**
500 SE Washington
Avenue, Chehalis WA
98532-3058.
206/740-8533.

**SPECIALTY
HOSPITALS**

**Tri-State Memorial
Hospital**
P.O. Box 189,
Clarkston WA 99403-
0189. 509/758-4650.

**MEDICAL
LABORATORIES**

**Pathology Associates
Medical Labs**
N5901 North
Lidgerwood Street,
Spokane WA 99207-
1123. 509/927-6282.

SPECIALTY OUTPATIENT FACILITIES

Community Memorial Hospital
P.O. Box 218, Enumclaw WA 98022-0218. 206/825-2505.

St Joseph's Hospital
P.O. Box 197, Chewelah WA 99109-0197. 509/935-8211.

Island Hospital
1211 24th Street, Anacortes WA 98221-2590. 206/293-3181.

SURGICAL AND MEDICAL INSTRUMENTS

Heart Technology
17425 NE Union Hill Road, Redmond WA 98052-3376. 206/869-6160.

ELECTROMEDICAL AND ELECTRO-THERAPEUTIC APPARATUS

Self Regulation Systems
14770 NE 95th Street, Redmond WA 98052-2554. 206/882-1101.

First Medical Devices Corporation
2445 140th Avenue NE, Bellevue WA 98005-1879. 206/641-4774.

Fukuda Denshi America Corporation
7102 180th Avenue NE Suite 101 A, Redmond WA 98052-4961. 206/881-7737.

JJ&A Instruments-Ultra Check
17117 NE 84th Street, Redmond WA 98052-3972. 206/882-0466.

Lawrence Medical Systems Inc.
2869 152nd Avenue NE, Redmond WA 98052-5514. 206/881-7717.

MEDICAL, DENTAL AND HOSPITAL EQUIPMENT WHOLESALE

Independence Products Northwest
3018 South Mullen Street, Tacoma WA 98409-2346. 206/566-7015.

Burkhart Dental Supply Company
2502 South 78th Street, Tacoma WA 98409-5824. 206/474-7761.

Stein Dental Supply
946 North 127th Street, Seattle WA 98133-8031. 206/363-1044.

XRS Inc.
3602 South Madison Street, Tacoma WA 98409-2216. 206/272-6454.

HEALTH AND ALLIED SERVICES

Mount Carmel Hospital
P.O. Box 351, Colville WA 99114-0351. 509/684-2561.

OPHTHALMIC GOODS WHOLESALE

Western Optical Corporation
1200 Mercer Street, Seattle WA 98109-5511. 206/622-7627.

Kittitas Valley Community Hospital
603 South Chestnut Street, Ellensburg WA 98926-3875. 509/962-9841.

Prosser Memorial Hospital
723 Memorial Street, Prosser WA 99350-1593. 509/786-2222.

Sunnyside Community Hospital
P.O. Box 719, Sunnyside WA 98944-0719. 509/837-1500.

St. Mary Medical Center
P.O. Box 1477, Walla Walla WA 99362-0312. 509/525-3320.

Carondelet Psychiatric Care Center
1175 Carondelet Drive, Richland WA 99352-3396. 509/943-9104.

For more information on career opportunities in the health care industry:

Associations

AMERICAN ACADEMY OF FAMILY PHYSICIANS
8880 Ward Parkway, Kansas City MO 64114. 816/333-9700.

AMERICAN ACADEMY OF PHYSICIAN ASSISTANTS
950 North Washington Street, Alexandria VA 22314. 703/836-2272.

AMERICAN ASSOCIATION FOR CLINICAL CHEMISTRY
2101 Lovely Street NW, Suite 202, Washington, DC 20037-1526.

AMERICAN ASSOCIATION OF COLLEGES OF OSTEOPATHIC MEDICINE
6110 Executive Boulevard, Suite 405, Rockville MD 20852. 301/468-2037.

AMERICAN ASSOCIATION OF COLLEGES OF PODIATRIC MEDICINE
1350 Piccard Drive, Suite 322, Rockville MD 20850. 301/990-7400.

AMERICAN ASSOCIATION OF DENTAL SCHOOLS
1625 Massachusetts Avenue NW, Washington DC 20036. 202/667-9433.

AMERICAN ASSOCIATION OF MEDICAL ASSISTANTS
20 North Wacker Drive, Suite 1575, Chicago IL 60606. 312/899-1500.

AMERICAN ASSOCIATION OF NURSE ANESTHETISTS
222 South Prospect, Park Ridge IL 60068-4001. 708/692-7050.

AMERICAN ASSOCIATION OF RESPIRATORY CARE
11030 Ables Lane, Dallas TX 75229-4593. 214/243-2272.

AMERICAN CHIROPRACTIC ASSOCIATION
1701 Clarendon Boulevard, Arlington VA 22209. 703/276-8800.

AMERICAN COLLEGE OF HEALTHCARE ADMINISTRATORS
325 South Patrick Street, Alexandria VA 22314. 703/549-5822.

AMERICAN COLLEGE OF HEALTHCARE EXECUTIVES
840 North Lake Shore Drive, West 1103, Chicago IL 60611. 312/943-0544.

AMERICAN DENTAL ASSOCIATION
211 East Chicago Avenue, Chicago IL 60611. 312/440-2500.

AMERICAN DENTAL HYGIENISTS ASSOCIATION
Division of Professional Development, 444 North Michigan Avenue, Suite 3400, Chicago IL 60611. 312/440-8900.

AMERICAN DIETETIC ASSOCIATION
216 West Jackson Boulevard, Chicago IL 60606. 312/899-0040.

AMERICAN HEALTH CARE ASSOCIATION
1201 L Street NW, Washington DC 20005-4014. 202/842-4444.

AMERICAN MEDICAL ASSOCIATION
515 North State Street, Chicago IL 60610. 312/464-5000.

AMERICAN HEALTH INFORMATION MANAGEMENT ASSOCIATION
919 North Michigan Avenue, Suite 1400, Chicago IL 60611. 312/787-2672.

AMERICAN MEDICAL TECHNOLOGISTS
710 Higgins Road, Park Ridge IL 60068. 708/823-5169.

AMERICAN NURSES ASSOCIATION
600 Maryland Avenue SW, Suite 100W, Washington DC 20024-2571. 202/554-4444.

AMERICAN OCCUPATIONAL THERAPY ASSOCIATION
1383 Piccard Drive, P.O. Box 1725, Rockville MD 20849-1725. 301/948-9626.

AMERICAN OPTOMETRIC ASSOCIATION
243 North Lindbergh Boulevard, St. Louis MO 63141. 314/991-4100.

AMERICAN PHYSICAL THERAPY ASSOCIATION
1111 North Fairfax Street, Alexandria VA 22314. 703/684-2782. Must send small fee in return for information.

AMERICAN VETERINARY MEDICAL ASSOCIATION
1931 North Meacham Road, Suite 100, Schaumburg IL 60173-4360. 708/925-8070.

FLORIDA NURSES' ASSOCIATION
1235 East Concord Street, Box 536985, Orlando FL 32853. 407/896-3261.

NATIONAL MEDICAL ASSOCIATION
1012 Tenth Street NW, Washington DC 20001. 202/347-1895.

NATIONAL PHARMACEUTICAL COUNCIL
1894 Prewston White Drive, Reston VA 22091. 703/620-6390. FAX: 703/476-0904. Fax requests to the attention of Pat Adams, Vice President of Finance and Administration.

NATIONAL SOCIETY FOR CARDIOVASCULAR TECHNOLOGY
120 Falcon Drive, Unit 3, Fredricksburg VA 22408. Operates a jobline: 800/898-2393.

NATIONAL SOCIETY FOR PULMONARY TECHNOLOGY
120 Falcon Drive, Unit 3, Fredricksburg VA 22408.

Directories

BLUE BOOK DIGEST OF HMOs
National Association of Employers on Health Care Alternatives, P.O. Box 220, Fort Lauderdale FL 33310. 305/361-2810.

ENCYCLOPEDIA OF MEDICAL ORGANIZATIONS AND AGENCIES
Gale Research Inc., 835 Penobscot Building, Detroit MI 48226. 313/961-2242.

HEALTH ORGANIZATIONS OF THE UNITED STATES, CANADA, AND THE WORLD
Gale Research Inc., 835 Penobscot Building, Detroit MI 48226. 313/961-2242.

MEDICAL AND HEALTH INFORMATION DIRECTORY
Gale Research Inc., 835 Penobscot Building, Detroit MI 48226. 313/961-2242.

NATIONAL DIRECTORY OF HEALTH MAINTENANCE ORGANIZATIONS
Group Health Association of America, 1129 20th Street NW, Suite 600, Washington DC 20036. 202/778-3200.

Magazines

AMERICAN MEDICAL NEWS
American Medical Association, 515 North State Street, Chicago IL 60605. 312/464-5000.

CHANGING MEDICAL MARKETS
Theta Corporation, Theta Building, Middlefield CT 06455. 203/349-1054.

HEALTH CARE EXECUTIVE
American College of Health Care Executives, 840 North Lake Shore Drive, Chicago IL 60611. 312/943-0544.

MODERN HEALTHCARE
Crain Communications, 740 North Rush Street, Chicago IL 60611. 312/649-5374.

NURSEFAX
Springhouse Corporation, 1111 Bethlehem Pike, P.O. Box 908, Springhouse PA 19477.
This is a jobline service designed to be used in conjunction with *Nursing* magazine.

HOTELS AND RESTAURANTS

In the restaurant segment, the fastest growing sector of the market continues to be fast food-style establishments, although increased public concern over health has led industry leaders to develop new products and marketing strategies: McDonald's released its lower-fat "McLean Deluxe", and Kentucky Fried Chicken changed its name to "KFC" to de-emphasize the word "Fried". The take-out trend, spurred by changing demographics and eating habits, is changing the industry as a whole, not just at the fast food end. Managerial prospects are better than average, but the industry is hampered by a shortage of entry-level workers.

The hotel industry is tied closely to other segments of the travel industry, which in turn relies on the U.S. economy as a whole. International arrivals are the fastest-growing segment of the travel industry, so hotels in major American international destinations are better positioned. Look for greater specialization within the industry, with hotels advertising as "budget", "luxury", or "corporate/meeting", for example. Hotels will also need to respond to the growing number of working couples who take shorter vacations together.

AGGIES INN
602 East Front Street
Port Angeles WA 98362
206/457-0471
Contact: Human Resources
Description: An inn.

AZTECA RESTAURANTS
133 SW 158th Street
Seattle WA 98166
206/243-7021
Contact: Human Resources
Description: A Mexican restaurant company. **Common positions include:** Assistant Manager; Blue-Collar Worker Supervisor; Cashier; Chef/Cook/Kitchen Worker; Department Manager; General Manager; Payroll Clerk; Personnel/Labor Relations Specialist. **Educational backgrounds include:** Business Administration. **Benefits:** Dental Insurance; Employee Discounts; Medical Insurance. **Corporate headquarters location:** This Location. **Operations at this facility include:** Regional Headquarters.

FOOD MANAGEMENT CORPORATION
P.O. Box 98807
Seattle WA 98198-0807
206/824-0887
Contact: Human Resources Department
Description: A contract food services management company. **Common positions include:** Cashier; Chef/Cook/Kitchen Worker; Dietician/Nutritionist; Food and Beverage Service Worker; Restaurant/Food Service Manager. **Benefits:** Life Insurance; Meal Plan; Medical Insurance; Paid Vacation; Profit Sharing. **Corporate headquarters location:** This Location. **Other U.S. locations:** AL; ID; OR; UT. **Operations at this facility include:** Administration; Regional Headquarters; Sales; Service. **Listed on:** Privately held. **Number of employees at this location:** 25. **Number of employees nationwide:** 750.

FOUR SEASONS OLYMPIC HOTEL
411 University Street
Seattle WA 98101
206/621-1700
Contact: Human Resources Department
Description: A hotel.

KFC (KENTUCKY FRIED CHICKEN)
1203 NE 78th Street
Vancouver WA 98665
Contact: Human Resources
Description: A fast-food restaurant chain, specializing in chicken.

PIZZA HAVEN INC.
12860 Inter Urban Avenue South
Seattle WA 98168
206/241-2990
Contact: Personnel Department
Description: A chain of pizza restaurants, and Bean Pod Deli restaurants.

RED LION HOTEL BELLEVUE
300 112th Avenue SE
Bellevue WA 98004
206/455-1300
Contact: Human Resources
Description: A 355-room hotel. Ask for job hotline extension.

RED LION HOTEL/SEA-TAC
18740 Pacific Highway South
Seattle WA 98188
206/246-8600
Contact: Human Resources Department
Description: A hotel. Ask for job hotline extension.

RESTAURANTS UNLIMITED INC.
1818 North Northlake Way
Seattle WA 98103
206/634-0550
Fax: 206/632-3533
Contact: Tom Griffith, Director of Staffing
Description: Owners and operators of a chain of full-service dinner houses and the originator and operator of the Cinnabon Quick-Service Bakeries. **Common positions include:** Chef/Cook/Kitchen Worker; Restaurant/Food Service Manager. **Educational backgrounds include:** Business Administration; Communications; Economics; Hotel Administration; Liberal Arts; Restaurant Management. **Benefits:** 401K; Dental Insurance; Disability Coverage; Employee Discounts; Life Insurance; Medical Insurance. **Corporate headquarters location:** This Location. **Operations at this facility include:** Administration; Divisional Headquarters; Regional Headquarters.

SEA GALLEY STORES, INC.
7116 220th Street SW, Suite 200
Mountlake Terrace WA 98048
206/775-0411
Contact: Kyle J. Kumasaka, Vice President of Operations
Description: Sea Galley Stores, Inc. operates full-service restaurants in four states -- Alaska, Arizona, Idaho, and Washington. **Common positions include:** Accountant/Auditor; Assistant Manager; Chef/Cook/Kitchen Worker; Food and Beverage Service Worker; General Manager; Marketing/Advertising/PR Manager; Restaurant/Food Service Manager; Secretary. **Educational backgrounds include:** Accounting; Business Administration; Finance; Hospitality/Restaurant. **Benefits:** 401K; Employee Discounts; Life Insurance; Medical Insurance; Savings Plan. **Special Programs:** Internships; Training Programs. **Corporate headquarters location:** This Location. **Other U.S. locations:** AK; AZ; ID; WA. **Operations at this facility include:** Administration; Divisional Headquarters; Research and Development. **Listed on:** NASDAQ. **Annual Revenues:** $20,000,000. **Number of employees at this location:** 20. **Number of employees nationwide:** 800.

SEATTLE MARRIOT SEA-TAC AIRPORT
3201 South 176th Street
Seattle WA 98188
206/241-2000
Contact: Human Resources
Description: A 460-room hotel in close proximity to the Seattle-Tacoma International Aiport.

SEATTLE SHERATON HOTEL
1400 6th Avenue
Seattle WA 98101
206/621-9000
Contact: John Boulanger, Director of Human Resources
Description: A hotel. **Common positions include:** Chef/Cook/Kitchen Worker; Department Manager; Food and Beverage Service Worker; Hotel/Motel Clerk. **Benefits:** Employee Discounts; Life Insurance; Meal Discounts; Medical Insurance; Pension Plan; Tuition Assistance. **Corporate headquarters location:** Boston MA. **Parent company:** ITT Sheraton. **Operations at this facility include:** Administration; Sales; Service. **Listed on:** New York Stock Exchange. **Number of employees at this location:** 500.

SKIPPER'S INCORPORATED
1500 114th Avenue SE, Suite 150
Bellevue WA 98004
206/462-8400
Contact: Alison Deede, Human Resources Manager
Description: A fast-food seafood restaurant chain. **Common positions include:** Management Trainee. **Benefits:** Dental Insurance; Disability Coverage; Life Insurance; Medical Insurance; Profit Sharing; Stock Option; Tuition Assistance. **Special Programs:** Internships; Training Programs. **Corporate headquarters location:** This Location. **Other U.S. locations:** AK; CA; CO; ID; MT; OR; UT; WA; WY. **Parent company:** National Pizza Company. **Operations at this facility include:** Service. **Number of employees nationwide:** 3,000.

STARBUCKS CORPORATION
2203 Airport Way South
Seattle WA 98134
206/447-1575
Contact: Human Resources
Description: Starbucks Corporation purchases and roasts high-quality whole bean coffees, which it sells, along with fresh, rich-brewed coffees and Italian-style expresso beverages, primarily through more than 230 company-operated coffee shops. Company also sells a wide selection of coffee-making equipment, accessories, pastries, and confections.

STOUFFER MADISON HOTEL
515 Madison Street
Seattle WA 98104
206/583-0300
Contact: Jeanne Hartman, Human Resources Director
Description: A 550-room hotel. **Special Programs:** Internships. **Parent company:** Renaissance. **Number of employees at this location:** 365.

UNIVERSAL OGDEN SERVICES
520 Pike Street, Suite 2230
Seattle WA 98101
206/340-9200
Contact: Personnel Department
Description: A remote-site catering contractor, providing services to remote construction and offshore oil and drilling operations.

WESTCOAST HOTELS
Plaza 600 Building
600 Stewart Street, Suite 300
Seattle WA 98101
206/441-9856
Contact: Personnel Department
Description: Engaged in hotels, restaurants, and real estate. **Parent company:** Granaten AB. **Number of employees at this location:** 380.

WESTIN HOTEL SEATTLE
1900 5th Avenue
Seattle WA 98101
206/728-1000
Contact: Human Resources
Description: A 865-room hotel.

WESTIN HOTELS & RESORTS
The Westin Building
2001 Sixth Avenue
Seattle WA 98121
206/443-5000
Contact: Personnel Department
Description: Seattle office of the Westin hotels and resorts. **Corporate headquarters location:** This Location.

Note: Because addresses and telephone numbers of smaller companies change rapidly, we recommend you call each company and verify the information below before mailing to employers. Mass mailings are not recommended.

Additional employers with over 250 employees:

EATING PLACES

Falls Terrace Restaurant
106 Deschutes Way SW, Olympia WA 98501.

Robin Red Burgers & Spirits
2706 West Nob Hill Boulevard, Yakima WA 98902.

Additional employers with under 250 employees:

EATING PLACES

Chapter Eleven
E105 East Mission
Avenue, Spokane WA
99202-1816.
509/326-0466.

Dick's Drive Ins Ltd.
500 Queen Anne
Avenue North, Seattle
WA 98109-4520.
206/285-5155.

Ray's Boathouse
6049 Seaview Avenue
NW, Seattle WA
98107-2690.
206/789-3770.

Taco Time-Office
4429 6th Avenue,
Tacoma WA 98406-
3501. 206/752-1154.

The Salish Lodge
Fall City-Snoqualmie
Road, Snoqualmie WA
98065. 206/888-
2556.

Trattoria Mitchelli
84 Yesler Way,
Seattle WA 98104-
2529. 206/623-3883.

**Wendy's Old Fashion
Hamburgers**
E123 East 2nd
Avenue, Spokane WA
99202-1504.
509/747-5900.

Zip's Drive In
N10125 North
Division Street,
Spokane WA 99218-
1306. 509/466-6924.

Domino's Pizza
N1105 North Lincoln
Street, Spokane WA
99201-2138.
509/327-6142.

**HOTELS AND
MOTELS**

Days Inn Towncenter
2205 7th Avenue,
Seattle WA 98121-
1875. 206/448-3434.

**Alpental Ski Acres
Snoqualmie**
7900 SE 28th Street,
Mercer Island WA
98040-2968.
206/232-8182.

The Inn At Semiahmoo
9565 Semiahmoo
Parkway, Blaine WA
98230-9326.
206/371-2000.

Trendwest Resorts
4010 Lake
Washington Boulevard
NE, Kirkland WA
98033. 206/889-
2387.

For more information on career opportunities in hotels and restaurants:

Associations

**AMERICAN HOTEL AND MOTEL
ASSOCIATION**
1201 New York Avenue NW, Suite
600, Washington DC 20005-3931.
202/289-3100.

**THE EDUCATIONAL
FOUNDATION OF THE
NATIONAL RESTAURANT
ASSOCIATION**
250 South Wacker Drive, 14th
Floor, Chicago IL 60606. 312/715-
1010.

NATIONAL RESTAURANT ASSOCIATION
1200 17th Street NW, Washington DC 20036. 202/331-5900.

Directories

DIRECTORY OF CHAIN RESTAURANT OPERATORS
Business Guides, Inc., Lebhar-Friedman, Inc., 3922 Coconut Palm Drive, Tampa FL 33619-8321. 813/664-6700.

DIRECTORY OF HIGH-VOLUME INDEPENDENT RESTAURANTS
Lebhar-Friedman, Inc., 3922 Coconut Palm Drive, Tampa FL 33619-8321. 813/664-6700.

Magazines

CORNELL HOTEL AND RESTAURANT ADMINISTRATION QUARTERLY
Cornell University School of Hotel Administration, Statler Hall, Ithaca NY 14853. 607/255-9393.

HOTEL AND MOTEL MANAGEMENT
120 West 2nd Street, Duluth MN 55802.

INNKEEPING WORLD
Box 84108, Seattle WA 98124. 206/362-7125.

NATION'S RESTAURANT NEWS
3922 Coconut Palm Drive, Tampa, FL 33619. 212/756-5200.

INSURANCE

 *While individual life insurance and health insurance are still weak, jobseekers should look to companies that specialize in annuities, which will continue to be the industry's fastest growing segment. Premiums of property-casualty insurers should increase by about 7-9 percent in personal business, but commercial business will be tighter. Competition and mergers will increase, and life insurance companies are expected to experience further problems. The industry as a whole has been trimming back through layoffs, although the worst appears to be over.*

AETNA LIFE & CASUALTY
1501 4th Avenue, Suite 1000
Seattle WA 98101
206/467-2500
Contact: Shelley Jacobson, Human Resources Consultant
Description: Regional field operations of the national insurance firm.

AGENA CORPORATION
9709 Third Avenue NE
Seattle WA 98115
206/525-0005
Contact: Personnel Department
Description: An independent insurance agent of automation services.

ALLSTATE INSURANCE SEATTLE REGIONAL
19015 North Creek Parkway
Bothell WA 98111
206/489-9000
Contact: Human Resources
Description: A member of the Sears Financial Network. One of the nation's largest insurance companies.

BLUE CROSS OF WASHINGTON AND ALASKA
P.O. Box 327
Seattle WA 98111-0327
206/670-4791
Fax: 206/670-4773
Contact: Personnel
Description: A non-profit health care insurance organization.

FAMILY LIFE INSURANCE COMPANY
2101 4th Avenue, Suite 700
Seattle WA 98121
206/441-1942
Contact: Personnel Department
Description: Sells life and disability insurance. **Parent company:** Merrill Lynch & Company Inc. **Number of employees at this location:** 419.

FARMERS NEW WORLD LIFE INSURANCE
3003 77th Avenue South East
Mercer Island WA 98040
206/236-6540
Contact: Amy McCullough, Human Resources Manager
Description: Offers a complete line of life insurance services.

FEDERATED AMERICAN INSURANCE COMPANY
15300 Bothell Way NE
Seattle WA 98155
206/364-3010
Contact: Personnel Department
Description: An insurance company specializing in auto insurance.

FIREMAN'S FUND INSURANCE COMPANY
2101 4th Avenue, Suite 11
Seattle WA 98121
206/278-5250
Contact: Roxie Hislop, Human Resource Representative
Description: Offers a variety of commercial insurance products and services. **Common positions include:** Claim Representative; Loss Prevention Specialist; Underwriter/Assistant Underwriter. **Educational backgrounds include:** Business Administration; Communications; Economics; Liberal Arts; Marketing; Mathematics. **Benefits:** Dental Insurance; Disability Coverage; Life Insurance; Medical Insurance; Pension Plan; Savings Plan; Tuition Assistance. **Special Programs:** Training Programs. **Corporate headquarters location:** Novato CA. **Operations at this facility include:** Administration; Service.

GRANGE INSURANCE ASSOCIATION
200 Cedar Street
Seattle WA 98121
206/448-4911
Contact: Personnel Department
Description: A property and casualty insurance firm. **Common positions include:** Accountant/Auditor; Branch Manager; Claim Representative; Computer Programmer; Customer Service Representative; Department Manager; Marketing Specialist; Systems Analyst; Underwriter/Assistant

Underwriter. **Educational backgrounds include:** Accounting; Business Administration; Computer Science; Finance; Marketing. **Benefits:** Dental Insurance; Disability Coverage; Employee Discounts; Life Insurance; Medical Insurance; Pension Plan; Savings Plan; Tuition Assistance; Vision Insurance. **Corporate headquarters location:** This Location.

GREAT REPUBLIC LIFE INSURANCE
226 2nd Avenue West
Seattle WA 98119
206/285-1422
Contact: Personnel Department
Description: A health insurance underwriting company. **Common positions include:** Accountant/Auditor; Actuary; Adjuster; Collector; Computer Systems Analyst; Customer Service Representative; Investigator. **Educational backgrounds include:** Accounting; Business Administration; Computer Science; Marketing. **Benefits:** Life Insurance; Medical Insurance; Savings Plan. **Corporate headquarters location:** This Location.

GROUP HEALTH COOPERATIVE
P.O. Box 34586
Seattle WA 98128
206/448-2748
Contact: Personnel Department
Description: A health maintenance organization (HMO) and hospital operator. **Number of employees at this location:** 9,000.

MARSH & McLENNAN
720 Olive Way, Suite 1900
Seattle WA 98101
206/223-1240
Contact: Lois Struthers, Personnel
Description: Provides a wide variety of insurance products and services.

NATIONAL MERIT INSURANCE COMPANY
P.O. Box 55369
Seattle WA 98155
206/367-4888
Contact: Personnel Department
Description: A property and casualty insurance company.

NORTHERN LIFE
P.O. Box 12530
Seattle WA 98111-4530
206/292-1111
Contact: Ann Hetherington, Human Resources
Description: Provides long-term financial security products (primarily annuities) for people in educational and non-profit organization. **Common positions include:** Accountant/Auditor; Actuary; Administrative Services

Manager; Attorney; Budget Analyst; Computer Programmer; Computer Systems Analyst; Customer Service Representative; Financial Analyst; Personnel/Labor Relations Specialist; Technical Writer/Editor. **Educational backgrounds include:** Business Administration; Economics; Liberal Arts. **Benefits:** 401K; Dental Insurance; Disability Coverage; Life Insurance; Medical Insurance; Pension Plan; Profit Sharing; Savings Plan; Tuition Assistance. **Corporate headquarters location:** Minneapolis MN. **Parent company:** Northwestern National Life Insurance. **Operations at this facility include:** Administration; Sales; Service. **Number of employees at this location:** 280.

PEMCO
P.O. Box 778
Seattle WA 98111
206/628-4000
Contact: Personnel Department
Description: A company involved in casualty property and auto insurance underwriting.

PRUDENTIAL INSURANCE COMPANY OF AMERICA
3400 188th Street SW, Suite 601
Lynnwood WA 98037
206/775-7258
Contact: William R. Decker, District Manager
Description: Nationally, the firm is one of the world's largest multiline insurance companies.

SAFECO INSURANCE CORPORATION
Safeco Plaza
Seattle WA 98185
206/545-5000
Contact: Personnel Director
Description: A diversified financial services company, headquartered in Seattle, whose operations include property and liability, and life and health insurance, pension plans, mutual funds, commercial credit and real estate development. **Common positions include:** Accountant/Auditor; Actuary; Administrator; Advertising Clerk; Attorney; Buyer; Claim Representative; Computer Programmer; Customer Service Representative; Purchasing Agent and Manager; Systems Analyst; Technical Writer/Editor; Underwriter/Assistant Underwriter. **Educational backgrounds include:** Accounting; Business Administration; Computer Science; Economics; Finance; Liberal Arts; Marketing; Mathematics. **Benefits:** Daycare Assistance; Disability Coverage; Life Insurance; Medical Insurance; Pension Plan; Tuition Assistance. **Special Programs:** Internships; Training Programs.

SAFECO LIFE AND HEALTH INSURANCE COMPANY
P.O. Box 34690
Seattle WA 98124-1690
206/867-8000
Contact: Human Resources Department
Description: An insurance company.

SUNSET LIFE INSURANCE COMPANY
3200 Capitol Boulevard South
Olympia WA 98501-3304
206/943-1400
Contact: Human Resources
Description: A life insurance company.

TRANSAMERICA TITLE INSURANCE COMPANY
DIVISION HEADQUARTERS
320 108th Avenue NE
Bellevue WA 98004
206/628-4650
Contact: Louise Condon, Personnel Administrator
Description: Nationally, the firm is one of the nation's leading providers of title insurance.

THE TRAVELERS COMPANIES
P.O. Box 91026
Seattle WA 98111-9126
206/464-3400
Contact: Personnel Manager
Description: Nationally, the firm is one of the largest investor-owned insurance and financial service institutions in the world. Writes every principal form of life, accident, health, and casualty/property insurance. Offers a broad range of pension and other investment management services. Operates more than 375 field offices throughout the country, and has assets of over $20 billion and more than $100 billion of life insurance in force. **Corporate headquarters location:** Hartford CT. **Listed on:** New York Stock Exchange.

UNIGARD INSURANCE COMPANY
15805 NE 24th Street
Bellevue WA 98008
206/644-5236
Contact: Angela Hawkins, Employment Specialist
Description: An insurance company specializing in property and casualty insurance. **Common positions include:** Accountant/Auditor; Actuary; Attorney; Branch Manager; Claim Representative; Computer Programmer; Customer Service Representative; Systems Analyst; Underwriter/Assistant Underwriter. **Educational backgrounds include:** Accounting; Business

Administration; Communications; Finance; Mathematics. **Benefits:** Dental Insurance; Disability Coverage; Life Insurance; Medical Insurance; Pension Plan; Profit Sharing; Savings Plan; Tuition Assistance. **Other U.S. locations:** AZ; CA; ID; NC; NY; UT. **Parent company:** Winterthur Group. **Number of employees at this location:** 500. **Number of employees nationwide:** 630.

UNITED PACIFIC LIFE INSURANCE COMPANY
P.O. Box 490
Seattle WA 98111
Contact: Personnel Department
Description: Toll free phone: 800/428-8511. A life insurance company.

WESTERN NATIONAL ASSURANCE INC.
9706 4th Avenue NE, Suite 200
Seattle WA 98115
206/526-5900
Contact: Personnel Department
Description: An insurance brokerage company.

WILLIS CORROON CORPORATION OF SEATTLE
701 Fifth Avenue, Suite 4200
Seattle WA 98104
206/386-7400
Contact: Diana R. Guild, Assistant Vice President of Administration
Description: An international commercial insurance broker, engaged in commercial property, liability, fidelity, security, and life insurance, and group benefits. **Common positions include:** Claim Representative; Customer Service Representative; Insurance Agent/Broker. **Educational backgrounds include:** Business Administration. **Benefits:** Credit Union; Dental Insurance; Disability Coverage; Employee Discounts; Life Insurance; Medical Insurance; Pension Plan; Profit Sharing; Savings Plan; Tuition Assistance. **Special Programs:** Internships; Training Programs. **Corporate headquarters location:** Nashville TN. **Parent company:** Willis Corron Group plc. (London, England). **Operations at this facility include:** Regional Headquarters; Sales; Service. **Listed on:** New York Stock Exchange.

Note: Because addresses and telephone numbers of smaller companies change rapidly, we recommend you call each company and verify the information below before mailing to employers. Mass mailings are not recommended.

Additional employers with over 50 employees:

INSURANCE COMPANIES

Commonwealth Insurance Company-USB
P.O. Box C34069, Seattle WA 98124-1069. 206/382-6670.

General Insurance Company Of America
Safeco Plaza, Seattle WA 98185. 206/545-5000.

Pacific Eagle Insurance Company
P.O. Box 47088, Seattle WA 98146-7088. 206/993-5200.

For more information on career opportunities in insurance:

Associations

ALLIANCE OF AMERICAN INSURERS
1501 Woodfield Road, Suite 400 West, Schaumburg IL 60173-4980. 708/330-8500.

HEALTH INSURANCE ASSOCIATION OF AMERICA
1025 Connecticut Avenue NW, Suite 1200, Washington DC 20036-3998. 202/223-7780.

INSURANCE INFORMATION INSTITUTE
110 William Street, 24th Floor, New York NY 10038. 212/669-9200.

SOCIETY OF ACTUARIES
475 North Martingale Road, Suite 800, Schaumburg IL 60173-2226. 708/706-3500.

Directories

INSURANCE ALMANAC
Underwriter Printing and Publishing Co., 50 East Palisade Avenue, Englewood NJ 07631. 201/569-8808.

INSURANCE MARKET PLACE
Rough Notes Company, Inc., P.O. Box 564, Indianapolis IN 46206. 317/634-1541.

INSURANCE PHONE BOOK AND DIRECTORY
121 Chanlon Road, New Providence NJ 07974. 800/521-8110.

Magazines

BEST'S REVIEW
A.M. Best Co., A.M. Best Road, Oldwick NJ 08858-9988. 908/439-2200.

INSURANCE JOURNAL
9191 Towne Centre Drive, Suite 550, San Diego, CA 92122 619/455-7717.

INSURANCE TIMES
M & S Communications, 20 Park Plaza, Suite 1101, Boston MA 02116. 617/292-7117.

LEGAL SERVICES

The legal profession is undergoing a major adjustment, largely due to the rapid rise in the number of lawyers over the past two decades. In the '70s the number of lawyers doubled, and in the '80s the number rose by another 48 percent. Meanwhile, a decline in civil litigation, coupled with the recent economic downturn, has led to a "produce or perish" climate. Law schools are reporting a 10-20 percent decline in placements, and firms are laying off associates, freezing rates, and firing unproductive partners. Graduates of prestigious law schools and those who rank high in their classes will have the best opportunities.

Paralegals, or legal assistants, have a bright future. According to the U.S. Department of Labor, paralegal employment is expected to grow much faster than the average for all occupations during the next decade. As employers become aware that legal work can be done by a paralegal for less than an attorney, employment should rise sharply.

GARVEY, SCHUBERT & BARER
1191 2nd Avenue, Suite 1800
Seattle WA 98101-2933
206/464-3939
Contact: Human Resources
Description: A legal services firm.

MUNDT, MACGREGOR & HAPPEL
First Interstate Center, 999 3rd Avenue
Seattle WA 98104
206/624-5950
Contact: Human Resources
Description: A legal services firm.

SHORT, CRESSMAN & BURGESS
Suite 3000, First Interstate Center
999 3rd Avenue
Seattle WA 98104
206/682-3333
Contact: Human Resources
Description: A legal services firm.

For more information on careers in the legal services industry:

Associations

AMERICAN BAR ASSOCIATION
750 North Lake Shore Drive,
Chicago IL 60611. 312/988-5000.

FEDERAL BAR ASSOCIATION
1815 H. Street NW, Suite 408,
Washington DC 20006-3697.
202/638-0252.

**NATIONAL ASSOCIATION OF
LEGAL ASSISTANTS**
1516 South Boston, Suite 200,
Tulsa OK 74119-4013. 918/587-
6828.

**NATIONAL FEDERATION OF
PARALEGAL ASSOCIATIONS**
P.O. Box 33108, Kansas City MO
64114-0108. 816/941-4000.

**NATIONAL PARALEGAL
ASSOCIATION**
P.O. Box 629, 6186 Honey Hollow
Road, Doylestown PA 18901.
215/297-8333.

MANUFACTURING AND WHOLESALING: MISCELLANEOUS CONSUMER

Because the consumer products industry is so diversified, industry outlooks depend more on specific product categories. Here's a sampling.

Soaps and Detergents: One of the biggest trends in this category has been to move away from the environmentally damaging phosphates used in detergents. In fact, about 40 percent of the nation has banned phosphates altogether, instead using natural soaps made of tallow and tropical oils. Overall, employment in this area will be increasing.

Household Durables: The short-term prognosis depends on consumer confidence. Although disposable incomes have risen slightly, many consumers are replenishing savings and paying off debts instead of buying expensive new items. A recovery in housing and the aging baby-boom generation should contribute to the long-term health of this segment.

DERBY CYCLE CORPORATION
22710 72nd Avenue South
Kent WA 98032
206/395-1100
Contact: Director of Human Resources
Description: A national manufacturer and distributor of Raleigh and Nishiki bicycles and related parts and accessories. **Common positions include:** Accountant/Auditor; Credit Manager; Customer Service Representative; Financial Analyst; Industrial Engineer; Manufacturer's/Wholesaler's Sales Rep.; Mechanical Engineer; Purchasing Agent and Manager. **Educational backgrounds include:** Accounting; Engineering; Finance; Marketing. **Benefits:** Dental Insurance; Employee Discounts; Life Insurance; Medical Insurance; Pension Plan; Tuition Assistance. **Corporate headquarters location:** This Location. **Operations at this facility include:** Administration; Manufacturing; Sales. **Number of employees at this location:** 200. **Number of employees nationwide:** 285.

EZ LOADER BOAT TRAILERS INC.
P.O. Box 3263
Spokane WA 99220
509/489-0181
Contact: Tarol Mueller, Personnel Director

Description: A manufacturer of boat trailers. **Common positions include:** Accountant/Auditor; Administrator; Blue-Collar Worker Supervisor; Buyer; Civil Engineer; Computer Programmer; Credit Manager; Department Manager; Financial Analyst; Industrial Engineer; Manufacturer's/Wholesaler's Sales Rep.; Mechanical Engineer; Operations/Production Manager; Purchasing Agent and Manager. **Educational backgrounds include:** Accounting; Business Administration; Computer Science; Engineering; Finance; Marketing. **Benefits:** Dental Insurance; Disability Coverage; Life Insurance; Medical Insurance; Pension Plan; Profit Sharing. **Corporate headquarters location:** This Location. **Operations at this facility include:** Administration; Divisional Headquarters; Manufacturing; Research and Development.

JENSEN-BYRD COMPANY INC.
P.O. Box 3708-99220
Spokane WA 99220
509/624-1321
Contact: Personnel Coordinator
Description: A wholesale distributor of hardware goods.

K2 CORPORATION
19215 Vashon Highway SW
Vashon WA 98070
206/463-3631
Contact: Rob Moynan, Personnel Director
Description: A producer of camping and skiing equipment, including tents, skis, and bindings. **Common positions include:** Accountant/Auditor; Buyer; Chemical Engineer; Chemist; Department Manager; Industrial Engineer; Mechanical Engineer; Operations/Production Manager; Purchasing Agent and Manager; Quality Control Supervisor; Systems Analyst. **Educational backgrounds include:** Accounting; Business Administration; Engineering; Marketing. **Benefits:** Dental Insurance; Disability Coverage; Employee Discounts; Legal Services; Medical Insurance; Savings Plan; Tuition Assistance. **Corporate headquarters location:** This Location. **Number of employees nationwide:** 800.

NINTENDO OF AMERICA
P.O. Box 957
Redmond WA 98073
206/882-2040
Contact: Personnel Department
Description: An importer, wholesaler, and manufacturer of electronic games, home video systems, games and watches.

PACIFIC COAST FEATHER COMPANY INC.
1964 4th Avenue South
Seattle WA 98134
206/624-1057
Contact: Personnel Department
Description: A company engaged in the manufacture of house furnishings and features.

PRECOR U.S.A. INCORPORATED
P.O. Box 3004
Bothell WA 98041
Contact: Human Resources Department
Description: A manufacturer of high-tech aerobic exercise equipment. **Corporate headquarters location:** This Location. **Parent company:** Premark International.

SEALY MATTRESS COMPANY
121 North Boron
Seattle WA 98109
206/682-4472
Contact: Human Resources
Description: Manufactures mattresses.

THE SIMPSON DOOR COMPANY
P.O. Box 210, 400 Simpson Avenue
McCleary WA 98557
206/495-3291
Contact: Personnel Department
Description: A manufacturer of doors.

SKYWAY LUGGAGE COMPANY
10 Wall Street
Seattle WA 98121
206/441-5300
Contact: Personnel Department
Description: A manufacturer of luggage and other consumer products.

THAW CORPORATION
P.O. Box 3978, Terminal Station
Seattle WA 98124
206/624-4277
Contact: Personnel Department
Description: A manufacturer and importer of recreational products.

Note: Because addresses and telephone numbers of smaller companies change rapidly, we recommend you call each company and verify the information below before mailing to employers. Mass mailings are not recommended.

Additional employers with over 250 employees:

HOUSEHOLD FURNITURE

Thunderbird Furniture Company
P.O. Box 238, Spangle WA 99031-0238.
509/245-3285.

PHOTOGRAPHIC EQUIPMENT AND SUPPLIES WHOLESALE

Momentum Corporation
500 108th Avenue NE, Bellevue WA 98004-5500.
206/646-6550.

CLEANING, POLISHING, AND SANITATION PREPARATIONS

Zep Manufacturing Company
21019 77th Avenue South, Kent WA 98032-1360.
206/248-1900.

SPORTING GOODS

Jan Sport
10411 Airport Road, Everett WA 98204-3540. 206/353-0200.

HARDWARE WHOLESALE

RB&W Fastening Service
22415 68th Avenue South #A, Kent WA 98032-2444.
206/872-9645.

Additional employers with under 250 employees:

HARDWARE

Biaser Die Casting Company
P.O. Box 80286, Seattle WA 98108-0286. 206/767-7800.

ELECTRIC HOUSEWARES AND FANS

Cadet Manufacturing Company
2500 West Fourth Plain Boulevard, Vancouver WA 98660-1354.
206/693-2505.

HOUSEHOLD AUDIO AND VIDEO EQUIPMENT

Carver Corporation
P.O. Box 1237, Lynnwood WA 98046-1237.
206/775-1202.

SPORTING AND ATHLETIC GOODS

Allsop Inc.
4201 Meridian Street,
Bellingham WA
98226-5512.
206/734-9090.

Kidder Skis
3223 C Street NE,
Auburn WA 98002-
1720. 206/939-7100.

O'Brien International
14615 NE 91st Street
Redmond WA 98052-
3459. 206/881-5900.

**Yakima Bait
Company/Wordens
Lures**
P.O. Box 310, Granger
WA 98932-0310.
509/854-1311.

SPORTING AND RECREATIONAL GOODS WHOLESALE

Achilles USA Inc.
P.O. Box 2287,
Everett WA 98203-
0287. 206/353-7000.

**Columbia Cascade
Company**
1701 West 18th
Street, Vancouver WA
98660-1301.
206/693-8558.

Outdoor Research
1000 1st Avenue
South, Floor 5, Seattle
WA 98134-1200.
206/467-8197.

**Raleigh Cycle Of
America**
22710 72D South,
Kent WA 98032.
206/395-1100.

DURABLE GOODS WOOD HOUSEHOLD FURNITURE

All-Wood Components
P.O. Box 3068,
Yakima WA 98903-
0068. 509/452-7494.

UPHOLSTERED WOOD HOUSEHOLD FURNITURE

Simmons Upholstery
7401 NE 47th
Avenue, Vancouver
WA 98661-1327.
206/695-1542.

MATTRESSES, FOUNDATIONS AND CONVERTIBLE BEDS

Cascade Designs
4000 1st Avenue
South, Seattle WA
98134-2301.
206/583-0583.

PUBLIC BUILDING AND RELATED FURNITURE

Magna Design Inc.
5804 204th Street,
SW, Lynnwood WA
98036-7555.
206/776-2181.

OFFICE FURNITURE

Lunstead Inc.
8655 South 208th
Street, Kent WA
98031-1214.
206/872-8835.

DRAPERY HARDWARE AND WINDOW BLINDS

**Hunter Douglas
Northwest**
7015 South 212th
Street, Kent WA
98032-2396.
206/872-4109.

FURNITURE AND FIXTURES

BPI Inc.
21608 85th Avenue
South, Kent WA
98031-1926.
206/624-2277.

COMMERCIAL WHOLESALE

Gatco
21209 Snag Island
Drive, Sumner WA
98390-8705.
206/862-4393.

For more information on career opportunities in consumer manufacturing and wholesaling:

Associations

ASSOCIATION FOR MANUFACTURING TECHNOLOGY
7901 Westpark Drive, McLean VA 22102. 703/893-2900.

ASSOCIATION OF HOME APPLIANCE MANUFACTURERS
20 North Wacker Drive, Chicago IL 60606. 312/984-5800.

NATIONAL ASSOCIATION OF MANUFACTURERS
1331 Pennsylvania Avenue, NW, Suite 1500, Washington DC 20004. 202/637-3000.

NATIONAL HOUSEWARES MANUFACTURERS ASSOCIATION
6400 Schafer Court, Suite 650, Rosemont IL 60018. 708/292-4200.

SOAP AND DETERGENT ASSOCIATION
475 Park Avenue South, 27th Floor, New York NY 10016. 212/725-1262.

Directories

APPLIANCE MANUFACTURER ANNUAL DIRECTORY
Appliance Manufacturer, 5900 Harper Road, Suite 105, Solon OH 44139. 216/349-3060.

HOUSEHOLD AND PERSONAL PRODUCTS INDUSTRY BUYERS GUIDE
Rodman Publishing Group, 17 South Franklin Turnpike, Ramsey NJ 07446. 201/825-2552.

DIRECTORY OF TEXAS MANUFACTURERS
University of Texas at Austin, Bureau of Business Research, Box 7459, Austin TX 78713-7459. 512/471-1616.

TEXAS MANUFACTURERS REGISTER
Manufacturer's News, Inc., 1633 Central Street, Evanston IL 60201. 708/864-7000.

Magazines

APPLIANCE
1110 Jorie Boulevard, Oak Brook IL 60522-9019. 708/990-3484.

COSMETICS INSIDERS REPORT
Advanstar Communications, 7500 Old Oak Boulevard, Cleveland OH 44130. 216/243-8100.

MANUFACTURING AND WHOLESALING: MISCELLANEOUS INDUSTRIAL

In the machinery manufacturing segment, many of the biggest company names will continue to disappear due to mergers and buy outs. While hundreds of U.S. companies still make machine tools, materials-handling equipment, and compressors for American factories, the fastest-growing machinery markets are now overseas. This means that U.S. firms will have to build an overseas presence just to survive. In fact, foreign orders for a number of American-made tools remain strong.

Although mergers are often followed by layoffs, workers who survive these cuts should be better positioned for the long-term. Many manufacturers are giving workers a much greater degree of across-the-board involvement, with team-based product management allowing individual workers to gain training in a number of different job functions.

AIMSCO INCORPORATED
P.O. Box 80304
Seattle WA 98108
206/284-5563
Contact: Personnel Department
Description: A manufacturer of fasteners.

ANIXTER-SEATTLE
18435 Olympic Avenue South
Seattle WA 98188
206/251-5287
Contact: Gary Richardson, Operations Manager
Description: A diversified corporation with nationwide operations in communications equipment, shipbuilding, and related activities, as well as energy and natural resources operations. **Corporate headquarters location:** Skokie IL.

E.J. BARTELLS COMPANY
P.O. Box 4160
Renton WA 98057
206/228-4111
Contact: Personnel Director
Description: A manufacturer of industrial insulation products.

BELSHAW BROTHER, INC.
1750 22nd South
Seattle WA 98144
206/322-5474
Contact: Personnel Department
Description: A bakery equipment manufacturer. Products include Donut Robot, Type K, Multi-Matic, Batterboy, Cut-n-Fry, and Robot Fry.

BRUDI EQUIPMENT INC.
26709 NW 19th Avenue
Ridgefield WA 98642
206/887-4666
Contact: Human Resources
Description: Wholesalers of industrial machinery.

COLUMBIA MACHINE INC.
107 Grand Boulevard
Vancouver WA 98661
206/694-1501
Contact: Hiring Officer
Description: Manufactures a variety of industrial products.

FISHERIES SUPPLY COMPANY
1900 North Northlake Way
Seattle WA 98103
206/632-4462
Contact: Personnel Department
Description: A wholesaler of industrial hardware and supplies.

KEY INDUSTRIES INC.
dba LIBERTY EQUIPMENT & SUPPLY COMPANY
P.O. Box 24848
Seattle WA 98124
206/682-8700
Contact: Paula Fredell, Administrative Manager
Description: Wholesale distributor of industrial pipe, valves and fittings for commercial, industrial, marine and nuclear applications; also valve automation products. **Common positions include:** Accountant/Auditor; Blue-Collar Worker Supervisor; Branch Manager; Manufacturer's/Wholesaler's Sales Rep.; Purchasing Agent and Manager; Quality Control Supervisor. **Educational backgrounds include:** Business Administration; Finance. **Benefits:** Dental Insurance; Life Insurance; Medical Insurance; Profit Sharing; Savings Plan; Tuition Assistance. **Special Programs:** Training Programs. **Corporate headquarters location:** This Location. Operations at this facility include: Administration; Divisional Headquarters; Regional Headquarters; Sales.

MARCO SEATTLE
2300 West Commodore Way
Seattle WA 98199
206/285-3200
Contact: Hank Schlapp, Personnel Director
Description: A manufacturer of commercial marine machinery, fishing gear, equipment and vessels. Other operations include oil-spill management systems and related pollution control items. **Number of employees nationwide:** 600.

NC MACHINERY COMPANY
P.O. Box 3562
Seattle WA 98124
206/251-9800
Contact: Mrs. Hui Chong Hoge, Personnel Director
Description: A dealer of heavy equipment. **Number of employees nationwide:** 600.

NORTH STAR ICE EQUIPMENT CORPORATION
P.O. Box 80227
Seattle WA 98108
206/763-7300
Contact: Personnel Department
Description: A manufacturer of continuous flake ice-makers and mechanical ice-dispensing systems.

PACO PUMPS INC.
3215 South 116th Street
Seattle WA 98168
206/433-2600
Contact: Human Resources
Description: Manufactures pumps.

ROBBINS COMPANY
P.O. Box 97027
Kent WA 98064
206/872-0500
Contact: Human Resources Department
Description: A mining machinery and equipment company.

SEATTLE MARINE FISHING SUPPLY COMPANY
P.O. Box 99098
Seattle WA 98199
206/285-5010
Contact: Personnel Department
Description: A wholesaler of marine supplies and hardware.

TEMPRESS INC.
701 South Orchard
Seattle WA 98108
206/762-1419
Contact: Personnel Department
Description: A manufacturer of tools and die molds.

UTILX
22404 66th Avenue South
Kent WA 98032
206/395-0200
Contact: Personnel Department
Description: A cable and pipe installer. **Number of employees at this location: 438.**

Note: Because addresses and telephone numbers of smaller companies change rapidly, we recommend you call each company and verify the information below before mailing to employers. Mass mailings are not recommended.

Additional employers with over 250 employees:

AIR-CONDITIONING AND HEATING EQUIPMENT, AND REFRIGERATION EQUIPMENT

Red Dot Corporation
P.O. Box 58270,
Seattle WA 98138-1270. 206/575-3840.

METAL HARDWARE

Best Locking Systems
1701 Dexter Avenue North,
Seattle WA 98109-3022. 206/284-5252.

INDUSTRIAL MACHINE TOOLS

Tidland Corporation
P.O. Box 1008,
Camas WA 98607-0008. 206/834-2345.

FOOD PRODUCTS MACHINERY

The Lucks Company Manufactured
21112 72nd Avenue South,
Kent WA 98032-1339. 206/872-2180.

PRINTING MACHINERY AND EQUIPMENT

Enterprises International Inc.
P.O. Box 293,
Hoquiam WA 98550-0293.
206/533-6222.

SPECIAL INDUSTRIAL MACHINERY

Flow International Corporation
21440 68th Avenue South,
Kent WA 98032-2416. 206/872-4900.

Wagstaff Inc.
3910 North Flora
Road, Spokane WA
99216-1720.
509/922-1404.

**US Natural
Resources Inc.**
8000 NE Parkway
Drive, Suite 100
Vancouver WA
98662-6732.
206/892-2650.

**INDUSTRIAL
MACHINERY AND
EQUIPMENT
WHOLESALE**

Grainger
5706 East
Broadway Avenue,
Spokane WA
99212-0912.
509/535-9882.

**Cummins
Northwest Inc.**
926 NW Maryland
Avenue, Chehalis
WA 98532-1807.
206/748-8841.

Alled Safety Inc.
P.O. Box 80467,
Seattle WA 98108-
0467. 206/767-
4500.

Bearings Inc.
530 North Pearl
Street, Centralia
WA 98531-4698.
206/736-8233.

Packaging West
6838 South 190th
Street, Kent WA
98032-1033.
206/251-9155.

ENGINE PARTS

**Rexroth Corporation
Pneumatics**
4200 Fruit Valley
Road, Vancouver
WA 98660-1223.
206/750-8800.

**INDUSTRIAL
INSTRUMENTS**

**Pacific Electro
Dynamics Inc.**
P.O. Box 97045,
Redmond WA
98073-9745.
206/881-1700.

**HEATING AND A/C
EQUIPMENT
WHOLESALE**

Chromalox
1850 130th
Avenue NE,
Bellevue WA
98005-2244.
206/885-0372.

Additional employers with under 250 employees:

INDUSTRIAL VALVES

Technaflow Inc.
1400 NE 136th
Avenue, Vancouver
WA 98684-0818.
206/944-1400.

**GT Development
Corporation**
6437 South 144th
Street, Seattle WA
98168-4608.
206/244-1305.

**CONSTRUCTION
MACHINERY AND
EQUIPMENT**

RA Hanson Company
P.O. Box 7400,
Spokane WA 99207-
0400. 509/467-0770.

Young Corporation
P.O. Box 3522,
Seattle WA 98124-
3522. 206/624-1071.

**INTERNAL
COMBUSTION
ENGINES**

Hatch & Kirk Inc.
5111 Leary Avenue
NW, Seattle WA
98107-4820.
206/783-2766.

VALVES AND PIPE FITTINGS

Romac Industries
1064 4th Avenue
South, Seattle WA
98134-1303.
206/624-6491.

CONVEYORS AND CONVEYING EQUIPMENT

Thermoguard Equipment
5303 East Desmet
Avenue, Spokane WA
99212-0915.
509/535-0356.

INDUSTRIAL TRUCKS, TRACTORS AND TRAILERS

Neil F. Lampson Inc.
P.O. Box 6510,
Kennewick WA
99336-0502.
509/586-0411.

INDUSTRIAL PATTERNS

Ovalstrapping Inc.
P.O. Box 704,
Hoquiam WA 98550-
0704. 206/532-9101.

Precision Pattern
2620 East G Street,
Tacoma WA 98421-
1907. 206/572-4333.

RA Pearson Company
8120 West Sunset
Highway, Spokane
WA 99204-9048.
509/838-6226.

Tacoma Rubber Stamp
919 Market Street,
Tacoma WA 98402-
3604. 206/383-5433.

CUTTING TOOLS AND MACHINE TOOL ACCESSORIES

Tidland Corporation
P.O. Box 1008,
Camas WA 98607-
0008. 206/834-2345.

WOODWORKING MACHINERY

Acrowood Corporation
4425 South 3rd
Avenue, Everett WA
98203-2515.
206/258-3555.

Globe Machine Manufacturing Company
701 East D Street,
Tacoma WA 98421-
1811. 206/383-2584.

Schurman Machine
P.O. Box 310,
Woodland WA 98674-
0310. 206/225-8267.

FOOD PRODUCTS MACHINERY

Baxter Manufacturing Company
P.O. Box 729, Orting
WA 98360-0729.
206/893-5554.

SPECIAL INDUSTRY MACHINERY

Global Equipment
10807 East
Montgomery Drive #4,
Spokane WA 99206-
4777. 509/924-9496.

PUMPS AND PUMPING EQUIPMENT

Micropump Corporation
P.O. Box 8975,
Vancouver WA
98668-8975.
206/253-2008.

Rogers Machinery Company Inc.
7800 5th Avenue
South, Seattle WA
98108-4304.
206/763-2530.

INDUSTRIAL PROCESS FURNACES AND OVENS

Willard Smith Inc.
Tarco
27124 78th Avenue
South, Kent WA
98032-7340.
206/850-9730.

OFFICE MACHINES

North American Morpho Systems
1145 Broadway, Suite
300, Tacoma WA
98402-3523.
206/383-3617.

INDUSTRIAL AND COMMERCIAL MACHINERY AND EQUIPMENT

Airsensors Inc.
708 Industry Drive,
Seattle WA 98188-
3408. 206/575-1594.

Allfab Inc.
Building C-19 Paine
Field, Everett WA
98204. 206/353-
8080.

American Boiler Works
1332 West Marine
View Drive, Everett
WA 98201-1645.
206/259-0834.

Mamco Manufacturing
P.O. Box 70645,
Seattle WA 98107-
0645. 206/789-1111.

Precision Machine Works
2024 Puyallup
Avenue, Tacoma WA
98421-2619.
206/272-5119.

Wayron Inc.
1133 California Way,
Longview WA 98632-
1628. 206/425-8600.

LABORATORY APPARATUS AND FURNITURE

Cellpro Inc.
22322 20th Avenue
SE, Bothell WA
98021-7426.
206/485-7644.

INDUSTRIAL INSTRUMENTS FOR MEASUREMENT AND DISPLAY

Ryan Instruments
8801 148th Avenue
NE, Redmond WA
98052-3492.
206/883-7926.

INSTRUMENTS FOR MEASUREMENT AND TESTING

Schweitzer Engineering Labs
2350 NE Hopkins
Court, Pullman WA
99163-5600.
509/332-1890.

LABORATORY ANALYTICAL INSTRUMENTS

Cascadia Technology
2877 152nd Avenue
NE, Redmond WA
98052-5572.
206/882-3500.

Scientific Instrument Company
12727 NE 20th
Street, #7, Bellevue
WA 98005-1906.
206/883-0721.

MEASURING AND CONTROLLING DEVICES

Paine Corporation
P.O. Box 3986,
Seattle WA 98124-
3986. 206/329-8600.

CONSTRUCTION AND MINING MACHINERY WHOLESALE

Economy Forms Corporation
P.O. Box 129, Kent
WA 98035-0129.
206/852-3800.

Spider Staging Corporation
4493 South 134th
Place, Seattle WA
98168-6204.
206/241-9304.

Smith Tractor & Equipment Company
3607 20th Street E,
Tacoma WA 98424-
1704. 206/922-8718.

INDUSTRIAL MACHINERY WHOLESALE

Ace Tank & Equipment Company
1143 Elliott Avenue
West, Seattle WA
98119-3102.
206/281-5000.

Bargreen-Ellingson
6266 Tacoma Mall
Boulevard, Tacoma
WA 98409-6827.
206/475-9201.

Packers Engineering
518A East 1st
Avenue, Kennewick
WA 99336-4058.
509/582-4717.

PBI Market Equipment
14940 NE 95th
Street, #C, Redmond
WA 98052-2526.
206/885-1060.

**INDUSTRIAL
SUPPLIES
WHOLESALE**

**Calkins Manufacturing
Company**
P.O. Box 14527,
Spokane WA 99214-
0527. 509/928-7420.

**McGuire Bearing
Company**
2111 Pacific Avenue,
Tacoma WA 98402-
3098. 206/572-2700.

Paul Munroe-Rucker
365 Upland Drive,
Seattle WA 98188-
3802. 206/575-3736.

**Ryco Packaging
Corporation**
5814 South 196th
Street, Kent WA
98032-2101.
206/872-0858.

**SERVICE
ESTABLISHMENT
EQUIPMENT
WHOLESALE**

Web Service Company
658 South 152nd
Street, Seattle WA
98148-1111.
206/242-7228.

**Viking Automatic
Sprinkler Company**
3434 1st Avenue
South, Seattle WA
98134-1805.
206/622-4656.

**SCRAP AND WASTE
MATERIALS
WHOLESALE**

Fibres International
1533 120th Avenue
NE, Bellevue WA
98005-2131.
206/455-9811.

**For more information on career opportunities in industrial manufacturing
and wholesaling:**

<u>Associations</u>

**APPLIANCE PARTS
DISTRIBUTORS ASSOCIATION**
228 East Baltimore Street, Detroit
MI 48202. 313/875-8455.

**ASSOCIATION FOR
MANUFACTURING
TECHNOLOGY**
7901 Westpark Drive, McLean VA
22102. 703/893-2900.

**NATIONAL ASSOCIATION OF
MANUFACTURERS**
1331 Pennsylvania Avenue, NW,
Suite 1500, Washington DC 20004.
202/637-3000.

**NATIONAL SCREW MACHINE
PRODUCTS ASSOCIATION**
6700 West Snowville Road,
Brecksville OH 44141. 216/526-
0300.

**NATIONAL TOOLING AND
MACHINING ASSOCIATION**
9300 Livingston Road, Fort
Washington MD 20744. 301/248-
1250.

<u>Special Programs</u>

**BUREAU OF APPRENTICESHIP
AND TRAINING**
U.S. Department of Labor, 200
Constitution Avenue, NW,
Washington, DC 20210. 202/219-
6540.

Directories

DIRECTORY OF TEXAS MANUFACTURERS
University of Texas at Austin, Bureau of Business Research, Box 7459, Austin TX 78713. 512/471-1616.

TEXAS MANUFACTURERS REGISTER
Manufacturer's News, Inc., 1633 Central Street, Evanston IL 60201. 708/864-7000.

MINING/GAS/PETROLEUM/ENERGY RELATED

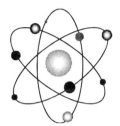

The short-term future for the petroleum industry depends upon the world economy, OPEC production, and world oil prices. U.S. crude and natural gas production is expected to remain flat, while demand for petroleum products is forecasted to rise slowly -- 1 percent annually, through 1997. Jobseekers, especially those with engineering backgrounds, should keep an eye out for the growing emphasis on the development of alternative fuels like methanol, and for growth in hydroelectric, geothermal, and other environmentally sound energy sources.

ARCO PRODUCTS
P.O. Box 8100
Blaine WA 98231
206/384-1500
Contact: Human Resources
Description: An energy products manufacturer engaged in the production of diesel and jet fuel, gasoline, and related petroleum products.

CASCADE NATURAL GAS CORPORATION
222 Fairview Avenue North
Seattle WA 98109
206/624-3900
Contact: Mr. Larry Rosok, Personnel Director
Description: Engaged in the distribution and transport of natural gas to customers. **Common positions include:** Accountant/Auditor; Attorney; Claim Representative; Computer Programmer; Credit Manager; Customer Service Representative; Department Manager; Draftsperson; Economist/Market Research Analyst; Marketing Specialist; Mechanical Engineer; Personnel/Labor Relations Specialist; Purchasing Agent and Manager; Statistician; Systems Analyst. **Educational backgrounds include:** Accounting; Business Administration; Economics; Engineering; Finance; Mathematics. **Benefits:** Dental Insurance; Disability Coverage; Life Insurance; Medical Insurance; Pension Plan; Tuition Assistance. **Operations at this facility include:** Administration. **Listed on:** New York Stock Exchange.

COMINCO AMERICAN INCORPORATED
P.O. Box 3087
Spokane WA 99220
509/747-6111
Contact: Personnel Director
Description: A natural resource company engaged in a wide variety of activities, including mineral development, metals mining and marketing, and fertilizer production.

SHELL OIL COMPANY
P.O. Box 700
Anacortes WA 98221
206/293-9119
Contact: Personnel Director
Description: A refinery engaged in the production of automobile and airplane fuels, including kerosene and diesel products. Nationally, the firm is involved in the exploration for, and the development, production, purchase, transportation, and marketing of, crude oil, natural gas, petroleum products, and related chemical products. **Corporate headquarters location:** Houston TX. **Listed on:** New York Stock Exchange.

SIEMENS NUCLEAR POWER CORPORATION
2101 Horn Rapids Road
Richland WA 99352
509/375-8344
Contact: Daniel D. Whitlow, Employee Relations Supervisor
Description: A manufacturer of nuclear fuel for commercial reactors. **Number of employees at this location:** 900.

TEXACO REFINING & MARKETING
P.O. Box 622
Anacortes WA 98221-0622
206/293-0800
Contact: Human Resources Department
Description: A petroleum refining company.

TIME OIL COMPANY
2737 West Commodore Way
Seattle WA 98199
206/285-2400
Contact: Personnel Department
Description: A company engaged in retail gasoline service stations, wholesale petroleum products, and retail fuel oil beaters.

TOSCO NORTHWEST COMPANY
P.O. Box 8
Ferndale WA 98248
206/384-1011
Fax: 206/384-8246
Contact: J.R. Eklund, Human Resources Manager
Description: A refiner of petroleum and related products. **Common positions include:** Accountant/Auditor; Buyer; Chemical Engineer; Chemist; Civil Engineer; Clerical Supervisor; Clinical Lab Technician; Computer Programmer; Computer Systems Analyst; Construction Contractor and Manager; Designer; Draftsperson; Electrical/Electronic Engineer; General Manager; Mechanical Engineer; Medical Record Technician; Metallurgical Engineer; Paralegal; Personnel/Labor Relations Specialist; Petroleum Engineer; Public Relations Specialist; Purchasing Agent and Manager; Registered Nurse; Technical Writer/Editor. **Educational backgrounds include:** Accounting; Business Administration; Chemistry; Engineering; Personnel Relations. **Benefits:** 401K; Dental Insurance; Disability Coverage; Life Insurance; Medical Insurance; Pension Plan; Profit Sharing; Savings Plan; Tuition Assistance. **Special Programs:** Internships. **Corporate headquarters location:** Seattle WA. **Other U.S. locations:** Martinez CA; Lynden NJ. **Parent company:** Tosco Corporation. **Operations at this facility include:** Administration; Manufacturing. **Listed on:** New York Stock Exchange. **Number of employees at this location:** 300. **Number of employees nationwide:** 2,000.

U.S. OIL AND REFINING
3001 Marshall Avenue
Tacoma WA 98421
206/383-1651
Contact: Human Resources
Description: A petroleum refinery.

Note: Because addresses and telephone numbers of smaller companies change rapidly, we recommend you call each company and verify the information below before mailing to employers. Mass mailings are not recommended.

Additional employers with over 250 employees:

PETROLEUM REFINING

BP Marine Americas
320 Dayton Street,
Suite 280, Edmonds
WA 98020.

ORE MINING

Pegasus Gold Inc.
North Nine Post,
Spokane WA 99201,
509/624-4653.

Additional employers with under 250 employees:

**PETROLEUM AND
PETROLEUM
PRODUCTS
WHOLESALERS**

Gull Industries Inc.
3404 4th Avenue
South, Seattle WA
98134-1905.
206/624-5900.

**ASPHALT FELTS AND
COATINGS**

Fields Products Inc.
2240 Taylor Way,
Tacoma WA 98421-
4303. 206/627-4098.

For more information on career opportunities in the mining, gas, petroleum and energy industries:

Associations

**AMERICAN ASSOCIATION OF
PETROLEUM GEOLOGISTS**
P.O. Box 979, Tulsa OK 7410-
0979. 918/584-2555.

**AMERICAN GEOLOGICAL
INSTITUTE**
4220 King Street, Alexandria VA
22302-1507. 703/379-2480.

AMERICAN NUCLEAR SOCIETY
555 North Kensington Avenue, La
Grange Park IL 60525. 708/352-
6611.

**AMERICAN PETROLEUM
INSTITUTE**
1220 L Street NW, Suite 900,
Washington DC 20005. 202/682-
8000.

**GEOLOGICAL SOCIETY OF
AMERICA**
3300 Penrose Place, P.O. Box
9140, Boulder CO 80301. 303/447-
2020.

**SOCIETY OF EXPLORATION
GEOPHYSICISTS**
P.O. Box 702740, Tulsa OK 74170-
2740. 918/493-3516.

Directories

**BROWN'S DIRECTORY OF
NORTH AMERICAN AND
INTERNATIONAL GAS
COMPANIES**
Advanstar Communications, 7500
Old Oak Boulevard, Cleveland OH
44130. 800/225-4569.

**NATIONAL PETROLEUM NEWS
FACT BOOK**
Hunter Publishing Co., 25 NW Point
Boulevard, Suite 800, Elk Grove
Village, IL 60007. 708/427-9512.

OIL AND GAS DIRECTORY
Geophysical Directory, Inc., P.O.
Box 130508, Houston TX 77219.
713/529-8789.

Magazines

AMERICAN GAS MONTHLY
1515 Wilson Boulevard, Arlington
VA 22209. 703/841-8686.

GAS INDUSTRIES
Gas Industries News, Inc., 6300
North River Road, Suite 505,
Rosemont IL 60018. 312/693-3682.

NATIONAL PETROLEUM NEWS
Hunter Publishing Co., 25 NW Point
Boulevard, Elk Grove IL 60007.
708/296-0770.

OIL AND GAS JOURNAL
PennWell Publishing Co., 1421
South Sheridan Road, P.O. Box
1260. Tulsa OK 74101. 918/835-
3161.

PAPER AND WOOD PRODUCTS

 *If the economy continues to strengthen and export markets regain the momentum lost during the last few years, the industry should see revenues grow about 10 percent by the end of 1996. Technological advances should strengthen the industry both at home and abroad. Environmental concerns voiced by the public should give the paper packaging segment an advantage over plastics, as companies move to become "green."*

Lumber and wood product shipments rose only slightly in 1993. Nationwide, the industry has been hit hard -- according to industry observers, more than 125 lumber and panel product mills in the Pacific Northwest, the heart of the U.S. lumber industry, have closed in the past three years due in part to poor log supplies.

ACRO-WOOD CORPORATION
P.O. Box 1028
Everett WA 98206
206/258-3555
Contact: Philip Hutmacher, Controller
Description: A pulp and paper mill offering a variety of services and products, including plywood, particle board, and machinery for the lumber industry. **Corporate headquarters location:** New York NY.

AMERICAN PLYWOOD ASSOCIATION
P.O. Box 11700
Tacoma WA 98411-0700
206/565-6600
Contact: Personnel Department
Description: Manufacturers construction and industrial panels, interior and exterior types and grades company.

BUFFELEN WOODWORKING COMPANY
P.O. Box 1383
Tacoma WA 98401
206/627-1191
Contact: Human Resources
Description: A large millwork manufacturing company. **Common positions include:** Accountant/Auditor; Administrator; Blue-Collar Worker Supervisor; Buyer; Computer Programmer; Credit Manager; Customer Service Representative; Department Manager; Financial Analyst; General Manager; Manufacturer's/Wholesaler's Sales Rep.; Operations/Production Manager; Personnel/Labor Relations Specialist; Purchasing Agent and Manager;

Transportation/Traffic Specialist. **Educational backgrounds include:** Accounting; Business Administration; Computer Science; Finance. **Benefits:** Dental Insurance; Disability Coverage; Employee Discounts; Life Insurance; Medical Insurance; Savings Plan. **Corporate headquarters location:** This Location. **Operations at this facility include:** Administration; Manufacturing; Sales; Service.

DAISHOWA AMERICA COMPANY LTD.
P.O. Box 271
Port Angeles WA 98362
206/457-4474
Contact: Dave Floodstrom, Personnel Director
Description: The mill facility of a large paper manufacturer.

DAISHOWA AMERICA COMPANY LTD.
701 Fifth Avenue, Suite 7200
Seattle WA 98104
206/623-1772
Contact: Personnel Department
Description: Engaged in the production and export of wood chips, and the production and sale of telephone directory paper.

GEORGIA PACIFIC CORP
P.O. Box 1236
Bellingham WA 98227
206/733-4410
Contact: Human Resources Department
Description: A sanitary paper products company.

JAMES RIVER CORPORATION
Northeast 4th & Adams
Camas WA 98607
206/834-3021
Contact: Mike Wendling, Personnel Director
Description: Manufactures paper products and related goods.

JEFFERSON SMURFIT/CONTAINER CORPORATION OF AMERICA
P.O. Box 479
Renton WA 98057
206/235-3300
Contact: Robert C. Jacobs, Employee Relations Manager
Description: A national producer of paperboard packaging. Manufacturing facilities are located throughout the United States and in foreign locations. Some major products include shipping containers, folding cartons, plastic drums, and many others. Soon to be publicly offered. **Common positions include:** Accountant/Auditor; Blue-Collar Worker Supervisor; Buyer; Customer Service Representative; Management Trainee; Manufacturer's/Wholesaler's Sales Rep.; Marketing Specialist; Mechanical Engineer; Operations/Production

Manager; Personnel/Labor Relations Specialist; Purchasing Agent and Manager. **Educational backgrounds include:** Accounting; Art/Design; Business Administration; Computer Science; Engineering; Finance; Marketing. **Benefits:** 401K; Dental Insurance; Disability Coverage; Life Insurance; Medical Insurance; Pension Plan; Savings Plan; Tuition Assistance. **Special Programs:** Training Programs. **Corporate headquarters location:** St. Louis MO. **Listed on:** NASDAQ.

K-PLY INC.
439 Marine Drive
Port Angeles WA 98362
206/457-4421
Contact: Pam Anderson, Personnel Director
Description: A manufacturer of forest products for use in home applications, including exterior siding. **Number of employees nationwide:** 300.

HENRY H. KETCHAM LUMBER COMPANY INC.
P.O. Box 22789
Seattle WA 98122
206/329-2700
Contact: Personnel Department
Description: A wholesale lumber company.

KINNEAR OF WASHINGTON
2001 Industrial Drive
Centralia WA 98531
206/736-7654
Contact: Richard Rowan, Personnel Director
Description: A manufacturer of garage doors and related wood items. **Corporate headquarters location:** Camp Hill PA. **Parent company:** Hardsco Corporation.

LONGVIEW FIBRE COMPANY
P.O. Box 639
Longview WA 98632
206/425-1550
Contact: Human Resources
Description: A pulp and paper manufacturer.

MANKE LUMBER COMPANY INC.
1717 Marine View Drive
Tacoma WA 98422
206/572-6252
Contact: Personnel Director
Description: A manufacturer of a variety of lumber products.

MERRILL & RING INC.
1411 4th Avenue Building, Suite 1415
Seattle WA 98101
Contact: Personnel Department
Description: A company engaged in logging.

MODULINE INTERNATIONAL INC.
5016 Lacey Boulevard SE
Lacey WA 98503
206/491-1130
Contact: Personnel Director
Description: A manufacturer of wooden storage and shelving products.

NORD COMPANY
P.O. Box 1187
Everett WA 98206
206/259-9292
Contact: Personnel Department
Description: Produces wood style and rail panel doors; louver products; columns and posts; and arch spindles.

PLUM CREEK LUMBER COMPANY INC.
999 3rd Avenue, Suite 2300
Seattle WA 98104
206/467-3600
Contact: Personnel Department
Description: A company engaged in the manufacture of softwood and hardwood, lumber, plywood, fiber bands, and laminates.

R.S.G. FOREST PRODUCTS
985 2nd Street NW
Kalama WA 98625
206/673-2825
Contact: Human Resources
Description: A forest products company.

SCOTT PAPER COMPANY
P.O. Box 925
Everett WA 98206
206/259-7333
Contact: Dorothy Beck, Staffing and Compensation Manager
Description: A processor of pulp and paper.

SHAKERTOWN CORPORATION
P.O. Box 400
Winlock WA 98596
206/785-3501
Contact: Personnel Department
Description: A manufacturer of cedar shingle siding panels and cedar shingle roofing panels.

SIMPSON INVESTMENT COMPANY
1201 3rd Avenue, Suite 4900
Seattle WA 98101
206/292-5000
Contact: Human Resources
Description: Produces label, offset, book, coated, writing, and fine papers. Offers high grade printing and technical specialties on 100 percent recycled printing and fine papers. **Number of employees at this location: 2,013.**

SUMMIT TIMBER COMPANY
P.O. Box 368
Darrington WA 98241
206/259-4181
Contact: Human Resources
Description: A logging company.

VAAGEN BROS. LUMBER INC.
565 West Fifth
Colville WA 99114
509/684-5071
Contact: Personnel Department
Description: A lumber producer. **Number of employees at this location: 480.**

WEATHERVANE WINDOW COMPANY
10819 120th Avenue Northeast
Kirkland WA 98033
206/827-9669
Contact: Human Resources Department
Description: Manufactures wooden windows.

WESTERN CABINET MILLWORK
P.O. Box 137
Woodinville WA 98072
206/823-4141
Contact: Human Resources
Description: Manufactures kitchen cabinets.

WEYERHAEUSER COMPANY
PCI-126
Tacoma WA 98477
206/924-2602
Fax: 206/924-4157
Contact: College Relations/Recruiting
Description: One of the world's largest forest products companies. **Common positions include:** Accountant/Auditor; Administrative Services Manager; Civil Engineer; Computer Programmer; Electrical/Electronic Engineer; Forester/Conservation Scientist; General Manager; Management Analyst/Consultant; Management Trainee; Mechanical Engineer; Personnel/Labor Relations Specialist; Public Relations Specialist; Reporter; Technical Writer/Editor. **Educational backgrounds include:** Accounting; Business Administration; Communications; Computer Science; Engineering; Finance; Marine Science. **Benefits:** Life Insurance; Pension Plan; Tuition Assistance. **Special Programs:** Internships. **Corporate headquarters location:** This Location. **Operations at this facility include:** Administration; Divisional Headquarters; Regional Headquarters; Research and Development; Sales; Service. **Listed on:** New York Stock Exchange. **Number of employees nationwide:** 40,000.

Note: Because addresses and telephone numbers of smaller companies change rapidly, we recommend you call each company and verify the information below before mailing to employers. Mass mailings are not recommended.

Additional employers with over 250 employees:

LOGGING

Anderson & Middleton Company
815 8th Street,
Hoquiam WA 98550.
206/533-2410.

Boise Cascade Corp.
P.O. Box 8, Ellensburg
WA 98926-0008.
509/925-5341.

WOOD MILLS

Boise Cascade Corp.
P.O. Box 51, Yakima
WA 98907-1459.
509/453-3131.

Cowlitz Stud Company
P.O. Box 219, Randle
WA 98377-0219.
206/497-5030.

Cowlitz Stud Company
P.O. Box P, Morton
WA 98356-0080.
206/496-5115.

Ione Division/Vaagen Brothers
P.O. Box 257, Ione
WA 99139-0257.
509/442-3511.

Omak Wood Products
729 Jackson Street,
Omak WA 98841.
509/826-1460.

Sonoco Products Company
P.O. Box 11368,
Spokane WA 99211-
1368. 509/535-1232.

Northwest Hardwoods
P.O. Box 7, Arlington
WA 98223-0007.
206/435-8502.

MILLWORK

**Northwest Windows &
Patio**
P.O. Box 886, Kent
WA 98035-0886.
206/854-3970.

SNE Enterprises Inc.
3808 NorthSullivan
Road Building 20,
Spokane WA 99216-
1616. 509/924-0300.

VENEER AND
PLYWOOD

**Fort Vancouver
Plywood Company**
P.O. Box 289,
Vancouver WA
98666-0289.
206/694-3368.

**Boise Cascade
Corporation**
110 S Boise Road,
Kettle Falls WA
99141-9625.
509/738-6421.

PAPER MILLS

ITT Rayonier Inc.
700 S Ennis Street,
Port Angeles WA
98362-6648.
206/457-3391.

**Boise Cascade
Corporation**
907 West 7th Street,
Vancouver WA
98660-3066.
206/690-7000.

**OJI Paper Company
Ltd.**
999 3rd Avenue Suite
2610, Seattle WA
98104-4050.
206/622-2820.

**Port Townsend Paper
Corporation**
P.O. Box 11500,
Bainbridge Is WA
98110-5500.
206/842-0611.

FIBER PRODUCTS

**Sonoco Products
Company**
P.O. Box 98330,
Tacoma WA 98498-
0330. 206/584-4164.

DIE-CUT PAPER AND
PAPER PRODUCTS

**Globe Ticket & Label
Company**
P.O. Box 11067,
Tacoma WA 98411-
0067. 206/474-0722.

PAPER PRODUCTS

Little Rapids Corp.
P.O. Box 2093,
Tacoma WA 98401-
2093. 206/627-3156.

Paragon Trade Brands
505 South 336th
Street, Federal Way
WA 98003-6328.
206/924-4509.

**Pacific Lumber &
Shipping Company**
P.O. Box 21785,
Seattle WA 98111-
3785. 206/682-7262.

INDUSTRIAL PAPER
AND RELATED
PRODUCTS
WHOLESALE

Boise Cascade Corp.
P.O. Box 300, Wallula
WA 99363-0300.
509/545-3202.

Additional employers with under 250 employees:

TIMBER TRACTS

Northwest Hardwoods
120 Industrial Way,
Longview WA 98632-
1004. 206/577-3887.

LOGGING

Browning Timber
579 Highway 141,
White Salmon WA
98672-8324.
509/493-3885.

Buse Timber & Sales
3812 28th Place NE,
Everett WA 98205-
3209. 206/258-2577.

Mayr Brothers Logging Company
P.O. Box 180,
Hoquiam WA 98550-
0180. 206/532-7490.

Morton Forest Products Company
P.O. Box I, Morton
WA 98356-0049.
206/496-6666.

Sedro Woolley Lumber Company
109 Jameson Street,
Sedro Woolley WA
98284-1572.
206/855-2125.

Tumwater Lumber Company
P.O. Box 4158,
Olympia WA 98501-
0158. 206/352-1548.

SAWMILLS AND PLANING MILLS

Brazier Forest Industries
701 5th Avenue Suite
4500, Seattle WA
98104-7090.
206/386-5800.

Caffall Brothers Forest
540 3rd Avenue,
Longview WA 98632-
1652. 206/636-5960.

Commencement Bay Mill Company
917 East 11th Street,
Tacoma WA 98421-
3039. 206/383-8858.

Cowlitz Stud Co.
P.O. Box P, Morton
WA 98356-0080.
206/496-5115.

Gram Lumber Co.
985 2nd Street NW,
Kalama WA 98625-
9648. 206/673-5231.

Louisiana-Pacific Corporation
P.O. Box 1575, Walla
Walla WA 99362-
0325. 509/529-0200.

Mary's River Lumber Company
P.O. Box 569,
Montesano WA
98563-0569.
206/249-5907.

Packwood Lumber Company
P.O. Box 229,
Packwood WA 98361-
0229. 206/494-5175.

SDS Lumber Company
P.O. Box 266, Bingen
WA 98605-0266.
509/493-2155.

Skookum Lumber Company
P.O. Box 1398,
Shelton WA 98584-
0919. 206/426-9721.

T&H Of Washington
S I P Building N-5,
Spokane WA 99216.
509/926-2726.

W-I Forest Products
P.O. Box 3344,
Spokane WA 99220-
3344. 509/534-1561.

Welco Lumber Company
P.O. Box 125,
Marysville WA 98270-
0125. 206/659-1261.

MILLWORK

Colville Indian Precision Pine
P.O. Box 3293, Omak
WA 98841-3293.
509/826-1921.

Dellen Wood Products
P.O. Box 510,
Veradale WA 99037-
0510. 509/928-1397.

Jeld-Wen Of Washington
P.O. Box 4364,
Spokane WA 99202-
0364. 509/534-0471.

Wood Magic
S1020 South Perry
Street, Spokane WA
99202-3465.
509/534-1061.

SPECIAL PRODUCT SAWMILLS

Miller Shingle Company
P.O. Box 29, Granite
Falls WA 98252-
0029. 206/691-7727.

WOOD KITCHEN CABINETS

Dewils Industries
6307 NE 127th
Avenue, Vancouver
WA 98682-5899.
206/892-0300.

Huntwood Industries
3808 North Sullivan,
Sip Building 26,
Spokane WA 99216.
509/924-5858.

Tacoma Fixture Company
1815 East D Street,
Tacoma WA 98421-
1505. 206/383-5541.

HARDWOOD DIMENSIONS AND FLOORING MILLS

Emco Wood Products
3927 300th Street
NW, Stanwood WA
98292-9670.
206/629-4511.

Nicholson Manufacturing Company
3670 East Marginal
Way South, Seattle
WA 98134-1152.
206/682-2752.

Ross Simmons Hardwood Lumber
P.O. Box 366,
Longview WA 98632-
7231. 206/423-8210.

HARDWOOD VENEER AND PLYWOOD

Hoquiam Plywood Company Inc.
1000 Woodlawn
Avenue, Hoquiam WA
98550-1140.
206/533-3060.

Mount Baker Plywood
2929 Roeder Avenue,
Bellingham WA
98225-2065.
206/733-3960.

Woodtape
P.O. Box 1234,
Seattle WA 98111-
1234. 206/821-2150.

Woodtape
11403 120th Avenue
NE, Kirkland WA
98033-4525.
206/821-2150.

STRUCTURAL WOOD MEMBERS

Roof Truss Supply
P.O. Box 532,
Woodinville WA
98072-0532.
206/481-0900.

WOOD CONTAINERS

Nepa Pallet & Container Company
P.O. Box 399,
Snohomish WA
98291-0399.
206/568-3185.

WOOD PRESERVING

McFarland Cascade
P.O. Box 1496,
Tacoma WA 98401-
1496. 206/572-3033.

Spokane Custom Wood Treating
P.O. Box 4595,
Spokane WA 99202-
0595. 509/535-5401.

RECONSTITUTED WOOD PRODUCTS

Portac Inc.
4215 East West Road,
Tacoma WA 98421-
3901. 206/922-9900.

WOOD PRODUCTS

Strauser Manufacturing
P.O. Box 991, Walla
Walla WA 99362-
0020. 509/529-6284.

West Coast Door Inc.
3102 South Pine
Street, Tacoma WA
98409-4715.
206/272-4269.

PULP MILLS

Alaska Pulp Corporation
3000 Rainier Bank
Tower, Seattle WA
98101. 206/682-
6400.

PAPER MILLS

Canadian Pacific Forest Products
1201 3rd Avenue #1110, Seattle WA 98101-3000. 206/224-7060.

Gregory Groth Paperworks
P.O. Box 273, Deer Harbor WA 98243-0273. 206/376-5155.

Hammermill Paper Company
33400 8th Avenue South Suite 230, Federal Way WA 98003-6382. 206/874-2777.

Inland Empire Paper Company
3320 North Argonne Road, Spokane WA 99212-2099. 509/924-1911.

Mead Fine Paper
31919 1st Avenue South, Federal Way WA 98003-5258. 206/946-5135.

Neenah Paper
10655 NE 4th Street, Bellevue WA 98004-5022. 206/637-9724.

Ponderay Newsprint Company
422767 Highway 20, Usk WA 99180-9770. 509/445-1511.

Tenma USA Inc.
1101 Seneca Street, Seattle WA 98101-2855. 206/340-0744.

CORRUGATED AND SOLID FIBER BOXES

Michelsen Packaging Company
P.O. Box 89, Yakima WA 98902. 509/248-6270.

Pac Services Inc.
17735 NE 65th Street, Redmond WA 98052-4903. 206/882-2121.

Seattle Box Company
23400 71st Place South, Kent WA 98032-2905. 206/854-9700.

Seattle Packaging Corporation
3701 South Norfolk Street, Seattle WA 98118-5639. 206/725-3000.

Sheets Unlimited
301 SW 27th Street, Renton WA 98055-4081. 206/251-5959.

Spokane Packaging
Spokane Industrial Pk Building 21, Spokane WA 99216. 509/924-7623.

FIBER CANS, TUBES AND DRUMS

Portco Corporation
4200 East Columbia Way, Vancouver WA 98661-5528. 206/696-1641.

CONVERTED PAPER AND PAPERBOARD PRODUCTS

Convert Pac Inc.
18000 Pacific Highway South, Suite 109, Seattle WA 98188-4205. 206/244-0905.

Nelson-Ball Paper Products Inc.
P.O. Box 3016, Longview WA 98632. 206/423-3420.

VMG Enterprises
801 SE Assembly Avenue, Vancouver WA 98661-5500. 206/693-6688.

FOLDING PAPERBOARD BOXES

Seattle Tacoma Box
2826 Kauffman Avenue, Vancouver WA 98660-2042. 206/693-2610.

COATED AND LAMINATED PAPER

Box Maker Inc.
6412 South 190th
Street, Kent WA
98032-2191.
206/251-5428.

DIE-CUT PAPER AND PAPERBOARD

Globe Ticket & Label
6002 East McKinley
Avenue, Tacoma WA
98404-2333.
206/474-0722.

INDUSTRIAL AND PERSONAL SERVICE PAPER WHOLESALE

Allpak Container Inc.
1100 SW 27th Street,
Renton WA 98055-
2624. 206/227-0400.

Company Wholesale Building Materials
N911 Thierman Road,
Spokane WA 99212.
509/535-1414.

Shurgard Storage Center
2233 East Valley
Road, Renton WA
98055-4016.
206/255-9383.

The Unisource Corporation
P.O. Box 3506, Kent
WA 98032-0209.
206/575-0220.

West Coast Paper Company Spokane
3808 North Sullivan
Road, Spokane WA
99216-1608.
509/928-4644.

ENVELOPES

American Envelope Company
401 Andover Park E,
Seattle WA 98188-
7605. 206/575-1400.

SANITARY FOOD CONTAINERS

Tetra-Pak Materials
P.O. Box 1826,
Vancouver WA
98668-1826.
206/693-3664.

STATIONERY, TABLETS AND RELATED PRODUCTS

Everett Pad & Paper Company Inc.
2216 36th Street,
Everett WA 98201-
4504. 206/259-2133.

STATIONERY AND OFFICE SUPPLIES WHOLESALE

Labels West
17629 130th Avenue
NE, Woodinville WA
98072-5747.
206/486-8484.

For more information on career opportunities in the paper and wood products industries:

Associations

AMERICAN FOREST AND PAPER ASSOCIATION
1111 19th Street NW, Suite 700,
Washington DC 20036. 202/463-2700.

AMERICAN FOREST AND PAPER ASSOCIATION
260 Madison Avenue, New York NY
10016. 212/340-0600.

AMERICAN FOREST AND PAPER ASSOCIATION
1250 Connecticut Avenue NW,
Washington DC 20036. 202/463-2700.

FOREST PRODUCTS RESEARCH SOCIETY
2801 Marshall Court, Madison WI 53705. 608/231-1361.

NATIONAL PAPER TRADE ASSOCIATION
111 Great Neck Road, Great Neck NY 11021. 516/829-3070.

PAPERBOARD PACKAGING COUNCIL
888 17th Street NW, Suite 900, Washington DC 20006. 202/289-4100.

TECHNICAL ASSOCIATION OF THE PULP AND PAPER INDUSTRY
P.O. Box 105113, Atlanta GA 30348. 404/446-1400.

Directories

DIRECTORY OF THE FOREST PRODUCTS INDUSTRY
Miller Freeman Publications, Inc., 600 Harrison Street, San Francisco CA 94107. 415/905-2200.

LOCKWOOD-POST'S DIRECTORY OF THE PAPER AND ALLIED TRADES
Miller Freeman Publications, Inc., 600 Harrison Street, San Francisco CA 94107. 415/905-2200.

POST'S PULP AND PAPER DIRECTORY
Miller Freeman Publications, Inc., 600 Harrison Street, San Francisco CA 94107. 415/905-2200.

Magazines

PAPERBOARD PACKAGING
Advanstar Communications, 131 West First Street, Duluth MN 55802. 218/723-9200.

PULP AND PAPER WEEK
Miller Freeman Publications, Inc., 600 Harrison Street, San Francisco CA 94107. 415/905-2200.

WOOD TECHNOLOGIES
Miller Freeman Publications, Inc., 600 Harrison Street, San Francisco CA 94107. 415/905-2200.

PRINTING AND PUBLISHING

Cuts in print advertising have hurt the printing industry in recent years, but as the U.S. economy improves and more money is spent on advertising, things will improve for printers. They will still face tight profit margins because of rising supply costs -- the price of paper is expected to remain soft, with paper mill capacity outstripping demand; and the costs of other materials, like film, chemicals, and plates, are expected to gradually rise in response to an improving economy. But despite these pressures, increased sales should mean that after years of layoffs, printers will begin hiring again. Job opportunities for bindery workers and printing press operators will experience a growth rate similar to all other professions, while openings for prepress workers will be slightly below that average.

Newspaper and magazine publishers have also been suffering from shrinking advertising dollars, but they expected 1994 to be a good year, as the overall economy improved and clients increased their advertising budgets. For the long-term, look for newspaper companies to target specific readers in order to attract advertisers.

An improving economy will also help book publishers, who were hit hard by the recession of the early 1990s. As the economic recovery continues and disposable income increases, sales of adult trade books will climb. The expanding 5-14 year-old age group should also prompt a rise in sales of juvenile books. Employment in the book publishing industry was expected to jump to 77,000 in 1994, a gain of roughly 1,000 nationwide. Those jobs were expected in editorial, marketing and administrative positions.

BELLINGHAM HERALD
P.O. Box 1277
Bellingham WA 98227
206/676-2600
Contact: Personnel Director
Description: Operates a local evening newspaper.

THE CHRONICLE
P.O. Box 580
Centralia WA 98531
206/736-3311
Fax: 206/736-1568
Contact: Rosie O'Connor, Administrative Assistant

Description: Publishes a daily newspaper with a circulation of 15,500. **Common positions include:** Administrator; Advertising Clerk; Editor; Reporter; Services Sales Representative. **Educational backgrounds include:** English; Liberal Arts. **Benefits:** Dental Insurance; Life Insurance; Medical Insurance; Profit Sharing; Savings Plan. **Corporate headquarters location:** This Location. **Number of employees at this location:** 100.

COLUMBIA BASIN HERALD
P.O. Box 910
Moses Lake WA 98837
509/765-4561
Contact: Dan Black, Managing Editor
Description: A newspaper.

THE COLUMBIAN PUBLISHING COMPANY
701 West 8th Street, P.O. Box 180
Vancouver WA 98666-0180
206/694-3391
Contact: Ann Maxwell, Vice President of Human Resources
Description: A newspaper and information system. **Common positions include:** Customer Service Representative; Editor; Graphic Artist; Production Worker; Reporter; Services Sales Representative. **Educational backgrounds include:** Communications; Journalism; Liberal Arts; Marketing. **Benefits:** Dental Insurance; Disability Coverage; Employee Discounts; Life Insurance; Medical Insurance; Profit Sharing; Savings Plan; Tuition Assistance; Vision Insurance. **Corporate headquarters location:** This Location. **Operations at this facility include:** Manufacturing; Sales; Service. **Number of employees at this location:** 350.

CRAFTSMAN PRESS INC.
1155 Valley Street
Seattle WA 98109
206/682-8800
Contact: Personnel Director
Description: A commercial printing firm.

THE DAILY NEWS
107 South Grand, Suite B
Pullman WA 99163
509/334-6397
Contact: Managing Editor
Description: Publishes a daily newspaper.

DAILY RECORD
McLATCHY NEWSPAPER
401 North Maine
Ellensburg WA 98926
509/925-1414
Contact: Keith Love, Editor/Publisher
Description: Publishes a newspaper with a circulation of 5,000.

THE DAILY WORLD
P.O. Box 269
Aberdeen WA 98520
206/532-4000
Contact: Duane Langliers, General Manager
Description: Publishes a daily newspaper with a circulation of 15,000.

EMERALD CITY GRAPHICS
22223 68th Avenue South
Kent WA 98032
206/872-6874
Contact: Human Resources
Description: A book binding company.

FISHING AND HUNTING NEWS
OUTDOOR EMPIRE PUBLISHING
511 Eastlake Avenue East
Seattle WA 98109
206/624-3845
Contact: Human Resources
Description: A periodical.

THE HERALD
P.O. Box 930
Everett WA 98206
Contact: Human Resources Department
Description: Publishes a daily newspaper.

INTAQ KEY PANELS
2040 15th Avenue West
Seattle WA 98119
206/284-5475
Contact: Human Resources
Description: A printing company.

JOURNAL-AMERICAN
P.O. Box 90130
Bellevue WA 98009-9230
206/455-2222
Contact: Nick Chernock, Vice President of Employee Relations
Description: Publishes a daily newspaper with a circulation of approximately 28,000. A member of the McClelland Newspapers group.

K.P. CORPORATION
2001 22nd Avenue South
Seattle WA 98144
206/328-2770
Contact: Human Resources Department
Description: A commercial lithographic printer.

THE OLYMPIAN
P.O. Box 407
Olympia WA 98507
206/754-5491
Contact: Carol Achatz, Human Resources Director
Description: Publishes a newspaper with a circulation of over 25,000. **Common positions include:** Accountant/Auditor; Administrator; Blue-Collar Worker Supervisor; Commercial Artist; Computer Programmer; Credit Manager; Customer Service Representative; Department Manager; Editor; Manufacturer's/Wholesaler's Sales Rep.; Marketing Specialist; Operations/ Production Manager; Personnel/Labor Relations Specialist; Public Relations Specialist; Reporter; Technical Writer/Editor. **Educational backgrounds include:** Accounting; Art/Design; Business Administration; Communications; Computer Science; Finance; Marketing. **Benefits:** Dental Insurance; Disability Coverage; Employee Discounts; Life Insurance; Medical Insurance; Pension Plan; Savings Plan; Tuition Assistance. **Corporate headquarters location:** Rosslyn VA. **Parent company:** Gannett Newspapers. **Listed on:** New York Stock Exchange.

PEANUT BUTTER PUBLISHING
226 2nd Avenue West
Seattle WA 98119
206/281-5965
Contact: Administrative Assistant
Description: A publisher specializing in cookbooks and dining guides. **Common positions include:** Administrator; Commercial Artist; Marketing Specialist; Technical Writer/Editor. **Educational backgrounds include:** Art/Design, Liberal Arts; Marketing **Special Programs:** Internships. **Corporate headquarters location:** This Location. **Operations at this facility include:** Administration; Service.

PENINSULA DAILY NEWS
P.O. Box 1330
Port Angeles WA 98362
206/452-2345
Contact: Editor
Description: A daily newspaper. **Common positions include:** Accountant/ Auditor; Advertising Clerk; Credit Manager; Editor; Graphic Artist; Photographer/Camera Operator; Printing Press Operator; Reporter. **Educational backgrounds include:** Accounting; Art/Design; Communications; Journalism. **Benefits:** Dental Insurance; Life Insurance; Medical Insurance; Pension Plan; Profit Sharing; Tuition Assistance. **Corporate headquarters location:** Bellevue WA. **Parent company:** Northwest Media. **Operations at this facility include:** Divisional Headquarters. **Number of employees at this location:** 68. **Number of employees nationwide:** 350.

SEATTLE DAILY JOURNAL OF COMMERCE
P.O. Box 11050
Seattle WA 98111
206/622-8272
Contact: John Mihalyo, General Manager
Description: Publishes a daily newspaper with a circulation of approximately 5,000.

SEATTLE FILMWORKS
1260 16th Aveue West
Seattle WA 98119
206/281-1390
Fax: 206/284-5357
Contact: Annette Mack, Human Resources
Description: Processes and sells (via mail-order) 35mm film. **Common positions include:** Accountant/Auditor; Blue-Collar Worker Supervisor; Buyer; Chemist; Computer Programmer; Computer Systems Analyst; Software Engineer. **Educational backgrounds include:** Marketing. **Benefits:** 401K; Dental Insurance; Disability Coverage; Employee Discounts; Life Insurance; Medical Insurance; Profit Sharing; Tuition Assistance. **Corporate headquarters location:** This Location. **Operations at this facility include:** Administration; Manufacturing; Research and Development; Sales. **Number of employees at this location:** 400.

SEATTLE POST - INTELLIGENCER
P.O. Box 1909
Seattle WA 98111
206/448-8000
Contact: Don J. Smith, City Editor
Description: Publishes a daily newspaper as part of the Hearst Newspaper Group; weekday circulation exceeds 200,000. The Seattle Times conducts circulation, advertising, and production operations for this paper.

THE SEATTLE TIMES COMPANY
P.O. Box 70
Seattle WA 98111
206/464-2111
Contact: Personnel Department
Description: Publishers of The Seattle Times.

KAYE SMITH BUSINESS GRAPHICS INC.
P.O. Box 756
Renton WA 98057
206/228-8600
Contact: Human Resources Department
Description: A commercial lithographic printer.

THE SPOKESMAN-REVIEW & SPOKANE CHRONICLE
P.O. Box 2160
Spokane WA 99210
509/459-5000
Contact: Personnel Department
Description: A newspaper.

SUN NEWSPAPER
545 5th Street
Bremerton WA 98310
206/792-3331
Contact: Tim Lavin, Accounting/Human Resources Manager
Description: Publishes an evening newspaper with a circulation of 40,000.
Number of employees at this location: 242.

SUNNYSIDE DAILY SUN NEWS
P.O. Box 878
Sunnyside WA 98944
509/837-4500
Contact: Tom Lanctot, Publisher
Description: Publishes a daily newspaper.

TACOMA NEWS, INC.
P.O. Box 11000
Tacoma WA 98411
206/597-8575
Contact: Human Resources Department
Description: Publishes a morning newspaper seven days a week, with a circulation of 122,000 daily and 140,000 Sunday. **Common positions include:** Artist; Circulation Manager; Computer Programmer; Customer Service Representative; Editor; Layout Specialist; Printing Press Operator; Reporter; Services Sales Representative.

TIME-LIFE LIBRARIES
1900 North Northlake Way, Suite 135
Seattle WA 98103
206/632-8444
Contact: Human Resources
Description: A telemarketing office of the book publishing company.

TIMES COMMUNITY NEWSPAPERS
207 SW 150th Street, P.O. Box 66518
Seattle WA 98166
206/242-0100
Contact: Human Resources Manager
Description: A newspaper publisher of The Highline Times, DesMoines News, and Federal Way News. **Common positions include:** Accountant/Auditor; Advertising Account Executive; Advertising Clerk; Editor; Reporter. **Educational backgrounds include:** Accounting; Art/Design; Journalism. **Benefits:** 401K; Dental Insurance; Life Insurance; Medical Insurance. **Special Programs:** Internships. **Corporate headquarters location:** This Location. **Operations at this facility include:** Administration; Sales; Service.

TRI-CITY HERALD
P.O. Box 2608
Tri-Cities WA 99302
509/582-1500
Contact: Cyndy Miles, Human Resources Manager
Description: Publishes a newspaper with a circulation of over 40,000. **Common positions include:** Accountant/Auditor; Advertising Clerk; Editor; Graphic Artist; Marketing/Advertising/PR Manager; Payroll Clerk; Photographer/Camera Operator; Photographic Process Worker; Prepress Worker; Printing Press Operator; Reporter; Services Sales Representative; Technical Writer/Editor. **Educational backgrounds include:** Journalism. **Benefits:** Disability Coverage; Employee Discounts; Life Insurance; Medical Insurance; Pension Plan. **Special Programs:** Internships. **Corporate headquarters location:** Sacramento CA. **Parent company:** McClatchy Newspapers Group.

UNITED GRAPHICS INC.
21409 72nd Avenue South
Kent WA 98032
206/395-8080
Contact: Personnel Department
Description: Engaged in lithographic commercial printing.

VALLEY DAILY NEWS
P.O. Box 130
Kent WA 98035
206/872-6600
Contact: Georgie Heath, Secretary
Description: Publishers of the Valley Daily News newspaper. **Common positions include:** Advertising Clerk; Editor; Reporter. **Educational backgrounds include:** Art/Design; Liberal Arts. **Benefits:** Dental Insurance; Life Insurance; Medical Insurance; Stock Option. **Special Programs:** Internships. **Number of employees at this location:** 160.

Note: Because addresses and telephone numbers of smaller companies change rapidly, we recommend you call each company and verify the information below before mailing to employers. Mass mailings are not recommended.

Additional employers with over 250 employees:

NEWSPAPERS PUBLISHING & PRINTING

The Standard Register Company
P.O. Box 988, Tekoa WA 99033-0988.
509/284-5782.

BUSINESS FORMS

Data Documents Inc.
2501 South 35th Street, Tacoma WA 98409-7405.
206/475-2200.

Moore Business Forms & Systems
2702 South 42nd Street, Suite 212, Tacoma WA 98409-7315. 206/475-2944.

The Standard Register Company
6840 South Center Boulevard Suite 150, Seattle WA 98188-2555. 206/243-0890.

PERIODICALS PUBLISHING & PRINTING

Cowles Publishing Co.
P.O. Box 2160, Spokane WA 99210-2160. 509/459-5000.

COMMERCIAL PRINTING

Data Documents Inc.
1212 North Washington Street, Suite 320, Spokane WA 99201-2401.
509/325-6570.

Merrill Corporation
700 5th Avenue # 4040, Seattle WA 98104-5000.
206/441-5599.

Moore Business Forms & Systems
501 North Riverpoint Boulevard #111, Spokane WA 99202-1656. 509/624-3660.

BOOKBINDING AND RELATED WORK

RR Donnelly & Sons Company
10500 NE 8th Street, Suite 1750 Bellevue WA 98004-4351. 206/455-0755.

Additional employers with under 250 employees:

NEWSPAPER PUBLISHING

Bainbridge Island Review
221 Winslow Way West, Bainbridge Island, WA 98110-2509. 206/842-6613.

Bellingham Herald
1155 North State Street, Bellingham WA 98225-5024. 206/676-2600.

Northwest Guardian
9105 Bridgeport Way SW, Tacoma WA 98499-2406. 206/584-5818.

Yakima Herald Republic
P.O. Box 9668, Yakima WA 98909-0668. 509/248-1251.

PERIODICAL PUBLISHING

Shields Printing
1010 Rock Avenue, Yakima WA 98902-4630. 509/453-8200.

Sunset Magazine
500 Union Street, Suite 600, Seattle WA 98101-2385. 206/682-3993.

MISCELLANEOUS PUBLISHING

Teldon Calendars
P.O. Box 8110, Blaine WA 98231-8110. 206/945-1211.

COMMERICAL PRINTING, LITHOGRAPHIC

Color Control Inc.
3820 150th Avenue NE, Redmond WA 98052-5313. 206/881-5454.

Devon Editions
6015 6th Avenue South, Seattle WA 98108-3307. 206/763-7010.

Impression Northwest
2001 22nd Avenue South, Seattle WA 98144-4597. 206/328-2770.

Whidbey Press Inc.
7689 NE Day Road, Bainbridge Is WA 98110-1260. 206/842-8305.

TYPESETTING

Kinko's Copies
16815 Redmond Way, Redmond WA 98052-4449. 206/882-1949.

COMMERICAL PRINTING

Huntsman Packaging Products Corporation
8039 South 192nd Street, Kent WA 98032-1129. 206/872-2253.

MANIFOLD BUSINESS FORMS

Vanier Business Forms Cascade
13223 NE 16th Street Bellevue WA 98005-2305. 206/637-0900.

BOOKS, PERIODICALS AND NEWSPAPERS WHOLESALE

Pacific Pipline Inc.
8030 South 228th Street, Kent WA 98032-2900. 206/872-5523.

PHOTOFINISHING LABORATORIES

Qualex Inc.
169 Sturdevant Road, Chehalis WA 98532-8720. 206/748-8891.

Chroma Copy
123 NW 36th Street, Seattle WA 98107-4922. 206/728-0808.

Kits Cameras Lewis County Mall, Chehalis WA 98532. 206/748-1666.	**Prolab** 123 NW 36th Street, Seattle WA 98107- 4998. 206/547-5447.	**Prozone** 123 NW 36th Street, Seattle WA 98107- 4922. 206/547-5463.

For more information on career opportunities in printing and publishing:

Associations

AMERICAN INSTITUTE OF GRAPHIC ARTS
919 3rd Avenue, 22nd Floor, New York NY 10003-3004. 212/807-1990.

NEWSPAPER ASSOCIATION OF AMERICA
Newspaper Center, 11600 Sunrise Valley Drive, Reston VA 22091. 703/648-1000.

AMERICAN SOCIETY OF NEWSPAPER EDITORS
P.O. Box 4090, Reston VA 22090-1700. 703/648-1144.

ASSOCIATION OF GRAPHIC ARTS
330 7th Avenue, 9th Floor, New York NY 10001-5010. 212/279-2100.

BINDING INDUSTRIES OF AMERICA
70 East Lake Street, Suite 300, Chicago IL 60601. 312/372-7606.

THE DOW JONES NEWSPAPER FUND
P.O. Box 300, Princeton NJ 08543-0300. 609/520-4000.

GRAPHIC ARTISTS GUILD
11 West 20th Street, 8th Floor, New York NY 10011. 212/463-7730.

INTERNATIONAL GRAPHIC ARTS EDUCATION ASSOCIATION
4615 Forbes Avenue, Pittsburgh PA 15213. 412/682-5170.

MAGAZINE PUBLISHERS ASSOCIATION
575 Lexington Avenue, Suite 540, New York NY 10022. 212/752-0055.

NATIONAL ASSOCIATION OF PRINTERS AND LITHOGRAPHERS
780 Pallisade Avenue, Teaneck NJ 07666. 201/342-0700.

NATIONAL NEWSPAPER ASSOCIATION
1525 Wilson Boulevard, Arlington VA 22209. 703/907-7900.

NATIONAL PRESS CLUB
529 14th Street, NW, 13th Floor, Washington DC 20045. 202/662-7500.

THE NEWSPAPER GUILD
Research and Information Department, 8611 2nd Avenue, Silver Spring MD 20910. 301/585-2990.

PRINTING INDUSTRIES OF AMERICA
100 Dangerfield Road, Arlington VA 22314. 703/519-8100.

TECHNICAL ASSOCIATION OF THE GRAPHIC ARTS
Box 9887, Rochester NY 14623.
716/475-7470.

WRITERS GUILD OF AMERICA WEST
8955 Beverly Boulevard, West Hollywood CA 90048. 310/550-1000.

Directories

EDITOR & PUBLISHER INTERNATIONAL YEARBOOK
Editor & Publisher Co. Inc., 11 West 19th Street, New York NY 10011. 212/675-4380.

GRAPHIC ARTS BLUE BOOK
A.F. Lewis & Co., 79 Madison Avenue, New York NY 10016. 212/679-0770.

JOURNALISM CAREER AND SCHOLARSHIP GUIDE
The Dow Jones Newspaper Fund, P.O. Box 300, Princeton NJ 08543-0300. 609/520-4000.

Magazines

AIGA JOURNAL
American Institute of Graphic Arts, 1059 Third Avenue, New York NY 10021. 212/752-0813.

EDITOR AND PUBLISHER
Editor & Publisher Co. Inc., 11 West 19th Street, New York NY 10011. 212/807-1990.

GRAPHIC ARTS MONTHLY
249 West 49th Street, New York NY 10011. 212/463-6836.

GRAPHIS
141 Lexington Avenue, New York NY 10016. 212/532-9387.

PRINT
104 Fifth Avenue, 19th Floor New York NY 10011. 212/463-0600.

Special Book and Magazine Programs

THE NEW YORK UNIVERSITY SUMMER PUBLISHING PROGRAM
48 Cooper Square, Room 108, New York NY 10003. 212/998-7219.

THE RADCLIFFE PUBLISHING COURSE
77 Brattle Street, Cambridge MA 02138. 617/495-8678.

RICE UNIVERSITY PUBLISHING PROGRAM
Office of Continuing Studies, P.O. Box 1892, Houston TX 77251-1892. 713/520-6022.

UNIVERSITY OF DENVER PUBLISHING INSTITUTE
2075 South University Boulevard, #D-114, Denver CO 80208. 303/871-4868.

REAL ESTATE

 *Solid opportunities for job seekers are available for those looking to enter the real estate field. Residential and commercial land sales will help keep up employment opportunities for real estate agents, brokers and appraisers. The number of job openings in these occupations are expected to match the number of openings for most other careers nationwide. Most of these openings, however, will be replacement positions, as agents retire or leave the field, rather than new positions being created.*

Property and real estate managers will have even greater luck finding employment, as more openings appear for these positions than other occupations. The people with the most qualified backgrounds for these positions will be those with college degrees in business administration and other related fields.

BELL-ANDERSON REALTY INC.
P.O. Box 5640
Kent WA 98064-5640
206/852-8195
Contact: Jerry Anderson, Owner
Description: Provides real estate and related services.

BRYN MAWR PROPERTIES
11326 Rainier Avenue South
Seattle WA 98178
206/772-0299
Contact: Personnel Department
Description: Operators and real estate managers of multi-family housing units.

CB COMMERCIAL REAL ESTATE GROUP, INC.
U.S. Bank Centre
1420 5th Avenue, Suite 1700
Seattle WA 98101-2314
206/292-1600
Contact: Maureen Ottele, Administrative Manager
Description: Nationally, the firm is a real estate service company with more than 4,000 employees and 88 offices from coast to coast. Founded in San Francisco in 1906, the firm is a fully-integrated real estate and real estate-related service company with offices in major cities of the United States and Canada. **Common positions include:** Administrative Worker/Clerk; Real Estate Agent. **Educational backgrounds include:** Business Administration; Finance; Marketing. **Benefits:** Dental Insurance; Disability Coverage; Life Insurance;

Medical Insurance; Pension Plan; Profit Sharing; Savings Plan. **Special Programs:** Training Programs. **Corporate headquarters location:** Los Angeles CA. **Operations at this facility include:** Administration; Divisional Headquarters; Regional Headquarters; Sales.

CUSHMAN & WAKEFIELD OF WASHINGTON INC.
700 5th Avenue, Suite 2700
Seattle WA 98104-5027
206/682-0666
Contact: Susan Brookins, Office Administrator
Description: A real estate services firm offering sales, property management and appraisal services to a variety of clients.

DIAMOND PARKING INC.
3161 Elliott Avenue
Seattle WA 98121
206/284-6303
Contact: Personnel Department
Description: Owns parking facilities and engaged in real estate. **Number of employees at this location:** 200.

DICK FISCHER DEVELOPMENT INC.
937 Harvard Avenue East
Seattle WA 98102
206/328-2000
Contact: Personnel Department
Description: Engaged in real estate development.

GREENWOOD TRUST
P.O. Box 95430
Seattle WA 98145-2430
206/523-2029
Contact: Personnel Department
Description: A company that owns, operates, and leases property.

MAC PHERSONS BETTER HOMES AND GARDENS
18551 Aurora Avenue North
Seattle WA 98133
206/546-4124
Contact: Personnel Department
Description: A real estate company that also operates apartment buildings and provides related services.

MAC PHERSONS BETTER HOMES AND GARDENS
12729 Lake City Way NE
Seattle WA 98125
206/364-9977
Contact: Personnel Department
Description: A real estate company that also operates apartment buildings and provides related services.

NEYHART COMPANY
315 Seneca Street
Seattle WA 98101
206/623-5110
Contact: Personnel Department
Description: An apartment buildings operator.

WRIGHT RUNSTAD & COMPANY
1201 3rd Avenue, Suite 2000
Seattle WA 98101
206/447-9000
Contact: Personnel Department
Description: A commercial real estate developer.

Note: Because addresses and telephone numbers of smaller companies change rapidly, we recommend you call each company and verify the information below before mailing to employers. Mass mailings are not recommended.

Additional employers with under 250 employees:

OPERATORS OF APARTMENT BUILDINGS

Panorama City
150 Circle Drive SE,
Olympia WA 98503-2526. 206/456-0111.

Alaska House
4545 42nd Avenue SW, Seattle WA 98116-4237. 206/935-0520.

Cedar Gardens
W405 West Bellwood Drive, Spokane WA 99218-2805. 509/467-6955.

Cedar Point Apartments
N8821 North Hill North Dale Street, Spokane WA 99218-1142. 509/467-1805.

Charles Gate Apartments
2230 4th Avenue, Seattle WA 98121-2013. 206/443-1332.

Court Of Flags Apartments
22804 91st Way South, Kent WA 98031-2461. 206/850-3593.

Firwood Grove Apartments
5150 College Street, SE, Olympia WA 98503-5938.
206/438-6205.

Gallery Place Apartments
8935 160th Avenue NE, Redmond WA 98052-7501.
206/869-0644.

Gilman Meadows
360 NW Dogwood Street, Issaquah WA 98027-3272.
206/392-0570.

La Scala Apartments
2922 Western Avenue, Seattle WA 98121-1026.
206/441-2922.

Millwood Estate Apartments
508 164th Street, SW, Lynnwood WA 98037-8123.
206/743-5050.

Reanne Court Apartments
18534 52nd Avenue West, Lynnwood WA 98037-4561.
206/771-7032.

Santa Fe Ridge Apartments
1415 NW Santa Fe Lane, Silverdale WA 98383-7918.
206/692-5311.

Teal Pointe Apartments
10405 NE 9th Avenue, Vancouver WA 98685-5552.
206/573-3221.

Waterford Place
13305 NE 171st Street, Woodinville WA 98072-6914.
206/483-3444.

LAND SUBDIVIDERS AND DEVELOPERS

Hal Griffith & Assocs
Bay Pavillion-Pier 57th, Seattle WA 98101. 206/623-8600.

REAL ESTATE MANAGERS AND AGENTS

Windermere Real Estate
2300 East Valley Road Suite A, Renton WA 98055-4013.
206/277-5900.

Windermere Real Estate
5900 24th Avenue NW, Seattle WA 98107-3206.
206/789-7700.

Zaser & Longston
1802 136th Place NE Bellevue WA 98005-2319. 206/562-7997.

Lexford Properties
17202 NE 85th Place, Redmond WA 98052-6616. 206/885-9989.

For more information on career opportunities in real estate:

Associations

INSTITUTE OF REAL ESTATE MANAGEMENT
430 North Michigan Avenue, Chicago IL 60611. 312/661-1930.

INTERNATIONAL ASSOCIATION OF CORPORATE REAL ESTATE EXECUTIVES
440 Columbia Drive, Suite 100, P.O. Box 1408, West Palm Beach FL 33409. 407/683-8111.

Magazines

JOURNAL OF PROPERTY MANAGEMENT
Institute of Real Estate Management, 430 North Michigan Avenue, Chicago IL 60610. 312/661-1930.

NATIONAL REAL ESTATE INVESTOR
6151 Powers Ferry Road, Atlanta GA 30339. 404/955-2500.

REAL ESTATE FORUM
12 West 37th Street, New York NY 10018. 212/563-6460.

REAL ESTATE NEWS
3525 West Peterson, Suite 100, Chicago IL 60659. 312/465-5151.

RETAIL

 *Over the past few years, much of the retail industry has been struggling against low consumer confidence, but with many prices now coming down, sales of some big-ticket items, like computers, have risen. The housing rebound is also spurring sales of appliances, home electronics equipment and furniture. Meanwhile, discount department stores keep booming. This trend holds true for both merchandise and apparel stores, as well as for other broad product areas like health and beauty aides. Unfortunately for professionals, most new jobs will be entry-level, where there is currently a major labor shortage.*

ASSOCIATED GROCERS, INC.
P.O. Box 265
Burlington WA 98233
206/757-1211
Contact: Colleen Helgeson, Personnel Director
Description: Operates a chain of retail food stores.

BJ'S PAINT-N-PLACE, INC.
6528 Capitol Boulevard South
Olympia WA 98501
206/943-3232
Contact: Human Resources
Description: A retailer of paint.

BARTELL DRUG COMPANY
4727 Denver Avenue South
Seattle WA 98134
206/763-2626
Contact: Personnel Department
Description: Operates a chain of drug stores. **Number of employees nationwide:** 600.

EDDIE BAUER, INC.
14850 Northeast 36th Street
Redmond WA 98052
206/882-6341
Contact: Director/Human Resources
Description: A specialty retailer and mail order company offering outdoors gear and apparel to customers throughout the United States. **Educational**

backgrounds include: Accounting; Art/Design; Business Administration; Communications; Finance; Marketing. **Benefits:** Dental Insurance; Disability Coverage; Employee Discounts; Life Insurance; Medical Insurance; Pension Plan; Profit Sharing; Savings Plan; Tuition Assistance.

THE BON MARCHE
1601 Third Avenue
Seattle WA 98181
206/344-2121
Contact: Personnel Department
Description: Operates a retail department store. **Number of employees nationwide:** 3,750.

BEN BRIDGE CORPORATION
P.O. Box 1908
Seattle WA 98111
206/448-8800
Contact: Jonathan Bridge, Vice Chairman
Description: A retailer of jewelry. **Common positions include:** Credit Clerk and Authorizer; Services Sales Representative. **Benefits:** Dental Insurance; Disability Coverage; Employee Discounts; Life Insurance; Medical Insurance; Profit Sharing; Tuition Assistance. **Special Programs:** Training Programs. **Corporate headquarters location:** This Location. **Other U.S. locations:** AL; CA; HI; NV; OR; WA. **Operations at this facility include:** Administration; Sales; Service.

WILLIAM B. CLOES
8214 Greenwood North
Seattle WA 98103
206/782-3131
Contact: Personnel Department
Description: A retailer of women's ready to wear clothing.

COSTCO WHOLESALE CORPORATION
10809 120th Avenue NE
Kirkland WA 98083
206/828-8100
Contact: Personnel Department
Description: Runs a chain of membership warehouse stores. **Number of employees at this location:** 5,000.

EGGHEAD, INC.
P.O. Box 7004
Issaquah WA 98027-7004
206/391-5160
Contact: Personnel
Description: Egghead is a large specialty retailer of personal computer software.

FOOD GIANT STORES
1801 North 46th
Seattle WA 98103
206/632-9253
Contact: Ken Gilman, Assistant General Manager
Description: Operates a chain of food stores.

FREMONT CAR QUEST
744 North 34th Street
Seattle WA 98103
206/633-2323
Contact: Personnel Department
Description: An auto parts wholesaler and retailer.

HAGGEN, INC./TOP FOOD & DRUG
P.O. Box 9704
Bellingham WA 98227-9704
206/733-8720
Contact: Janel Ernster, Human Resources Manager
Description: A growing supermarket chain. **Common positions include:** Accountant/Auditor; Chef/Cook/Kitchen Worker; Computer Programmer; Department Manager; Grocery Clerk; Meat Cutter; Pharmacist. **Educational backgrounds include:** Accounting; Business Administration; Communications; Computer Science; Liberal Arts; Marketing. **Benefits:** Dental Insurance; Disability Coverage; Life Insurance; Medical Insurance; Pension Plan; Profit Sharing; Savings Plan; Tuition Assistance. **Special Programs:** Internships; Training Programs. **Corporate headquarters location:** This Location. **Operations at this facility include:** Administration.

INFOTECH
1511 6th Avenue
Seattle WA 98101
206/621-6600
Contact: Personnel Department
Description: Operates a line of department stores and retail stores selling drugs, cosmetics, hardware, tools, appliances, plants, flowers, and lumber. **Parent company:** Trump Group Ltd. **Number of employees nationwide:** 10,000.

JAY JACOBS, INC.
1530 5th Avenue
Seattle WA 98101
206/622-5400
Contact: Human Resources
Description: A company engaged in the retailing of women's and young men's clothing.

LAMONTS APPAREL, INC.
3650 131st Avenue SE
Bellevue WA 98006
206/644-5700
Contact: Personnel Department
Description: An apparel store. **Parent company:** Seattle Holding Corporation.
Number of employees nationwide: 1,200.

MAGNOLIA HI-FI INC.
3701 7th Avenue South
Seattle WA 98134
206/623-7872
Contact: Personnel Department
Description: A retailer of stereophonic video equipment and car stereos.

FRED MEYER, INC.
14300 First Avenue South
Seattle WA 98168
800/401-5627
Contact: Personnel Department
Description: Operates a chain of one-stop shopping centers. Accepts applications for advertised positions only. **Number of employees nationwide:** 2,440.

NORDSTROM
100 Bellevue Square
Bellevue WA 98004
206/455-5800
Contact: Human Resources Department
Description: A department store.

PACCAR AUTOMOTIVE INC.
1400 North 4th Street
Renton WA 98055
206/251-7600
Contact: Human Resources Department
Description: An automobile parts, tires, and accessories retailer with automotive repair facilities. **Common positions include:** Automotive Mechanic/Body Repairer; Management Trainee; Sales Manager. **Educational backgrounds include:** Business Administration. **Benefits:** 401K; Dental Insurance; Disability Coverage; Employee Discounts; Life Insurance; Medical Insurance; Pension Plan; Savings Plan. **Special Programs:** Internships. **Corporate headquarters location:** This Location. **Other U.S. locations:** Oakland CA. **Parent company:** Paccar Inc. **Operations at this facility include:** Divisional Headquarters; Service. **Number of employees at this location:** 120. **Number of employees nationwide:** 1,600.

PAYLESS DRUG STORES
14880 NE 24th Street
Redmond WA 98052
206/883-6432
Contact: Mark Matthews, Regional Recruiter
Description: Operates 550 retail drug stores in 12 western states; adds 30 to 40 new stores per year. Stores offer over 45,000 different items. **Common positions include:** Management Trainee; Pharmacist. **Educational backgrounds include:** Business Administration; Marketing; Pharmacology. **Benefits:** Daycare Assistance; Dental Insurance; Disability Coverage; Employee Discounts; Life Insurance; Medical Insurance; Pension Plan; Profit Sharing; Savings Plan. **Corporate headquarters location:** Wilsonville OR. **Parent company:** Kmart Corporation. **Operations at this facility include:** Sales. **Number of employees nationwide:** 15,000.

QUALITY FOOD CENTERS
10112 Northeast 10th Street
Bellevue WA 98004-4156
206/455-3761
Contact: Human Resources
Description: Operates retail supermarkets, emphasizing superior customer service, high-quality perishables, competitive prices, and convenient store locations. **Number of employees nationwide:** 2,600.

RECREATIONAL EQUIPMENT INC. (REI)
P.O. Box 1938
Sumner WA 98390
206/395-5965
Contact: Jobline: 206/395-4694, Retail Recruiter
Description: A retailer of outdoor clothing and equipment. Retail stores in major markets throughout the U.S. **Common positions include:** Accountant/Auditor; Administrator; Computer Programmer; Customer Service Representative; Instructor/Trainer; Operations/Production Manager; Personnel/Labor Relations Specialist; Public Relations Specialist; Purchasing Agent and Manager; Services Sales Representative; Systems Analyst; Technical Writer/Editor; Transportation/Traffic Specialist. **Educational backgrounds include:** Liberal Arts. **Benefits:** Dental Insurance; Disability Coverage; Employee Discounts; Life Insurance; Medical Insurance; Pension Plan; Profit Sharing; Savings Plan; Tuition Assistance. **Special Programs:** Training Programs. **Corporate headquarters location:** This Location. **Operations at this facility include:** Administration. **Annual Revenues:** $320,000,000. **Number of employees nationwide:** 3,000.

SAFEWAY STORES, INC.
1647 140th Avenue NE
Bellevue WA 98005
206/455-6336
Contact: Personnel Department
Description: A retail grocer and distributor. **Number of employees nationwide:** 10,200.

SCHUCKS AUTO SUPPLY
2401 West Valley Highway North
Auburn WA 98002
206/833-1115
Fax: 206/833-9533
Contact: Dale Strothers, Regional Recruiter
Description: Offices for the retail auto parts and access stores. **Common positions include:** Cashier; Customer Service Representative; Management Trainee; Retail Sales Worker. **Benefits:** Dental Insurance; Employee Discounts; Medical Insurance; Savings Plan; Tuition Assistance. **Corporate headquarters location:** Phoenix AZ. **Parent company:** Northern Automotive. **Operations at this facility include:** Regional Headquarters.

SEARS, ROEBUCK & COMPANY
15711 Aurora Avenue North
Seattle WA 98133
206/364-9000
Contact: Human Resources Department
Description: A national retailer.

SOUTHLAND CORPORATION
7-ELEVEN/HOAGY'S CORNER
1035 Andover Park West
Tukwila WA 98188
206/575-6711
Fax: 206/575-8022
Contact: Janet Henry, Human Resource Specialist
Description: Operator of deli and convenience stores. **Common positions include:** Buyer; Management Analyst/Consultant; Management Trainee; Personnel/Labor Relations Specialist. **Benefits:** 401K; Dental Insurance; Disability Coverage; Life Insurance; Medical Insurance; Profit Sharing; Savings Plan. **Corporate headquarters location:** Dallas TX. **Operations at this facility include:** Administration. **Listed on:** NASDAQ. **Number of employees at this location:** 875.

TENNYS TOYOTA INC.
13355 Lake City Way NE
Seattle WA 98125
206/367-0080
Contact: Personnel Department
Description: A retailer and wholesaler of automobile parts and services.

THRIFTWAY STORES INC.
P.O. Box 3753
Seattle WA 98124
206/767-8717
Contact: Personnel
Description: Operates a retail grocery chain. Over 100 outlets.

U.R.M. STORES, INC.
P.O. Box 3365
Spokane WA 99220
509/467-2620
Contact: Personnel Department
Description: A groceries and non-food general merchandise business. **Number of employees nationwide: 2,000.**

KEITH UDDENBERG, INC.
P.O. Box 444
Gig Harbor WA 98335
206/851-6688
Contact: Personnel Department
Description: Operates a chain of grocery stores. **Number of employees nationwide: 1,200.**

WEISFIELD'S JEWELERS
636 Southcenter Shopping Center
Seattle WA 98188
206/244-7440
Contact: Personnel Department
Description: A jewelry store.

Note: Because addresses and telephone numbers of smaller companies change rapidly, we recommend you call each company and verify the information below before mailing to employers. Mass mailings are not recommended.

Additional employers with over 250 employees:

GROCERY STORES

Johnny's Food Centers
25715 102nd Place SE, Kent WA 98031-6874. 206/852-2990.

Klauser Corporation
3625 Perkins Lane SW Suite 300, Tacoma WA 98499-4799. 206/581-3341.

APPAREL STORES

Lamonts Apparel Inc.
3650 131st Avenue SE, Bellevue WA 98006-1334. 206/562-8386.

DEPARTMENT STORES

Tri North Department Stores
5000 1st Avenue

South, Seattle WA 98134-2498. 206/767-7600.

LUMBER AND BUILDING MATERIALS RETAILERS

Pay-n-Pak Stores
10900 NE 8th Street, Suite 945, Bellevue WA 98004-4405. 206/854-5450.

Additional employers with under 250 employees:

LUMBER AND OTHER BUILDING MATERIALS DEALERS

Hardel Mutual Plywood Corporation
P.O. Box 365, Olympia WA 98507-0365. 206/754-6030.

Crawford Door Sales
E1325 East Francis Avenue, Spokane WA 99207-3648. 509/484-6610.

Braco Energy Services
200 1st Avenue West #503, Seattle WA 98119-4219. 206/282-3644.

Mutual Materials Company
E6721 East Trent Avenue, Spokane WA 99212-1227. 509/922-4100.

RETAIL NURSERIES AND GARDEN SUPPLY STORES

McGregor Company
Plaza, Spangle WA 99028. 509/523-6311.

GROCERY STORES

Fuller Market Basket
771 South Market Boulevard, Chehalis WA 98532-3419. 206/736-9328.

Martin & Scouten
1300 Tichenal Road, Cashmere WA 98815. 509/782-3801.

Olson's Food Stores
176th & Highway 99, Lynnwood WA 98037. 206/743-1127.

West Star Corporation
2404 Harrison Avenue NW, Olympia WA 98502-4545. 206/754-9595.

Wray's Thriftway
5605 Summitview Avenue, Yakima WA 98908-3099. 509/966-2660.

MISCELLANEOUS FOOD STORES

General Nutrition Center
Franklin Park Mall, Spokane WA 99207. 509/487-9594.

Ralph's Thriftway
1908 4th Avenue East, Olympia WA 98506-4632. 206/352-4426.

CAR DEALERS

Honda Of Renton
200 SW Grady Way,
Renton WA 98055.
206/271-3131.

GASOLINE SERVICE STATIONS

Chevron USA
1601 Marvin Road NE,
Olympia WA 98516-
3879. 206/493-2212.

Dissmore's Inc.
1205 North Grand
Avenue, Pullman WA
99163-3426.
509/332-2918.

Holiday Companies
N9720 North Division
Street, Spokane WA
99218-1301.
509/467-1319.

BOAT DEALERS

Christensen Motor Yacht
4400 East Columbia
Way, Vancouver WA
98661-5570.
206/695-7671.

WOMEN'S ACCESSORY AND SPECIALTY STORES

Smart Sizes
36 South Grady Way,
Renton WA 98055-
3206. 206/228-7827.

CHILDREN'S AND INFANTS' WEAR STORES

Gymboree
Alderwood Mall,
Lynnwood WA
98037. 206/771-
4558.

MISCELLANEOUS APPAREL AND ACCESSORY STORES

Special Tees
2225 Carillon Point,
Kirkland WA 98033-
7353. 206/828-0238.

FURNITURE STORES

United Buy & Sell Furniture warehouse
16929 Highway 99,
Lynnwood WA
98037-3114.
206/745-2660.

Levitz Furniture Corporation
17601 Southcenter
Parkway, Seattle WA
98188-3706.
206/575-0510.

HOMEFURNISHING STORES

Lechters
Northtown Mall,
Spokane WA 99207.
509/484-1048.

Seattle Lighting Fixture Company
Silverdale Plaza,
Silverdale WA 98383.
206/692-1551.

Colorel Blinds
2560 152nd Avenue
NE, Redmond WA
98052-5535.
206/867-5365.

Pacific Linen
10876 NW Myhre
Road, Silverdale WA
98383-7991.
206/692-7007.

Smith's Home Furnishings Inc.
N9610 North Newport
Highway, Spokane
WA 99218-1221.
509/468-1850.

Software Etc.
3000 184th Street
SW Suite 238,
Lynnwood WA
98037-4719.
206/670-2951.

USED MERCHANDISE STORES

Goodwill Industries
307 West Columbia
Street, Pasco WA
99301-5634.
509/547-7717.

SEWING AND PIECE GOODS STORES

Fabricland
19800 44th Avenue
West, Lynnwood WA
98036-6739.
206/776-3300.

JEWELRY STORES

Hudson Goodman Jewelers
Kitsap Mall, Silverdale
WA 98383. 206/692-8660.

Hudson Goodman Jewelers
Blue Mountain Mall,
Walla Walla WA
99362. 509/522-1686.

Piercing Pagoda
Northgate Mall,
Seattle WA 98125.
206/367-7710.

Piercing Pagoda
4502 South Steele
Street, Tacoma WA
98409-7247.
206/471-0717.

LUGGAGE AND LEATHER GOODS STORES

Leather Loft
1312 Lum Road,
Centralia WA 98531-1818. 206/736-0532.

AUTOMATIC MERCHANDISING MACHINE OPERATORS

Ace Vending
9308 Lakeview
Avenue SW, Tacoma
WA 98499-4349.
206/584-5938.

OPTICAL GOODS STORES

Everett Clinic Optical Center
3901 Hoyt Avenue,
Everett WA 98201-4988. 206/339-5436.

Lens Crafters
2701 184th Street
SW, Lynnwood WA
98037-4739.
206/775-2822.

Shopko
N9520 North Newport
Highway, Spokane
WA 99218-1219.
509/466-7136.

MISCELLANEOUS RETAIL STORES

Allied Safe & Vault Company Inc.
425 West 2nd
Avenue, Spokane WA
99204-1311.
509/624-3152.

ADT Security Systems
1916 Boren Avenue,
Seattle WA 98101-1406. 206/624-3103.

Natural Wonders
532 Northgate Mall,
Seattle WA 98125-7107. 206/364-7470.

For more information on career opportunities in retail:

Associations

INTERNATIONAL ASSOCIATION OF CHAIN STORES
3800 Moor Place, Alexandria VA
22305. 703/549-4525.

INTERNATIONAL COUNCIL OF SHOPPING CENTERS
665 Fifth Avenue, New York NY
10022. 212/421-8181.

NATIONAL AUTOMOTIVE DEALERS ASSOCIATION
8400 Westpark Drive, McLean VA
22102. 703/821-7000.

NATIONAL INDEPENDENT AUTOMOTIVE DEALERS ASSOCIATION
2521 Brown Boulevard, Suite 100, Arlington TX 76006. 817/640-3838.

NATIONAL RETAIL FEDERATION
325 7th Street NW, Suite 1000, Washington DC 20004. 202/783-7971.

Directories

AUTOMOTIVE NEWS MARKET DATA BOOK
Automotive News, Crain Communication, 1400 Woodbridge Avenue, Detroit MI 48207-3187. 313/446-6000.

STONE, CLAY, GLASS AND CONCRETE PRODUCTS

 Growth in stone, clay, glass, concrete and related materials is closely tied to the success of the construction industry. On one hand, analysts believe that 1995 will be a year of improvement for construction companies. On the other, the longer-term forecast is for much slower growth, since infrastructure construction is dependent on shrinking local government budgets. All in all, the stone, clay, glass and concrete industry should see revenue growth of about 1 to 2 percent annually.

BALL INCON GLASS PACKAGING
5801 East Marginal Way South
Seattle WA 98134
206/762-0660
Contact: Human Resources Department
Description: Produces flat glass.

CONCRETE TECHNOLOGY CORPORATION
1123 Port of Tacoma Road
Tacoma WA 98421-2259
206/383-3545
Contact: Personnel Director
Description: A producer of concrete for a variety of end applications.

HEMPHILL BROTHERS INC.
P.O. Box 80786
Seattle WA 98108
206/762-7622
Contact: Personnel Department
Description: A manufacturer of crushed limestone and silica sand.

PALMER G. LEWIS COMPANY, INC.
P.O. Box 1049
Auburn WA 98071-1049
206/941-2600
Contact: Director of Employee Relations
Description: A wholesale distributor of building materials. Primary customers include retail building material dealers. **Common positions include:** Accountant/Auditor; Branch Manager; Buyer; Computer Programmer; Credit Manager; Department Manager; Financial Analyst; Management Trainee;

Manufacturer's/Wholesaler's Sales Rep.; Marketing Specialist; Purchasing Agent and Manager. **Educational backgrounds include:** Accounting; Business Administration; Communications; Economics; Finance; Marketing. **Benefits:** Dental Insurance; Disability Coverage; Life Insurance; Medical Insurance; Profit Sharing; Savings Plan. **Corporate headquarters location:** This Location. **Operations at this facility include:** Administration; Divisional Headquarters; Regional Headquarters; Sales.

Note: Because addresses and telephone numbers of smaller companies change rapidly, we recommend you call each company and verify the information below before mailing to employers. Mass mailings are not recommended.

Additional employers with over 250 employees:

ASPHALT

Lakeside Industries
P.O. Box 1379,
Bellevue WA 98009-
1379. 206/883-1661.

TILE

Mutual Materials Company
P.O. Box 1, Mica WA
99023-0001.
509/924-2120.

GLASS CONTAINERS

Pacific Coast Container
11010 NE 37th Circle,
Vancouver WA
98682-7216.
206/892-3451.

Milgard Manufacturing
P.O. Box 11368,
Tacoma WA 98411-
0368. 206/922-6030.

Visador Company Path
7717 Portland Avenue
E, Tacoma WA
98404-3327.
206/535-4000.

MINERALS AND EARTHS

Advanced Silicon Materials Inc.
3322 Road NE, Moses
Lake WA 98837.
509/765-2106.

Associated Sand & Gravel Company Inc.
6300 Glenwood
Avenue, Everett WA
98203-4247.
206/355-2111.

CEMENT

Holnam Inc.
5400 West Marginal
Way SW, Seattle WA
98106-1517.
206/937-8025.

Holnam Inc.
P.O. Box 11707,
Spokane WA 99211-
1707. 509/924-0540.

CONCRETE

Central Pre-Mix Concrete Company
P.O. Box 3366,
Spokane WA 99220-
3366. 509/534-6221.

Kenmore Pre-Mix
P.O. Box 82224,
Kenmore WA 98028-
0224. 206/486-3281.

Additional employers with under 250 employees:

ASPHALT PAVING MIXTURES

U.S. Oil & Refining Company
P.O. Box 2255,
Tacoma WA 98401-2255. 206/383-1651.

FLAT GLASS

Spectrum Glass Company
P.O. Box 646,
Woodinville WA 98072-0646.
206/483-6699.

HYDRAULIC CEMENT

Ash Grove Cement
3801 East Marginal Way South, Seattle WA 98134-1147.
206/623-5596.

Pozzolanic International
7525 SE 24th Street #630, Mercer Island WA 98040-2300.
206/232-9320.

CONCRETE PRODUCTS

Bethlehem Services
P.O. Box 505,
Cashmere WA 98815-0505. 509/782-1001.

Central Pre-Mix/Prestress Corporation
5111 East Broadway Avenue, Spokane WA 99212-0928.
509/534-6221.

READY-MIX CONCRETE

Stoneway Concrete
1915 SE Maple Valley Highway, Renton WA 98055-3906.
206/226-1000.

MINERALS AND EARTHS

Heckett Division Harsco Corporation
S Spokane & Harbor Av SW, Seattle WA 98126. 206/937-6774.

NONCLAY REFRACTORIES

North American Refractories Company
1420 Maple Avenue SW #203, Renton WA 98055-3108.
206/228-2656.

GLASS PRODUCTS

Northwestern Industries
2500 West Jameson Street, Seattle WA 98199-1294.
206/285-3140.

BRICK, STONE AND RELATED CONSTRUCTION MATERIAL WHOLESALE

Miles Sand & Gravel Company
P.O. Box 130, Auburn WA 98071-0130.
206/833-3700.

Dal-Tile Corporation
E4000 East Broadway Avenue, Spokane WA 99202-4529.
509/534-0202.

Ash Grove Cement Company
N1312 North Thierman Road,
Spokane WA 99212-1125. 509/928-4343.

For more information on career opportunities in stone, clay, glass and concrete products:

Associations

NATIONAL GLASS ASSOCIATION
8200 Greensboro Drive, McLean VA 22102. 703/442-4890

Magazines

GLASS MAGAZINE
National Glass Association, 8200 Greensboro Drive, McLean VA 22102. 703/442-4890

THE NORTH AMERICAN CEMENT REVIEW
Douglas M. Queen, Inc., 2143 Old Spring Road, Williamstown MA 01267. 413/458-8364.

ROCK PRODUCTS
MacLean Hunter Publishing Co., Chicago IL 60606. 312/726-2805.

TRANSPORTATION

All four major transportation segments -- airlines, railroad, trucking and water transport -- expect modest growth as the nation's economy slowly recovers. According to analysts, airline traffic should continue to grow both domestically and abroad, but carriers will still have to balance costs and fares. Regional carriers will continue to outpace larger airlines. According to the U.S. Labor Department, the hiring picture of airlines will improve over the long-term.

On the railroads, the use of both freight and passenger rail will climb. On the road, truckers will see an increase in opportunities, but a jump in operating costs will squeeze profit margins. Job opportunities should be good for truck drivers and mechanics, as the number of trucking and warehouse jobs are projected to grow by 25 percent over the next several years. And according to the U.S. Commerce Department, increased trade and stronger freight rates should help the performance of U.S. flag liner companies operating in the Asian markets. Domestic use of water transportation should also increase, especially between Alaska and the lower 48 states.

AAA TRAVEL
330 Sixth Avenue North
Seattle WA 98109
206/448-5353
Contact: Human Resources
Description: A travel services organization.

AIR VAN LINES
P.O. Box 3447
Bellevue WA 98009
206/453-5560
Contact: Personnel Director
Description: A freight-forwarding company with operations in domestic moving services.

AIRBORNE EXPRESS
P.O. Box 662
Seattle WA 98115
206/285-4600
Fax: 206/281-3890
Contact: Lee Rousseau, Manager, Recruiting and Placement
Description: A domestic and international air express, air, and ocean freight

services. **Common positions include:** Aircraft Mechanic/Engine Specialist; Computer Programmer; Computer Systems Analyst; Customer Service Representative; Driver; Industrial Engineer; Quality Control Supervisor; Services Sales Representative; Software Engineer; Supervisor; Telemarketer. **Educational backgrounds include:** Business Administration; Computer Science; Engineering; Liberal Arts; Marketing. **Benefits:** 401K; Dental Insurance; Disability Coverage; Employee Discounts; Life Insurance; Medical Insurance; Pension Plan; Profit Sharing; Savings Plan; Tuition Assistance; Vision Insurance. **Corporate headquarters location:** This Location. **Number of employees at this location:** 1,300. **Number of employees nationwide:** 16,500.

ALASKA AIR GROUP, INC.
ALASKA AIRLINES
P.O. Box 68900
Seattle WA 98168-0900
206/431-7040
Contact: Personnel Department
Description: A holding company for Alaska Airlines, Inc., and Horizon Air Industries, Inc. **Number of employees nationwide:** 5,740.

ANGEL LEE INC.
P.O. Box 68925
Seattle WA 98168
206/243-8011
Contact: Personnel Department
Description: A transportation company specializing in daily car rentals and airport parking.

BAYLINER MARINE CORPORATION
17825 59th Avenue NE
Arlington WA 98223
206/435-5571
Contact: Personnel Department
Description: Manufactures fiberglass pleasure boats as a subsidiary of Brunswick Corp. **Number of employees nationwide:** 1,550.

BEKINS MOVING & STORAGE COMPANY
P.O. Box 30728
Seattle WA 98103-0728
206/527-7600
Contact: Personnel Director
Description: Services include the transportation and warehousing of household goods, office and industrial equipment, electronics, business records, and air freight forwarding. **Corporate headquarters location:** This Location.

BUDGET CAR AND TRUCK RENTAL
2001 Westlake Avenue
Seattle WA 98121
206/448-4859
Contact: Human Resources
Description: A truck renting and leasing firm.

CONSOLIDATED FREIGHTWAYS
P.O. Box 3585
Seattle WA 98124
206/763-1517
Contact: Gene Owen, Office Manager
Description: Provides freight forwarding services.

CONTINENTAL VAN LINES INC.
P.O. Box 3963
Seattle WA 98124
206/937-2261
Contact: Personnel Department
Description: A transportation company engaged in interstate moving and storage.

DANZAS CORPORATION
P.O. Box 53370
Bellevue WA 98015
206/649-9339
Contact: Personnel Department
Description: An air freight forwarding company. **Number of employees at this location:** 500.

DUWAMISH SHIPYARD INC.
5658 West Marginal Way SW
Seattle WA 98106
206/767-4880
Contact: Human Resources
Description: Engaged in ship building and repair.

EXPEDITORS INTERNATIONAL OF WASHINGTON, INC.
P.O. Box 69620, 19119 16th Avenue South
Seattle WA 98168
206/246-3711
Contact: Personnel
Description: Engaged in the business of international freight fowarding, for both air and ocean freight. The company also acts as a customs broker in its domestic overseas offices. It offers domestic fowarding services in conjunction with international shipment but does not compete for domestic overnight business.

FOSS MARITIME
660 West Ewing
Seattle WA 98119
206/281-3800
Contact: Personnel Department
Description: A maritime carrier, deepsea forum, domestic, coastwide and intercoastal transportation, ship repair, and wholesaler of wire and rope.

HOLLAND AMERICA LINE WESTOURS
300 Elliott Avenue West
Seattle WA 98119
206/281-3535
Contact: Personnel Department
Description: A tour and cruise operator.

HORIZON AIR
P.O. Box 48309
Seattle WA 98148
206/241-6757
Contact: Kathleen Thompson, Employment Specialist
Description: A passenger/freight company. **Common positions include:** Transportation/Traffic Specialist. **Benefits:** Dental Insurance; Disability Coverage; Employee Discounts; Life Insurance; Medical Insurance; Profit Sharing; Savings Plan. **Listed on:** New York Stock Exchange.

INCO EXPRESS INC.
3600 South 124th
Seattle WA 98168
206/248-2700
Contact: Personnel Department
Description: A primary long distance trucking company.

INTERSTATE DISTRIBUTOR COMPANY
P.O. Box 45999
Tacoma WA 98445-0999
206/537-9455
Contact: George N. Payne, Executive Vice President
Description: Engaged in trucking and related transport activities.

LAIDLAW TRANSIT INC.
P.O. Box 27186
Seattle WA 98125-1586
206/365-7300
Contact: Human Resources Department
Description: A transportation service.

METRO-MUNICIPALITY-METRO SEATTLE
821 2nd Avenue
Seattle WA 98104
206/684-2100
Contact: Human Resources Department
Description: A bus line.

PORT OF SEATTLE
Pier 69, 2711 Alaskan Way
Seattle WA 98121
206/728-3286
Contact: Human Resources
Description: Manages the commercial activities of the port of Seattle.

PRINCESS TOURS
2815 2nd Avenue, Suite 400
Seattle WA 98121
206/728-4202
Contact: Manager, Human Resources
Description: Operates rail and motorcoach tours in Alaska and the Canadian Rockies, for land-only touring or in conjunction with ship cruises. Also owns and operates seasonal and year-round hotels in Alaska. **Common positions include:** Accountant/Auditor; Customer Service Representative; Public Relations Specialist; Purchasing Agent and Manager; Reservationist. **Educational backgrounds include:** Accounting; Communications; Marketing. **Benefits:** 401K; Dental Insurance; Disability Coverage; Life Insurance; Medical Insurance; Tuition Assistance. **Corporate headquarters location:** This Location. **Other U.S. locations:** AK. **Operations at this facility include:** Administration; Sales. **Number of employees at this location:** 150. **Number of employees nationwide:** 300.

PUGET SOUND FREIGHT LINES INC.
P.O. Box 24526
Seattle WA 98124-0526
206/623-1600
Contact: Personnel Department
Description: A regional common carrier operating in Washington and Oregon utilizing both company drivers and owner/operators in truckload operations. **Benefits:** Dental Insurance; Medical Insurance; Pension Plan; Profit Sharing. **Corporate headquarters location:** This Location.

SEA-LAND SERVICE INC.
3600 Port of Tacoma Road
4th Floor, World Trade Center
Tacoma WA 98424
800/426-4512
Contact: Personnel Manager
Description: A large container shipping company.

SOCIETY EXPEDITIONS, INC.
2001 Western Avenue, Suite 710
Seattle WA 98121
206/728-9400
Contact: Human Resources
Description: An ocean cruise line.

TACOMA BOATBUILDING COMPANY
1840 Marine View Drive
Tacoma WA 98422
206/572-3600
Contact: Charles Holmes, Human Resources Director
Description: Engaged in ship construction and repair for the US Navy, US Coast Guard, commercial, and foreign countries. **Common positions include:** Accountant/Auditor; Computer Programmer; Draftsperson; Electrical/ Electronic Engineer; Mechanical Engineer; Naval Architect; Personnel/Labor Relations Specialist; Purchasing Agent and Manager. **Educational backgrounds include:** Accounting; Business Administration; Computer Science; Finance; Liberal Arts. **Benefits:** Dental Insurance; Disability Coverage; Life Insurance; Medical Insurance; Tuition Assistance. **Corporate headquarters location:** This Location.

TODD PACIFIC SHIPYARDS CORPORATION
SEATTLE DIVISION
P.O. Box 3806
Seattle WA 98124
206/623-1635
Contact: Michael Marsh, Personnel Director
Description: Engaged in the construction and maintenance/repair of commercial ships, both domestic and foreign, and of ships for the U.S. Navy and other governmental agencies. Shipyards are strategically located in some of the nation's busiest ports where they meet the needs of the international trade industry.

TOLLYCRAFT YACHTS CORPORATION
2200 Clinton Avenue
Kelso WA 98626
206/423-5160
Contact: Personnel Department
Description: A corporation specializing in the manufacturing of inboard motor yachts and cruisers.

U.S. MARINE CORPORATION
P.O. Box 9029
Everett WA 98206
206/435-5571
Contact: Bob Teague, Human Resources
Description: Engaged in boat building activities.

UNITED MARINE SHIPBUILDING INC.
1441 North Northlake Way
Seattle WA 98103
206/632-1441
Contact: Sally Bergmann, Executive Administrator
Description: Engaged in ship building and repairing wholesale transportation equipment and supplies.

WESTOURS-MOTOR COACHES INC.
300 Elliott Avenue West
Seattle WA 98119
206/281-3535
Contact: Personnel Department
Description: A motor coach transportation company.

Note: Because addresses and telephone numbers of smaller companies change rapidly, we recommend you call each company and verify the information below before mailing to employers. Mass mailings are not recommended.

Additional employers with over 250 employees:

SHIP/BOAT BUILDING AND REPAIRING

Tektronix Inc.
11814 115th Avenue NE, Kirkland WA 98034-6923.
206/821-9100.

RAILROAD TRANSPORTATION

Union Pacific Railroad
402 S Dawson Street, Seattle WA 98108-2257. 206/764-1430.

TRUCKING

Oak Harbor Freight Lines
P.O. Box 1469, Auburn WA 98071-1469. 206/246-2600.

Quality Transportation
P.O. Box 28, Yakima WA 98907-0028.
509/248-2996.

System Transport
P.O. Box 3456, Spokane WA 99220-3456. 509/623-4000.

ASC Pacific Inc.
2141 Milwaukee Way, Tacoma WA 98421-2705. 9163726851.

WATER TRANSPORTATION OF FREIGHT

Norton Lilly International
33400 8th Avenue South, Federal Way WA 98003-6382.
206/874-2940.

OOCL-Usa Inc.
1218 3rd Avenue
Suite 710, Seattle WA
98101-3082.
206/624-8914.

AIR
TRANSPORTATION
AND SERVICES

Alaska Airlines Inc.
P.O. Box 68900,
Seattle WA 98168-
0900. 206/433-3200.

American Airlines
Seattle-Tacoma
International Airport,
Seattle WA 98158.
206/433-3951.

Continental Airlines
2580 S 156th Street,
Building A-207,
Seattle WA 98158-
1133. 206/433-6572.

**Delta Air Lines
Airfreight**
16745 Aircargo Road
Sea-Tac International,
Seattle WA 98158-
1109. 206/433-4900.

Delta Air Lines Inc.
717 West Sprague
Avenue, Suite 808,
Spokane WA 99204-
0419. 509/455-9390.

Hawaiian Airlines Inc.
Seattle-Tacoma Intl
Airport, Seattle WA
98158. 206/431-
7713.

**Lufthansa German
Airlines**
1200 5th Avenue
Suite 1205, Seattle
WA 98101-1127.
206/624-6244.

Northwest Airlines
Sea-Tac International
Airport, Seattle WA
98158. 206/433-
3587.

**Scandinavian Airlines
System**
1301 5th Avenue
Suite 2727, Seattle
WA 98101-2603.
206/682-5250.

**Scandinavian Airlines
System**
Avia Cargo Building 2,
Sea-Tac International,
Seattle WA 98158.
206/433-5151.

USAir
Sea-Tac Airport,
Seattle WA 98158.
206/433-7858.

Emery Worldwide
2625 South 161st
Street, Seattle WA
98158. 206/433-
5067.

Flightcraft Inc.
8285 Perimeter Road
South, Seattle WA
98108-3824.
206/764-6100.

Tramco Inc.
11323 30th Avenue
West, Everett WA
98204-3556.
206/347-3030.

TRANSPORTATION
EQUIPMENT AND
SUPPLIES
WHOLESALE

Bowman Distribution
P.O. Box 1678,
Auburn WA 98071-
1678. 206/833-9198.

Additional employers with under 250 employees:

SHIP BUILDING AND
REPAIR

AK-WA Company
P.O. Box 872, Tacoma
WA 98401-0872.

**JM Martinac
Shipbuilding
Corporation**
401 East 15th Street,
Tacoma WA 98421-
1601. 206/572-4005.

Mar Com Inc.
3001 SE Columbia
Way, Vancouver WA
98661-8002.
206/693-9916.

**Marine Industries
Northwest**
P.O. Box 1275,
Tacoma WA 98401-
1275. 206/627-9136.

Maritime Contractors
201 Harris Avenue,
Bellingham WA
98225-7018.
206/647-0080.

**Nichols Brothers Boat
Builders**
P.O. Box 580,
Freeland WA 98249-
0580. 206/331-5500.

**BOAT BUILDING AND
REPAIRS**

**Delta Marine
Industries**
1608 South 96th
Street, Seattle WA
98108-5115.
206/763-2383.

LOCAL TRUCKING

ASC Pacific Inc.
2141 Milwaukee Way,
Tacoma WA 98421-
2705. 206/383-4955.

Commercial Carriers
P.O. Box 810, Kent
WA 98035-0810.
206/854-5950.

LTI Inc.
8631 Depot Road,
Lynden WA 98264-
9301. 206/354-2101.

Navajo Northwest
1108 54th Avenue
East, Tacoma WA
98424-2733.
206/922-0400.

Jensen & Grove Inc.
Hayes Route, Box 18,
Woodland WA 98674.
206/225-8360.

**TNT United Truck
Lines**
E3901 East Broadway
Avenue, Spokane WA
99202-4526.
509/535-2382.

**Eagle Transfer
Company**
1751C North
Wenatchee Avenue,
Wenatchee WA
98801-1166.
509/662-2114.

Easley Hauling Service
3710 Gun Club Road,
Yakima WA 98901-
9531. 509/248-2996.

**REFRIDGERATED
WAREHOUSING AND
STORAGE**

Rainier Cold Storage
6004 Airport Way
South, Seattle WA
98108-2716.
206/762-8800.

Seattle Cold Storage
303 South River
Street, Seattle WA
98108-3255.
206/767-7733.

**GENERAL
WAREHOUSING AND
STORAGE**

Fritz Companies Inc.
6805 South 217th
Street, Kent WA
98032-2400.
206/872-4200.

Public Storage
23010 Highway 99,
Edmonds WA 98026-
8738. 206/771-0969.

**Shurgard Storage
Centers**
1715 228th Street
SE, Bothell WA
98021-8445.
206/485-7921.

**SPECIAL
WAREHOUSING AND
STORAGE**

**Haulaway Storage
Containers**
18680 142nd Avenue
NE, Woodinville WA
98072-8521.
206/483-0550.

**DEEP SEA AND
DOMESTIC FREIGHT
TRANSPORTATION**

Western Pioneer Inc.
4601 Shilshole
Avenue NW, Seattle
WA 98107-4716.
206/789-1930.

WATER TRANSPORTATION OF FREIGHT

American President Lines Ltd.
3443 West Marginal Way SW #5, Seattle WA 98106-1021.
206/933-4646.

Tidewater Barge Lines
6 Beach Drive, Vancouver WA 98661-7198.
206/693-1491.

MARINE CARGO HANDLING

Stevedoring Services
3415 11th Avenue SW, Seattle WA 98134-1092.
206/623-0304.

TOWING AND TUGBOAT SERVICES

Crowley Marine Services
2501 SE Columbia Way Suite 200, Vancouver WA 98661-8001.
206/694-6772.

WATER TRANSPORTATION SERVICES

Westcoast Marine Cleaning Inc.
455 C Street, Washougal WA 98671-2149.
206/835-3780.

SCHEDULED AIR TRANSPORTATION

Alaska Airlines Inc.
1301 4th Avenue, Seattle WA 98101-2503. 206/433-3100.

British Airways
2330 South 156th Street, Seattle WA 98158-1144.
206/433-6722.

Canadian Airlines International Ltd.
2345 South 156th Street, Seattle WA 98158-1143.
206/433-5090.

Continental Airlines
10630 8th Avenue NE, Seattle WA 98125-7214.
206/624-1740.

Delta Air Lines Inc.
3105 South Oregon Street, Seattle WA 98108-1638.
206/625-0469.

Markair Inc.
18000 Pacific Highway South, Seattle WA 98188-4205. 206/248-9412.

Markair Inc.
16215 Air Cargo Road, Seattle WA 98158-1301.
206/431-9593.

North Coast Airlines
679 Strander Boulevard, Seattle WA 98188-2922.
206/575-4629.

Northwest Airlines
17900 Pacific Highway South, Seattle WA 98188-4231. 206/433-3678.

Northwest Airlines
402 University Street, Seattle WA 98101-2508. 206/433-3500.

Northwest Airlines
10630 8th Avenue NE, Seattle WA 98125-7214.
206/433-3500.

United Airlines
1225 4th Avenue, Seattle WA 98101-3005. 206/441-3700.

United Airlines
10630 8th Avenue NE, Seattle WA 98125-7214.
206/441-3700.

US Air
10630 8th Avenue NE, Seattle WA 98125-7214.
206/587-6229.

AIR COURIER SERVICES

Combined Transport Service
16234 42D South, Seattle WA 98188.
206/242-6811.

TRAVEL AGENCIES

Central Park Travel
1204 13th Street,
Bellingham WA
98225-7108.
206/647-2550.

**PACKING AND
CRATING**

Diversified Industrial
P.O. Box 1919,
Everett WA 98206-
1919. 206/355-1253.

ANI America Inc.
2889 152nd Avenue
NE, Redmond WA
98052-5514.
206/883-2786.

Pacific Rim Transport
910 South 96th
Street, Seattle WA
98108-4915.
206/763-6860.

**ARRANGEMENT OF
FREIGHT AND CARGO
TRANSPORTATION**

**Carmichael
International**
2701 1st Avenue,
Suite 450, Seattle WA
98121-1123.
206/441-0600.

**George S. Bush &
Company**
821 2nd Avenue
Suite, Seattle WA
98104-1580.
206/623-2593.

Seino America Inc.
1511 3rd Avenue,
Suite 808, Seattle WA
98101-1671.
206/623-1023.

For more information on career opportunities in transportation:

Associations

**AMERICAN BUREAU OF
SHIPPING**
2 World Trade Center, 106th Floor,
New York NY 10048. 212/557-
9520.

**AMERICAN MARITIME
ASSOCIATION**
485 Madison Avenue, 15th Floor,
New York NY 10022. 212/319-
9217.

**AMERICAN SOCIETY OF TRAVEL
AGENTS**
1101 King Street, Alexandria VA
22314. 703/739-2782. For
information, send a SASE with $.75
postage to the attention of
Fulfillment Department.

**AMERICAN TRUCKING
ASSOCIATION**
2200 Mill Road, Alexandria VA
22314-4677. 703/838-1700.

**ASSOCIATION OF AMERICAN
RAILROADS**
50 F Street NW, Washington DC
20001. 202/639-2100.

**INSTITUTE OF
TRANSPORTATION ENGINEERS**
525 School Street SW, Suite 410,
Washington DC 20024. 202/554-
8050.

MARINE TECHNOLOGY SOCIETY
1828 L Street NW, Suite 906,
Washington DC 20036. 202/775-
5966.

NATIONAL MARINE MANUFACTURERS ASSOCIATION
401 North Michigan Avenue, Suite 1150, Chicago IL 60611. 312/836-4747. Subscription to job listing publication available for a fee.

NATIONAL MOTOR FREIGHT TRAFFIC ASSOCIATION
2200 Mill Road, Alexandria VA 22314. 703/838-1810.

NATIONAL TANK TRUCK CARRIERS
2200 Mill Road, Alexandria VA 22314. 703/838-1700.

Directories

MOODY'S TRANSPORTATION MANUAL
Moody's Investors Service, Inc., 99 Church Street, New York NY 10007. 212/553-0300.

NATIONAL TANK TRUCK CARRIER DIRECTORY
2200 Mill Road, Alexandria VA 22314. 703/838-1700.

OFFICIAL MOTOR FREIGHT GUIDE
1700 West Courtland Street, Chicago IL 60622. 312/278-2454.

Magazines

AMERICAN SHIPPER
P.O. Box 4728, Jacksonville FL 32201. 904/355-2601.

TRAFFIC WORLD MAGAZINE
741 National Press Building, Washington DC 20045. 202/383-6140.

FLEET OWNER
707 Westchester Avenue, White Plains NY 10604-3102. 914/949-8500.

HEAVY DUTY TRUCKING
Newport Communications, P.O. Box W, Newport Beach CA 92658. 714/261-1636.

MARINE DIGEST AND TRANSPORTATION NEWS
P.O. Box 3905, Seattle WA 98124. 206/682-3607.

SHIPPING DIGEST
51 Madison Avenue, New York NY 10010. 212/689-4411.

TRANSPORT TOPICS
2200 Mill Road, Alexandria VA 22314. 703/838-1772.

UTILITIES: ELECTRIC, GAS AND SANITATION

The major forces shaping the U.S. utilities industry are decreased regulation and competition from newly emerging alternative energy sources. Job prospects for those entering the utilities industry vary by sector; the best sector right now is electric, and at the bottom is the stagnant nuclear industry.

LAKESIDE ELECTRIC
13127 NE 137th Place
Kirkland WA 98034
206/823-4009
Contact: Human Resources
Description: An electric utility.

PUBLIC UTILITY DIST. NO. 1 OF SNOHOMISH COUNTY
P.O. Box 1107
Everett WA 98206
206/258-8211
Contact: Karen Grimsley, Director, Labor Relations
Description: Provides electric and water utilities. **Number of employees nationwide: 782.**

PUBLIC UTILITY DIST. NO. 2 OF GRANT COUNTY
P.O. Box 878
Ephrata WA 98823
509/754-3541
Contact: Personnel Department
Description: Engaged in hydroelectric transmission and distribution. **Number of employees nationwide: 531.**

PUGET SOUND POWER & LIGHT COMPANY
10608 NE 4th Avenue
Bellevue WA 98004
206/462-3875
Contact: Dorothy Graham, Director of Human Resources
Description: An investor-owned electric utility serving more than 1.4 million people within a 4,500 square mile service area that includes eight counties bordering Puget Sound in western Washington and one county in central Washington. **Corporate headquarters location:** This Location.

SEATTLE CITY LIGHT DEPARTMENT
1015 Third Avenue
Seattle WA 98104
206/625-3000
Contact: Personnel Department
Description: A municipal electric utility.

WASHINGTON NATURAL GAS COMPANY
915 Mercer Street
Seattle WA 98109
206/622-6767
Contact: Personnel Department
Description: A natural gas distributor.

WASHINGTON PUBLIC POWER SUPPLY
P.O. Box 968
Richland WA 99352
509/372-5000
Contact: Human Resources
Description: A utility.

WASHINGTON WATER POWER
P.O. Box 3727
Spokane WA 99220
509/482-4281
Fax: 509/482-4922
Contact: Elizabeth Nelson, Human Resources Consultant
Description: WWP, a diversified energy services company provides natural gas and electricity to customers in eastern Washington and northern Idaho and natural gas in parts of Oregon and northern California through an operating division known as WP Natural Gas. WWP is an equal opportunity employer committed to attaining a highly qualified workforce that reflects the diversity of the communities we serve. **Common positions include:** Accountant/Auditor; Civil Engineer; Construction and Building Inspector; Construction Contractor and Manager; Customer Service Representative; Draftsperson; Economist/Market Research Analyst; Electrician; Financial Analyst; Forester/Conservation Scientist; Manufacturer's/Wholesaler's Sales Rep.; Mechanical Engineer; Personnel/Labor Relations Specialist; Public Relations Specialist; Wholesale and Retail Buyer. **Educational backgrounds include:** Business Administration; Engineering; Finance; Marketing. **Benefits:** 401K; Dental Insurance; Disability Coverage; Employee Discounts; Life Insurance; Medical Insurance; Pension Plan; Profit Sharing; Savings Plan; Tuition Assistance. **Special Programs:** Internships. **Corporate headquarters location:** This Location. **Other U.S. locations:** South Lake Tahoe CA; Medford CT; Klammatli OR. **Operations at this facility include:** Administration. **Listed on:** New York Stock Exchange. **Number of employees at this location:** 900. **Number of employees nationwide:** 1,400.

WESTERN UTILITIES SUPPLY COMPANY
10013 Martin Luther King Way
Seattle WA 98178
206/722-4800
Contact: Personnel Department
Description: A company engaged in the wholesale of industrial water works supplies. **Common positions include:** Services Sales Representative. **Educational backgrounds include:** Marketing. **Benefits:** Dental Insurance; Disability Coverage; Life Insurance; Medical Insurance; Pension Plan; Profit Sharing; Tuition Assistance. **Corporate headquarters location:** This Location. **Operations at this facility include:** Administration; Sales; Service.

Note: Because addresses and telephone numbers of smaller companies change rapidly, we recommend you call each company and verify the information below before mailing to employers. Mass mailings are not recommended.

Additional employers with over 250 employees:

REFUSE SYSTEMS

Northwest Enviroservice Inc.
P.O. Box 24443, Seattle WA 98124-0443. 206/622-1090.

Pacific Nuclear Systems
1010 S 336th Street, 220, Federal Way WA 98003-6385. 206/874-2235.

Parametrix Inc.
P.O. Box 460, Sumner WA 98390-0080. 206/863-5128.

Additional employers with under 250 employees:

ELECTRICAL SERVICES

Centralia Light Department
1100 North Tower Avenue, Centralia WA 98531-5044. 206/736-7611.

Pac Power & Light Centralia
913A Big Hanaford Road, Centralia WA 98531-9101. 206/736-9901.

COMBINATION UTILITIES

Nepco
18578 NE 67th Court, Redmond WA 98052-6711. 206/869-3000.

REFUSE SYSTEMS

HDR Engineering Inc.
500 108th Avenue NE Suite 1200 Bellevue WA 98004-5500. 206/453-1523.

Seattle Disposal Company
P.O. Box 24625, Seattle WA 98124-0625. 206/763-2700.

Waste Management Northwest
1821 180th Street SE, Bothell WA 98012-6454. 206/337-1197.

Waste Management Northwest Inc.
1301 South Anacortes Street, Burlington WA 98233-3037. 206/757-8446.

For more information on career opportunities in the utilities industry:

Associations

AMERICAN PUBLIC GAS ASSOCIATION
P.O. Box 11094D, Vienna VA
22183. 703/352-3890.

AMERICAN PUBLIC POWER ASSOCIATION
2301 M Street NW, Washington DC
20037. 202/467-2970.

AMERICAN RURAL ELECTRIC COOPERATIVE ASSOCIATION
1800 Massachusetts Avenue NW,
Washington DC 20036. 202/797-
5441.

AMERICAN WATER WORKS ASSOCIATION
6666 West Quincy Avenue, Denver
CO 80235. 303/794-7711.

Directories

MOODY'S PUBLIC UTILITY MANUAL
Moody's Investors Service, Inc., 99
Church Street, New York NY
10007. 212/553-0300.

Magazines

PUBLIC POWER
2301 M Street NW, Washington DC
20037. 202/467-2900.

EMPLOYMENT SERVICES

EMPLOYMENT AGENCIES AND TEMPORARY SERVICES OF SEATTLE

NOTE: While every effort is made to keep the addresses and phone numbers of these companies up-to-date, smaller-sized companies and employment services often move or change hands and are therefore more difficult to track. Please notify the publisher if you find any discrepancies.

A.S.A.P. EMPLOYMENT SERVICES
4171 Wheaton Way, Suite 7, Bremerton WA 98310. 206/479-4310. **Contact:** Roberta I. Long, Owner. Employment agency; temporary help service. Appointment requested. Founded 1973. Nonspecialized. **Positions commonly filled include:** Accountant; Administrative Assistant; Advertising Worker; Bank Officer/Manager; Bookkeeper; Buyer; Civil Engineer; Claim Representative; Clerk; Computer Operator; Computer Programmer; Credit Manager; Customer Service Representative; Data Entry Clerk; Demonstrator; Draftsperson; EDP Specialist; Electrical Engineer; General Manager; Hotel Manager; Legal Secretary; Industrial Engineer; Mechanical Engineer; Medical Secretary; Nurse; Office Worker; Public Relations Worker; Purchasing Agent; Quality Control Supervisor; Receptionist; Reporter/Editor; Sales Representative; Secretary; Stenographer; Systems Analyst; Technical Writer/Editor; Technician; Word Processing Specialist. Company pays fee; individual pays fee. **Number of placements per year:** 201-500.

ABLE PERSONNEL SERVICE
NT Office Building, North 4407 Division, Suite 625, Spokane WA 99207. 509/487-2734. **Contact:** William "Jay" Kinzer, Owner/Manager. Employment agency. No appointment required. Founded 1964. **Specializes in the areas of:** Accounting and Finance; Clerical; Engineering; Sales and Marketing. **Positions commonly filled include:** Accountant; Administrative Assistant; Bookkeeper; Buyer; Claim Representative; Clerk; Credit Manager; Customer Service Representative; Data Entry Clerk; Draftsperson; General Manager; Legal Secretary; Marketing Specialist; Medical Secretary; Office Worker; Purchasing Agent; Receptionist; Sales Representative; Secretary; Stenographer; Typist; Word Processing Specialist. Individual pays fee.

CAREER SERVICES
677 George Washington Way, Richland WA 99352. 509/946-0643. **Contact:** Jean B. McKee, Owner. **Specializes in the area of:** Temporary services (accounting/bookkeeping; professional; industrial; sales; secretaries; technical; word processing).

GILMORE TEMPORARY PERSONNEL

2722 Colby Avenue, Suite 414, Everett WA 98201. 206/252-1195. **Contact:** Colleen Ellingson, Manager. Temporary help service. Appointment requested. Founded 1969. Nonspecialized. **Positions commonly filled include:** Administrative Assistant; Bookkeeper; Clerk; Computer Operator; Data Entry Clerk; Demonstrator; Factory Worker; Legal Secretary; Light Industrial Worker; Medical Secretary; Office Worker; Receptionist; Secretary; Statistician; Stenographer; Typist; Word Processing Specialist. Company pays fee. **Number of placements per year:** 1001+.

HALLMARK SERVICES

520 Pike Street, Suite 1450, Seattle WA 98101. 206/587-5360. **Contact:** Dolores Gohndron, Manager. Employment agency; temporary help service. No appointment required. Founded 1981. **Specializes in the areas of:** Clerical; Legal. **Positions commonly filled include:** Administrative Assistant; Bookkeeper; Clerk; Data Entry Clerk; Demonstrator; Office Worker; Receptionist; Secretary; Stenographer; Typist; Word Processing Specialist. Company pays fee; individual pays fee.

HOUSER, MARTIN, MORRIS & ASSOCIATES

P.O. Box 90015, Bellevue WA 98009. 206/453-2700. **Contact:** Bob Holbert, President. Employment agency. Appointment requested. Founded 1974. **Specializes in the areas of:** Accounting and Finance; Banking; Computer Hardware and Software; Engineering; Insurance; Manufacturing; MIS/EDP; Sales and Marketing. **Positions commonly filled include:** Accountant; Actuary; Aerospace Engineer; Bank Officer/Manager; Computer Programmer; Credit Manager; EDP Specialist; Electrical Engineer; Financial Analyst; General Manager; Industrial Engineer; Insurance Agent/Broker; MIS Specialist; Mechanical Engineer; Metallurgical Engineer; Purchasing Agent; Underwriter. Company pays fee.

JOBS CO.

East 8900 Sprague Avenue, Spokane WA 99212. 509/928-3151. **Contact:** Clark E. Hager, Sr., Owner. Employment agency. Appointment required. Founded 1973. Largest agency in Spokane - nationwide professional placement and search. Includes Med/Search, Pro/Search. Sales/Search, and EDP/Search divisions. **Specializes in the areas of:** Accounting; Banking and Finance; Computer Hardware and Software; Engineering; Health and Medical; Manufacturing; MIS/EDP; Sales and Marketing; Secretarial and Clerical; Technical and Scientific. **Positions commonly filled include:** Accountant; Administrative Assistant; Aerospace Engineer; Agricultural Engineer; Bank Officer/Manager; Biochemist/Chemist; Biomedical Engineer; Civil Engineer; Computer Programmer; Dietician/Nutritionist; EDP Specialist; Electrical Engineer; Executive Secretary; Financial Analyst, Industrial Designer; Industrial Engineer; Legal Secretary; Management Consultant; Mechanical Engineer; Medical Secretary; Metallurgical Engineer; Mining Engineer; Nurse; Personnel

Director; Petroleum; Physicist; Receptionist; Sales Representative; Secretary; Stenographer; Systems Analyst; Typist; Word Processor. Company pays fee. **Number of placements per year:** 501-1000.

OLSTEN KIMBERLY QUALITY CARE

3680 South Cedar, Suite A, Tacoma WA 98409. 206/475-6862. **Contact:** Blanche Jones, Branch Manager. Appointment required. Founded 1971. Full service Medicare/Medicaid provider. Services include: RN, PT, OT, ST, MSW, HHA. Private program includes RN, LPN, HHA and Homehelper services 2-24 hours/day, seven days/week. **Positions commonly filled include:** Accountant; Administrative Assistant; Bookkeeper; Data Entry Clerk; Dietician/Nutritionist; Medical Secretary; Nurse; Public Relations Worker; Typist, etc. Individual pays fee.

PERSONNEL UNLIMITED INC.

West 25 Nora, Spokane WA 99205. 509/326-8880. **Contact:** Gary Desgrosellier, President. Employment agency. Appointment requested. Founded 1978. **Specializes in the areas of:** Accounting and Finance; Clerical; Computer Hardware and Software; Engineering; Food Industry; Health and Medical; Insurance; Legal; MIS/EDP; Sales and Marketing. **Positions commonly filled include:** Accountant; Administrative Assistant; Agricultural Engineer; Bank Officer/Manager; Bookkeeper; Buyer; Claim Representative; Clerk; Computer Operator; Computer Programmer; Credit Manager; Customer Service Representative; Data Entry Clerk; Draftsperson; EDP Specialist; Electrical Engineer; Financial Analyst; General Manager; Hotel Manager/Assistant Manager; Industrial Engineer; Legal Secretary; MIS Specialist; Marketing Specialist; Mechanical Engineer; Medical Secretary; Metallurgical Engineer; Office Worker; Operations/Production Specialist; Public Relations Worker; Purchasing Agent; Quality Control Supervisor; Receptionist; Sales Representative; Secretary; Statistician; Stenographer; Systems Analyst; Technical Writer/Editor; Technician; Typist; Underwriter; Word Processing Specialist. Company pays fee; individual pays fee. **Number of placements per year:** 501-1000.

SNELLING & SNELLING OF SEATTLE

Post Office Box 66552, Seattle WA 98166. 206/246-6610. **Contact:** Sue & Tom Truscott, Owners/Managers. Employment agency. Appointment requested. Founded 1966. **Specializes in the areas of:** Banking; Clerical; Insurance; Retail Management; Sales and Marketing. **Positions commonly filled include:** Accountant; Administrative Assistant; Bank Officer/Manager; Bookkeeper; Claim Representative; Advertising Worker; Clerk; Computer Operator; Credit Manager; Customer Service Representative; Data Entry Clerk; Financial Analyst; Insurance Agent/Broker; Legal Secretary; Medical Secretary; Office Worker; Receptionist; Sales Representative; Secretary; Stenographer; Typist; Underwriter; Word Processing Specialist. Company pays fee; individual pays fee. **Number of placements per year:** 201-500.

STAFF BUILDERS, INC. OF WASHINGTON

10740 Meridian Avenue North, Suite 102, Seattle WA 98133. 206/364-0535 or 800/258-1059. Temporary help service. Appointment requested. Founded 1961. Branch offices located in: Arizona; California; Connecticut; District of Columbia; Florida; Georgia; Illinois; Indiana; Kansas; Louisiana; Maryland; Massachusetts; Michigan; Minnesota; Missouri; Nevada; New Jersey; New Mexico; New York; Ohio; Oklahoma; Oregon; Pennsylvania; Rhode Island; Tennessee; Texas; Virginia; Washington. Nonspecialized. **Positions commonly filled include:** Accountant; Administrative Assistant; Bookkeeper; Clerk; Companion; Computer Operator; Computer Programmer; Customer Service Representative; Data Entry Clerk; Demonstrator; Draftsperson; Driver; EDP Specialist; Factory Worker; General Laborer; Health Aide; Legal Secretary; Light Industrial Worker; Medical Secretary; Nurse; Office Worker; Public Relations Worker; Receptionist; Sales Representative; Secretary; Stenographer; Technician; Typist; Word Processing Specialist. Company pays fee. **Number of placements per year:** 1001+.

THE THOMAS COMPANY

Post Office Box 58155, Renton WA 98058. 206/255-7637. **Contact:** Thomas J. Yankowski, F.L.M.I., Executive Director. Employment agency. Appointment required. Founded 1979. Nationwide search firm specializing in the Insurance industry. **Specializes in the areas of:** Banking and Finance; Computer Hardware and Software; Insurance; MIS/EDP; Sales and Marketing. **Positions commonly filled include:** Accountant; Actuary; Administrative Assistant; Advertising Executive; Attorney; Bookkeeper; Claims Representative; Computer Programmer; Customer Service Rep; Data Entry Clerk; EDP Specialist; Economist; Financial Analyst; General Manager. Insurance Agent/Broker; Management Consultant; Marketing Specialist; Personnel Director; Statistician; Systems Analyst; Technical Writer/Editor; Technician; Underwriter, etc. Company pays fee. **Number of placements per year:** 51-100.

EXECUTIVE SEARCH FIRMS OF WASHINGTON

COMPUSEARCH OF SEATTLE
2510 Fairview Avenue East, Seattle WA 98102. 206/328-0936; **Fax:** 206/328-7221. **Contact:** Dan Jilka, General Manager. Executive search firm. Appointment required; no phone calls; unsolicited resumes accepted. Founded 1965. World's largest contingency search firm. Five hundred offices nationwide, doing business under the names "Management Recruiters", "Sales Consultants", "CompuSearch" and "OfficeMates5". Specializes in mid-management/professional positions, $25,000-75,000. **Specializes in the areas of:** Accounting; Administration, MIS/EDP; Advertising; Affirmative Action; Architecture; Banking and Finance; Communications; Computer Hardware and Software; Construction; Electrical; Engineering; Food Industry; General Management; Health and Medical; Human Resources; Industrial and Interior Design; Insurance; Legal; Manufacturing; Operations Management; Printing and Publishing; Procurement; Real Estate; Retailing; Sales and Marketing; Technical and Scientific; Textiles; Transportation. Contingency.

CONSULTANT CONNECTION, INC.
400 108th NE #600, Bellvue WA 98004. 206/455-2770. **FAX:** 206/454-1702. **Contact:** Howard Robboy, President. An executive search firm. Appointment required. Founded in 1982. **Specializes in the areas of:** Food Industry, Sales and Marketing. Company pays fee. **Number of placements per year:** 50-99.

KATHY EVANS EXECUTIVE SEARCH, INC.
400 108th N.E., #310, Bellevue WA 98004. 206/453-5548. **Contact:** Kathy Evans, President. Executive search firm. Appointment required. Founded 1980. **Specializes in the areas of:** Health and Medical; Sales and Marketing. **Positions commonly filled include:** Sales Representative. Company pays fee. **Number of placements per year:** 0-50.

THE KNAPP AGENCY
1904 3rd Avenue, Suite 1011, Seattle WA 98101. 206/623-2323. **Contact:** Odessa F. Frost, Owner. Executive search firm. Appointment requested; unsolicited resumes accepted. Founded 1955. Nonspecialized. Contingency; noncontingency. Number of searches conducted per year: 51-100.

MANAGEMENT RECRUITERS OF MERCER ISLAND
9725 SE 36th Street, Globe Building, Suite 312, Mercer Island WA 98040-3896. 206/232-0204. **Contact:** James J. Dykeman, Manager. Executive search firm. Appointment required; no phone calls; unsolicited resumes accepted. Founded 1965. World's largest contingency search firm. Five hundred offices nationwide, doing business under the names "Management Recruiters", "Sales Consultants", "CompuSearch" and "OfficeMates5". Specializes in mid-management/

professional positions, $25,000-75,000. **Specializes in the areas of:** Accounting; Administration, MIS/EDP; Advertising; Affirmative Action; Architecture; Banking and Finance; Communications; Computer Hardware and Software; Construction; Electrical; Engineering; Food Industry; General Management; Health and Medical; Human Resources; Industrial and Interior Design; Insurance; Legal; Manufacturing; Operations Management; Printing and Publishing; Procurement; Real Estate; Retailing; Sales and Marketing; Technical and Scientific; Textiles; Transportation. Contingency.

MANAGEMENT RECRUITERS OF SEATTLE

2510 Fairview Avenue East, Seattle WA 98102. 206/328-0936. **FAX:** 206/328-3256. **Contact:** Dan Jilka, General Manager. Executive search firm. Appointment required; no phone calls; unsolicited resumes accepted. Founded 1965. World's largest contingency search firm. Five hundred offices nationwide, doing business under the names "Management Recruiters", "Sales Consultants", "CompuSearch" and "OfficeMates5". Specializes in mid-management/professional positions, $25,000-75,000. **Specializes in the areas of:** Accounting; Administration, MIS/EDP; Advertising; Affirmative Action; Architecture; Banking and Finance; Communications; Computer Hardware and Software; Construction; Electrical; Engineering; Food Industry; General Management; Health and Medical; Human Resources; Industrial and Interior Design; Insurance; Legal; Manufacturing; Operations Management; Printing and Publishing; Procurement; Real Estate; Retailing; Sales and Marketing; Technical and Scientific; Textiles; Transportation. Contingency.

MANAGEMENT RECRUITERS OF TACOMA

1019 Pacific Avenue, Suite 806, Tacoma WA 98402-4403. 206/627-1972. **Contact:** Dennis Johnson, Manager. Executive search firm. Appointment required; no phone calls; unsolicited resumes accepted. Founded 1965. World's largest contingency search firm. Five hundred offices nationwide, doing business under the names "Management Recruiters", "Sales Consultants", "CompuSearch" and "OfficeMates5". Specializes in mid-management/professional positions, $25,000-75,000. **Specializes in the areas of:** Accounting; Administration, MIS/EDP; Advertising; Affirmative Action; Architecture; Banking and Finance; Communications; Computer Hardware and Software; Construction; Electrical; Engineering; Food Industry; General Management; Health and Medical; Human Resources; Industrial and Interior Design; Insurance; Legal; Manufacturing; Operations Management; Printing and Publishing; Procurement; Real Estate; Retailing; Sales and Marketing; Technical and Scientific; Textiles; Transportation. Contingency.

PERSONNEL UNLIMITED INC.

West 25 Nora, Spokane WA 99205. 509/326-8880. **Contact:** Gary Desgrosellier, President. Employment agency. Appointment requested. Founded 1970. **Specializes in the areas of:** Accounting and Finance; Clerical; Computer Hardware and Software; Engineering; Food Industry; Health and Medical; Insurance; Legal; MIS/EDP; Sales and Marketing. **Positions commonly filled include:** Accountant; Administrative Assistant; Agricultural Engineer; Bank Officer/Manager; Bookkeeper; Buyer; Claim Representative; Clerk; Computer

Operator; Computer Programmer; Credit Manager; Customer Service Representative; Data Entry Clerk; Draftsperson; EDP Specialist; Electrical Engineer; Financial Analyst; General Manager; Hotel Manager/Assistant Manager; Industrial Engineer; Legal Secretary; MIS Specialist; Marketing Specialist; Mechanical Engineer; Medical Secretary; Metallurgical Engineer; Office Worker; Operations/Production Specialist; Public Relations Worker; Purchasing Agent; Quality Control Supervisor; Receptionist; Sales Representative; Secretary; Statistician; Stenographer; Systems Analyst; Technical Writer/Editor; Technician; Typist; Underwriter; Word Processing Specialist. Company pays fee; individual pays fee. **Number of placements per year:** 501-1000.

SALES CONSULTANTS OF SEATTLE

275 1018th Avenue SE, Suite 125, Bellevue WA 98005. 206/455-1805. **Contact:** Paul Komorner, Manager. Executive search firm. Appointment required; no phone calls; unsolicited resumes accepted. Founded 1965. World's largest contingency search firm. Five hundred offices nationwide, doing business under the names "Management Recruiters", "Sales Consultants", "CompuSearch" and "OfficeMates5". Specializes in mid-management/professional positions, $25,000-75,000. **Specializes in the areas of:** Accounting; Administration, MIS/EDP; Advertising; Affirmative Action; Architecture; Banking and Finance; Communications; Computer Hardware and Software; Construction; Electrical; Engineering; Food Industry; General Management; Health and Medical; Human Resources; Industrial and Interior Design; Insurance; Legal; Manufacturing; Operations Management; Printing and Publishing; Procurement; Real Estate; Retailing; Sales and Marketing; Technical and Scientific; Textiles; Transportation. Contingency.

INDEX OF PRIMARY EMPLOYERS

NOTE: *Below is an alphabetical index of primary employer listings included in this book. Those employers in each industry that fall under the headings "Additional employers" are not indexed here.*

Your Job Hunt
Your Feedback

Comments, questions, or suggestions? We want to hear from you. Please complete this questionnaire and mail it to:

The JobBank Staff
c/o Bob Adams Inc.
260 Center Street
Holbrook, MA 02343

Did this book provide helpful advice and valuable information which you used in your job search? Was the information easy to access?

Recommendations for improvements. How could we improve this book to help in your job search? No suggestion is too small or too large.

Would you recommend this book to a friend beginning a job hunt?

Name: _____

Occupation: _____

Which JobBank did you use? _____

Address: _____

Daytime phone: _____

AVAILABLE AT YOUR LOCAL BOOKSTORE

Knock 'em Dead
The Ultimate Job Seeker's Handbook
The all-new 1994 edition of Martin Yate's classic now covers the entire job search. The new edition features a special section on what to do when a layoff is imminent. *Knock 'em Dead* also includes the best overall advice on mounting a successful job search campaign and Yate's famous great answers to tough interview questions. When it comes to proven tactics that give readers the competitive advantage, Martin Yate is the authority to turn to. 6x9", 304 pages, $8.95.

Resumes That Knock 'em Dead
Martin Yate reviews the marks of a great resume: what type of resume is right for each applicant, what always goes in, what always stays out, and why. Every single resume in *Resumes That Knock 'em Dead* was actually used by a job hunter to successfully obtain a job. No other book provides the hard facts for producing an exemplary resume. 8-1/2x11", 216 pages, $7.95.

Cover Letters That Knock 'em Dead
The final word on not just how to write a "correct" cover letter, but how to write a cover letter that offers a powerful competitive advantage in today's tough job market. *Cover Letters That Knock 'em Dead* gives the essential information on composing a cover letter that wins attention, interest, and job offers. 8-1/2x11", 204 pages, $7.95.

ALSO OF INTEREST...

The JobBank Series
There are now 20 *JobBank* books, each providing extensive, up-to-date employment information on hundreds of the largest employers in each job market. Recommended as an excellent place to begin your job search by *The New York Times, The Los Angeles Times, The Boston Globe, The Chicago Tribune,* and many other publications, *JobBank* books have been used by hundreds of thousands of people to find jobs.

Books available: *The Atlanta JobBank--The Boston JobBank--The Carolina JobBank--The Chicago JobBank--The Dallas-Ft. Worth JobBank--The Denver JobBank--The Detroit JobBank--The Florida JobBank--The Houston JobBank--The Los Angeles JobBank--The Minneapolis JobBank--The New York JobBank--The Ohio JobBank--The Philadelphia JobBank--The Phoenix JobBank--The St. Louis JobBank--The San Francisco JobBank--The Seattle JobBank--The Tennessee JobBank--The Washington DC JobBank.* Each book is 6x9", over 300 pages, paperback, $15.95.

If you cannot find a book at your local bookstore, you may order it directly from the publisher. Please send payment including $4.50 for shipping and handling (for the entire order) to: Bob Adams, Inc., 260 Center Street, Holbrook, MA 02343. Credit card holders may call 1-800/USA-JOBS (in Massachusetts, 617/767-8100). Please check first at your local bookstore.